OUR PLASTIC PROBLEM AND HOW TO SOLVE IT

Plastic pollution is a global problem that defies a singular solution. *Our Plastic Problem and How to Solve It* considers plastic's harm to the environment, from its production to its disposal, and offers a spectrum of solutions that require action by local and federal governments, businesses and non-profits, and individuals. Using specific examples and case studies, the book describes the history and chemistry of plastic, illustrates its harms, and identifies specific legislation and policies to offer concrete solutions. Plastic pollution is ubiquitous and impacts our soil, food, air, and water. To solve our plastic problem, collaboration across disciplines will be critical; innovations in science, law, and design will be essential. The book demonstrates the need to approach environmental problems from an interdisciplinary lens, and will benefit anyone interested in learning more about the harms and solutions associated with plastic pollution.

Sarah J. Morath is a lawyer, a writer, an educator, and a scientist. Her interdisciplinary scholarship has appeared in a variety of publications and is widely read and cited. She is the editor of *From Farm to Fork: Perspectives on Growing Sustainable Food Systems in the Twenty-First Century* (University of Akron Press, 2016). Professor Morath holds degrees from Vassar College, Yale University, and the University of Montana School of Law. She is currently a law professor at Wake Forest University School of Law.

Our Plastic Problem and How to Solve It

Sarah J. Morath
Wake Forest University

CAMBRIDGE
UNIVERSITY PRESS

University Printing House, Cambridge CB2 8BS, United Kingdom

One Liberty Plaza, 20th Floor, New York, NY 10006, USA

477 Williamstown Road, Port Melbourne, VIC 3207, Australia

314–321, 3rd Floor, Plot 3, Splendor Forum, Jasola District Centre, New Delhi – 110025, India

103 Penang Road, #05–06/07, Visioncrest Commercial, Singapore 238467

Cambridge University Press is part of the University of Cambridge.

It furthers the University's mission by disseminating knowledge in the pursuit of education, learning, and research at the highest international levels of excellence.

www.cambridge.org
Information on this title: www.cambridge.org/9781108841801
DOI: 10.1017/9781108895026

First published 2022

A catalogue record for this publication is available from the British Library.

ISBN 978-1-108-84180-1 Hardback
ISBN 978-1-108-79537-1 Paperback

CONTENTS

ACKNOWLEDGMENTS

In pursuing this project, I have benefited greatly from conversations and engagement with my academic colleagues at both the University of Houston Law Center and Wake Forest University School of Law, particularly the deans of research, Dave Fagundes (University of Houston Law Center) and Ronald Wright (Wake Forest University School of Law). In addition, I benefited from the feedback I received from the faculty at the University of Richmond School of Law, specifically the helpful responses of Noah M. Sachs. Finally, I benefited from the comments and support I received from the junior faculty group at Wake Forest University School of Law and my Lawyering Skills and Strategies colleagues at the University of Houston Law Center.

I wish to recognize the support of Leonard Baynes, the dean of the University of Houston Law Center, and Jane Aiken, the dean of the Wake Forest University School of Law, as well as the law librarians at both institutions. I am appreciative of the research assistance I received from Rebecca Jordan, Amanda Thompson, and Samantha Hamilton. Additionally, I would like to thank the editors at Cambridge University Press for their careful and thoughtful attention. Any mistakes are my own.

This book provides many examples from the private sphere, and I have never accepted any funding from any of the businesses or individuals mentioned in this book.

Above all else, I must acknowledge the support of my family. This book would not have been possible without them. This undertaking was truly a family effort – from the wonderful artwork of my sister-in-law Abby Maier Johnson to the cover art of my daughter to the thoughtful edits of my aunt Lucia Leith to the words of encouragement from my siblings, mother, in-laws, husband, and children. Your patience and understanding were remarkable, and your love kept me moving forward during the most challenging time of my life.

May we all leave this world a bit better.

ABBREVIATIONS

BPA	bisphenol A
CAA	Clean Air Act
CERCLA	Comprehensive Environmental Response, Compensation, and Liability Act
CO2e	carbon dioxide equivalents
CSO	combined sewage overflows
CSR	corporate social responsibility
CWA	Clean Water Act
DOE	Department of Energy
DOJ	Department of Justice
EAC	East African Community
EMS	environmental management system
EPA	Environmental Protection Agency
EPR	extended producer responsibility
EPS	expanded polystyrene
FDA	Food and Drug Administration
GAO	Government Accountability Office
GPGP	Great Pacific garbage patch
GPML	Global Partnership on Marine Litter
HDPE	high-density polyethylene
IMDCC	Interagency Marine Debris Coordinating Committee
IMO	International Maritime Organization
ISO	International Organization for Standardization
LDPE	low-density polyethylene
MARPOL	International Convention for the Prevention of Pollution from Ships

MDP	Marine Debris Program
MDRPRA	Marine Debris Research, Prevention, and Reduction Act
MFWA	Microbead-Free Waters Act
MPPRCA	Marine Plastic Pollution Research and Control Act
MPRSA	Marine Protection, Research, and Sanctuaries Act
MRC	materials recovery center
MSC	Marine Stewardship Council
MSW	municipal solid waste
MT	metric ton
NGO	nongovernmental organization
NOAA	National Oceanic and Atmospheric Administration
NPDES	National Pollutant Discharge Elimination System
OCS	Operation Clean Sweep
PCB	polychlorinated biphenyl
PE	polyethylene
PET	polyethylene terephthalate
PHAs	polyhydroxyalkanoates
PLA	polylactic acid
POP	persistent organic pollutants
PP	polypropylene
PS	polystyrene
PTF	plastic-to-fuel
PTP	plastic-to-plastic
PVC	polyvinyl chloride
RCRA	Resource Conservation and Recovery Act
RIC	Resin Identification Code
SOS	Save Our Seas
TRI	Toxics Release Inventory
UNCLOS	United Nations Convention on the Law of the Sea
UNEP	United Nations Environment Programme
UNESCO	United Nations Educational, Scientific, and Cultural Organization
WWF	World Wildlife Fund for Nature (formerly the World Wildlife Federation)

INTRODUCTION

Today, plastic pollution, like climate change, is part of everyday conversation. Plastic pollution and its associated harms dominate the news, scientific research, and environmental activism. Plastic-induced deaths of whales, seabirds, and turtles are reported regularly, and microplastics have been detected in drinking water and food.

Plastic waste discoveries occur in the most remote areas of the globe and in surprising amounts. A 2020 survey of microplastics in Pennsylvania waterways, for example, found that 100 percent of the sites sampled had plastic microfibers leading conservationists to proclaim that no waterbody is safe from this common contaminant.

The mounting evidence of plastic's devastation has escalated action by individuals. "Single-use" was the 2018 word of the year and plastic straws became the "poster child" for plastic pollution. Companies, too, are pledging to reduce their plastic use, and cities, states, and nations are agreeing to ban plastic altogether. Individuals, governments, NGOs, and businesses are working together to detect, study, and reduce plastic in our environment. With the growing realization of plastic's harm have also come exciting discoveries – a plastic-eating bacteria and a fungus that can break down polyester polyurethane – and innovative projects like turning plastic into clothing, sneakers, and even a form of currency.

Our Plastic Problem analyzes both the problem of plastic pollution and the promising solutions undertaken. As with many environmental problems, eliminating plastic pollution will require a comprehensive and integrated approach. As a result, this book discusses both traditional methods of addressing environmental harms through regulations or public governance, but also efforts to change social norms and individual behavior. In addition, because solving our plastic problem will require cooperation from businesses and industries that rely heavily on plastics, the book also examines private governance and design thinking. The benefits and challenges of these different solutions are discussed.

The book is divided into three parts. Part I comprises three chapters and discusses plastic in the environment. It traces the growth of plastic from a new discovery to a nuisance material. The chapters also discuss numerous studies that examine the origins of plastic in our environment and the harm it causes.

Part II comprises four chapters and looks at existing and potential actions that a cross section of actors can take to address plastic pollution. The chapters discuss federal statutes, statewide bans, international agreements, voluntary action by businesses and individuals, and educational campaigns by nonprofits. Throughout this section, readers are reminded that there is no silver bullet to solving our plastic problem. Collaboration and information sharing will be critical, and regulatory and nonregulatory tools must be employed.

Part III concludes by looking at innovative solutions that exist in how we design and reuse plastic. The chapters are devoted to bioplastics, recycling, and the circular economy. The book ends by offering the circular economy – where waste is designed out of manufacturing processes – as the optimal way forward.

The goal of this book is to help readers understand the complexity of plastic pollution and the need for a multimodal approach to solving this problem. Readers will learn about the formal and informal tools available to manage environmental harms and will understand that solving our plastic problem will require collective action from governments, businesses, nongovernmental organizations, industries, and individuals.

Readers should recognize that many scientists and policymakers believe that plastic's impact on the environment is just beginning to be realized. Some say we are in the "first inning" of understanding plastic pollution. Consequently, the development of effective solutions, be it through regulations, voluntary business actions, or innovative technological advances is in its infancy and is ongoing. A former EPA official, Judith Enrick, stated in 2019, “Where we are on plastics is where we were fifteen years ago on climate change. We’re just beginning to get the picture.” While there is much work to be done to solve our plastic problem, there is also infinite opportunity.

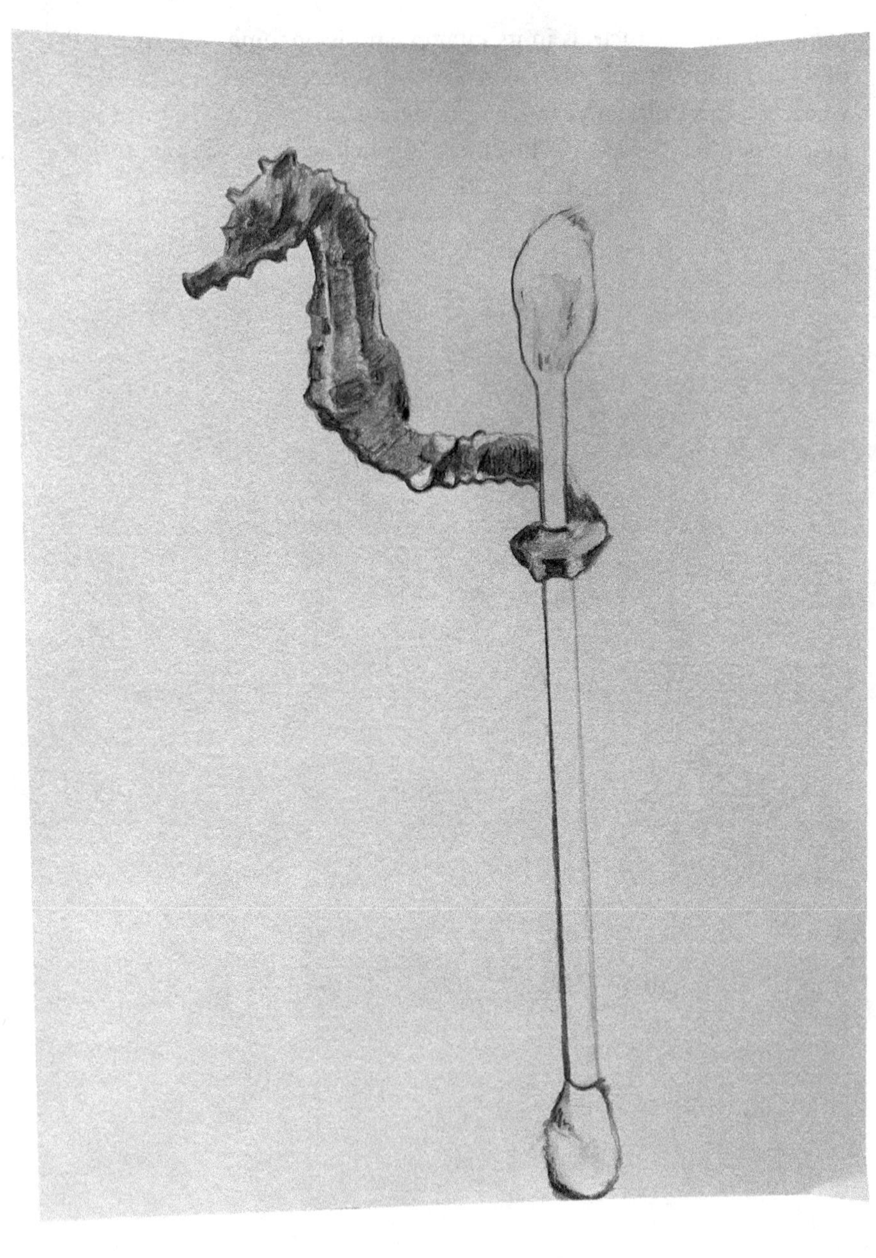

PART I

Plastic in the Environment

This part provides the groundwork necessary for an in-depth look at solving our plastic problem. Using three case studies, Chapter 1 reveals the ubiquitous nature of plastic in our environment and briefly traces the growth and development of the plastic industry. Chapter 2 describes how plastic in the environment is measured and offers insight into why plastic persists in the environment. Chapter 3 discusses plastic's impact on our ecosystem, health, and economy.

1 THE PROLIFERATION OF PLASTIC

MR. MCGUIRE: I want to say one word to you. Just one word.
BENJAMIN: Yes, sir.
MR. MCGUIRE: Are you listening?
BENJAMIN: Yes, I am.
MR. MCGUIRE: Plastics.
BENJAMIN: Exactly how do you mean?
MR. MCGUIRE: There's a great future in plastics. Think about it. Will you think about it?[1]

Mr. McGuire was onto something when, in 1967, he told Benjamin Braddock in *The Graduate* that there was a great future in plastics. Although mass production of plastics was just taking off in the 1960s, plastic is ubiquitous today. The material is inexpensive, lightweight, and durable, making it useful to almost any industry – from construction to electronics to transportation to packaging. The characteristics that make plastic so useful, however, also make it a problem.

Plastic is everywhere. Recent reports have found plastic in the ocean's deepest trench[2] and in the mountain air of the French Pyrenees.[3] How does plastic turn up in such remote locations? This chapter provides some answers, briefly tracing the development and growth of mass-produced plastics from the beginning of the twentieth

[1] *The Graduate* (Embassy Pictures 1967).

[2] Damian Carrington, Plastic pollution discovered at deepest point of ocean, *The Guardian* (December 2018) (available at www.theguardian.com/environment/2018/dec/20/plastic-pollution-mariana-trench-deepest-point-ocean) (last accessed October 31, 2021).

[3] Stephan Leahy, Microplastics are raining down from the sky, *National Geographic* (April 2019) (available at www.nationalgeographic.com/environment/article/microplastics-pollution-falls-from-air-even-mountains) (last accessed October 31, 2021).

century to this day. It lays the foundation for a discussion of measuring the plastic in our environment in Chapter 2 and the impact of plastic on our health, ecosystem, and economy presented in Chapter 3.

Ubiquitous is a word often associated with plastic. The term describes something that is everywhere, and, indeed, plastic has been found all over our globe. Today, no place is beyond the reach of plastic. It has been discovered in some of the most isolated places on Earth. Unfortunately, scientists who study plastic in the environment caution that their calculations are conservative, suggesting that there is in fact more plastic in our environment than we realize. This underscores the urgency of the need to address our plastic problem.

I THREE EXAMPLES: ISLANDS, OCEANS, AND MOUNTAINS

A remote island, an ocean trench, and a mountaintop provide three examples of plastic's ubiquity.

A A Remote Island

The Cocos (Keeling) Islands (CKI) – "Australia's last unspoilt [*sic*] paradise"[4] – are located in the Indian Ocean about 1,300 miles from the northwest coast of Australia. Two small atolls comprising twenty-seven islands make up the CKI. Their coral reefs were of particular interest to naturalist Charles Darwin, who described the scenery as "very curious and rather pretty," where "living coral darkens the emerald green water."[5] The total land area is 14 km^2, but most of the CKI are only a few acres in size. Around 600 people live on two of the islands; the remaining islands are uninhabited. This island chain is home to coconut trees, seabirds, including the endangered buff-banded rail, and the Pulu Keeling National Park. Tourism websites

[4] J. L. Lavers, L. Dicks, M. R. Dicks, and A. Finger, Significant plastic accumulation on the Cocos (Keeling) Islands, Australia, *Scientific Reports* (May 2019).

[5] https://theboar.org/2019/06/cocos-islands-drowing-in-sea-of-plastic/ (last accessed October 6, 2021).

tout the "spectacular snorkeling, world-class diving, excellent fishing and the adrenalin-rush of kitesurfing."[6] But these attractions are increasingly threatened by plastic debris.

A 2017 study examined debris on seven of these islands (88 percent of the landmass of the CKI). The study results published in *Scientific Reports* in 2019 found an estimated 413.6 million pieces of debris weighing 238 tons.[7] Plastic accounted for 95 percent of all debris recorded on the shores of the CKI. The study, which investigated both surface and buried debris, found that the amount of plastic debris buried a few centimeters below the beach surface is about twenty-six times greater than the amount of debris visible on the surface of the beach. The beaches of CKI are already fouled by an estimated 373,000 toothbrushes and 977,000 shoes – equivalent to what the CKI community would produce as waste in ~4,000 years. Dr. Jennifer Lavers, the scientist leading the study, explained that "remote islands can give a good view of the volume of plastic debris globally – acting like canaries in a coal mine."[8]

B An Ocean Trench

The Mariana Trench, seven miles deep and located in the Pacific Ocean, is the Earth's deepest ocean trench. In 1960, US Navy Lieutenant Don Walsh, along with scientist Jacques Picard, took the seven-mile journey to the bottom of the Mariana Trench. Walsh describes the forty-minute dive as occurring in "absolute darkness," except for the bioluminescent invertebrates flickering outside the pair's vessel.[9] The ocean floor, a "diatomaceous ooze, the skeletons of diatoms," was stirred up into a big cloud when they landed. The ooze

[6] www.cocoskeelingislands.com.au/

[7] Lavers et al., Significant plastic accumulation on the Cocos (Keeling) Islands, Australia.

[8] www.abc.net.au/news/science/2019-05-17/cocos-islands-millions-pieces-plastic-rubbish/11112784 (last accessed October 31, 2021).

[9] Jim Clash, What does the deepest point on the planet look like?, *Forbes* (May 4, 2017) (available at www.forbes.com/sites/jimclash/2017/05/04/what-does-the-deepest-point-on-the-planet-look-like/?sh=3750974445e1) (accessed October 31, 2021).

never settled, and, as a result, the explorers were unable to get a good picture of the ocean bottom.

While unmanned vessels have repeated this trip, only two other people have traveled into the Mariana Trench: film director James Cameron, in 2012, and retired naval officer and explorer Victor Vescovo, who, in May 2019, reached a depth of 11,000 m (almost 36,000 ft) – a world record. In addition to seeing a holothurian, a translucent sea cucumber, Vescovo recounted seeing trash, which was "man-made" and "probably plastic."[10]

Vescovo's speculation that he had seen plastic is probably correct. Until recently, there was limited information about plastic in the deep sea, but the Deep-sea Debris Database is trying to fill the gap. A 2018 article in *Marine Policy* describes how the database was established in March 2017 to assist in the categorization of deep-sea plastic debris.[11] In preparing the database, scientists reviewed the video footage taken from submersibles and remotely operated vehicles starting with the year 1983 and ending in 2017. A total of 5,010 dives were reviewed, and anthropogenic (man-made) debris was analyzed and classified into seven categories: plastic, glass, metal, rubber, cloth/paper/lumber, fishing gear, and other. Plastic debris was further categorized into single-use products (bags, bottles, and packages) and other plastics. From the 5,010 dives, 3,425 anthropogenic debris items were detected, with plastic accounting for 33 percent of all anthropogenic debris items, followed by metal (26 percent), rubber (1.8 percent), fishing gear (1.7 percent), glass (1.4 percent), cloth/paper/lumber (1.3 percent), and other (35 percent). Of the plastic items, 89 percent were single-use products. The deepest record of plastic debris was a plastic bag at 10,898 m in the Mariana Trench. While Vescovo is not positive he saw plastic, based on the database entries, he most likely did.

[10] Jim Clash, Victor Vescovo Finds Life, but Trash Too, at the Bottom of the Mariana Trench, *Forbes* (May 15, 2019) (available at www.forbes.com/sites/jimclash/2019/05/15/victor-vescovo-finds-life-but-trash-too-at-the-bottom-of-the-mariana-trench/?sh=c229f0b465f6) (last accessed October 16, 2021). There were reports that Vescovo saw a plastic bag and a candy wrapper, but an interview in *Forbes* magazine disputed this.

[11] Sanea Chiba, Hideaki Saito, Ruth Fletchner, and Takayuki Yogi, Human footprint in the abyss: 30 year records of deep-sea plastic debris, *Marine Policy* (October 2018).

C A Mountaintop

More than 7,000 miles east of the Mariana Trench lie the Pyrenees Mountains, a 270-mile-long chain that serves as a natural border between France and Spain. The snowcapped mountain peaks of the central ranges are 10,000 ft above sea level. The area is considered pristine wilderness due to its limited development, sparse population, and distance from industrial centers. Several national parks protect the hills, valleys, waterfalls, and cliffs of the region, making it an ideal place for alpine skiing, mountaineering, and the Tour de France.

Recently, in one of the first studies to detect traces of plastic in a remote terrestrial location, scientists recorded atmospheric deposition of microplastics – plastic fragments less than 5 mm in length – in the Pyrenees Mountains. The results of the study were published in May 2019 in *Nature Geoscience.*[12] Atmospheric deposition collectors from the monitored site in southwestern France, located more than 100 km from the nearest city, received large numbers of microplastic particles over a five-month winter period in 2017 and 2018. During this time, an average of 365 plastic particles dropped from the atmosphere into the collection devices. While computer simulators of wind patterns corroborated the argument that these plastic particles floated 100 km before falling back to earth, the researchers believe that the wind can carry these tiny particles even greater distances.

Today, plastic's appearance on a remote island beach, an isolated ocean trench, or a single mountain range is not unusual. The researchers of these three studies all note that their estimates are conservative and that, undoubtedly, there are other beaches, ocean trenches, and mountains where toothbrushes, plastic bags, and microplastics have accumulated. Furthermore, these three studies offer just a sampling of the research that chronicles the omnipresent nature of plastic in the environment. For example, several studies have found plastic in Arctic sea ice, beneath the Arctic Ocean's surface, and deep in Arctic sediment.[13] Similarly, recent studies of the waters of Antarctica have found

[12] Steve Allen, Deonie Allen, Vernon R. Phoenix et al., Atmospheric transport and deposition of microplastics in a remote mountain catchment, *Nature Geoscience* (April 2019).

[13] I. Peeken, Microplastics in the marine realms of the Arctic with special emphasis on sea ice, in 2018 *Arctic Report Card,* National Oceanic and Atmospheric Administration

plastic in both surface water and deep-sea sediments in the southern polar region.[14] Scientists studying microplastic concentrations at various depths in California's Monterey Bay found nearly identical concentrations of microplastic particles near the surface and in the deepest waters surveyed, 1,000 m below sea level.[15] Perhaps more startling was the fact that, at the midwater range (200–600 m deep), microplastic concentrations were nearly four times greater than in waters near the surface. Plastic has also been found in freshwater ecosystems[16] and in soils, with recent studies estimating that microplastic contamination on land is four to twenty-three times greater than in the oceans.[17] Collectively, these studies illustrate that no part of our globe is immune from plastic's reach. Indeed, plastic is ubiquitous.

II A BRIEF HISTORY OF PLASTICS IN AMERICA

To understand how the Earth has become inundated with plastic requires an understanding of plastic's chemistry and its development as an industry.

A The First Plastics

Plastic's prevalence in our environment is a result of both its chemistry and its growth as an industry. Today, plastic is the material of choice, replacing raw materials such as wood, metals, and fibers. Man-made plastics are synthetic polymers derived from petroleum, natural gas, or

(NOAA) (2018) (available at www.arctic.noaa.gov/Portals/7/ArcticReportCard/Documents/ArcticReportCard_full_report2018.pdf) (last accessed October 31, 2021).

14 Catherine L. Waller, Huw J. Griffiths, Claire M. Waluda et al., Microplastics in the Antarctic marine system: An emerging area of research, *Science of the Total Environment* (November 2017).

15 C. Anela Choy, The vertical distribution and biological transport of marine microplastics across the epipelagic and mesopelagic water column, *Scientific Reports* (June 2019).

16 Martin Wagner, Christian Scherer, Diana Alvarez-Muñoz et al., Microplastics in freshwater ecosystems: What we know and what we need to know, *Environmental Sciences Europe* (2014).

17 Susanna Gionfra, Plastic pollution in soil (Institute for European Environmental Policy, May 2018).

coal. *Polymers* are long chains of identical, repeating molecular units called monomers. All polymers are not plastic, but all plastics are polymers.

There are thousands of naturally occurring polymers. Complex carbohydrates are polymers made up of repeating units of a sugar monomer such as glucose ($C_6H_{12}O_6$). DNA and RNA are polymers of nucleotide monomers. Feathers, hair, and fingernails are all polymers made of the structural protein keratin, which is rich in the amino acid (monomer) cysteine. The most common natural polymer, however, is cellulose, an important structural component of the cell walls of plants.

And it is cellulose from which the first man-made plastic, Parkesine, was created. Discovered by Alexander Parkes, an inventor from Birmingham, England, nitrocellulose (patented as Parkesine in 1862) was created by chemically modifying cellulose with nitric acid and a solvent, something that dissolves substances. Parkes's discovery was never mass-produced, but it was improved upon by John Hyatt, an American inventor who, in 1869, developed the plastic material called celluloid by mixing nitrocellulose with camphor, an organic solid. Celluloid quickly replaced ivory in products like combs and billiard balls, but it was also used in shirt collars, toys, photographic films, and denture plates. While celluloid is still used in some products today, it has largely been supplanted by newer synthetic material.

The first fully synthetic plastic derived from fossil fuels, instead of from cellulose, is called Bakelite after its inventor, Leo Baekeland, a Belgium chemist who relocated to the United States in the late 1800s. In 1907, Baekeland discovered that when carbolic acid, phenol (a derivative of coal tar), and formaldehyde reacted under pressure, the result was a hard, insoluble resin. Bakelite is the first plastic that could be molded and shaped, giving rise to the term *plastic* (derived from the Latin "plasticus" and the Greek "plastikos"), which means capable of being molded or shaped.

Bakelite quickly became a popular material for household goods like telephones, clocks, and jewelry. It was durable, lightweight, and an excellent insulator, which allowed for its integration into the automotive and electrical industries. Because of his discovery of Bakelite, Baekeland is considered the founder of the modern plastic industry.

1 Thermosetting and Thermosoftening Plastics The earliest plastics, including Bakelite, are called thermosetting plastics. *Thermosetting plastics* cannot be reshaped after their initial formation. This is because, during the curing or manufacturing process, polymer chains become cross-linked to form a three-dimensional network of strong intermolecular bonds called van der Waals bonds. As a result of these strong chemical bonds, thermosetting polymers are generally hard and strong and cannot be melted or reshaped after they have been cured. Their resistance to heat makes them ideal for high-heating applications such as electronics and appliances. Thermosetting plastics, however, are not recyclable, though there are increasing efforts to incorporate thermosetting plastics into new products.

Some examples of thermosetting plastics include polyurethane, unsaturated polyester, epoxy and acrylic resins, and silicone. Polyurethane often appears as flexible foam used in furniture, bedding, and carpets. Epoxy resins are used for surface-coating applications, for circuit boards, and in the building sector. Acrylic resins are used in automotive finishes as well as in artificial teeth. Silicone has a wide range of uses, including lubricants, adhesives, gaskets and seals, dishware, and medical equipment.

Unlike thermosetting plastics, *thermosoftening plastics* melt with the application of heat. Thermosoftening polymers have linear molecular chains that soften when heated and harden when cooled. Unlike thermosetting polymers, thermosoftening polymers have weak intermolecular forces, which means they come apart easily when reheated. Thermoplastics can be reheated and molded again, making this kind of plastics a good candidate for recycling and reuse.

About 92 percent of all plastics today are thermosoftening plastics. Some examples include polyethylene (PE), polypropylene (PP), polystyrene (PS), polyethylene terephthalate (PET), and polyvinyl chloride (PVC). Polyethylene can be both high-density polyethylene (HDPE) and low-density polyethylene (LDPE). These plastics are distinguished by the polymer that makes up the plastic. These polymers are, by themselves, harmless. But all plastics on the marketplace have additives, such as plasticizers, colorants, ultraviolet absorbers, and flame retardants, that improve the performance and end use of the plastic.

HDPE has a chemical resistance that makes it well suited as a container for household chemicals and detergents. Its sturdy nature also makes it a good material for milk, juice, and water containers. In contrast, LDPE is transparent and flexible. It is used to make bottles that require extra flexibility, as well as grocery bags and garbage bags, shrink-and-stretch film, and coating for milk cartons. Polypropylene has high tensile strength, making it ideal for use in caps and lids that must secure threaded openings. Because of its high melting point, polypropylene can be filled with hot products designed to cool in bottles, including ketchup and syrup. It is also used for products that need to be incubated, such as yogurt. Polystyrene, in its crystalline form, is a colorless plastic that can be clear and hard. In its foamed or expanded form, it can be used for meat trays, egg cartons, and coffee cups. It is also used for insulation for secondary packaging to protect appliances, electronics, and other sensitive products during transport. Polyethylene terephthalate is a clear, tough polymer that can withstand the pressure of carbonated drinks, and it is used for packaging water, soft drinks, and soda. Vinyl (polyvinyl chloride, or PVC) provides excellent clarity, puncture resistance, and cling. As a film, vinyl can "breathe" just the right amount, making it ideal for packaging fresh meats that require oxygen to ensure a bright-red surface while maintaining an acceptable shelf life; it is also used in construction materials like pipes and siding.

This chemistry is important when considering solutions to plastic pollution such as recycling. First, thermosetting plastics are considered nonrecyclable, because their cross-linked bonds "set" when they harden. While the life span of thermosetting plastics is much longer than that of thermosoftening plastics, thermosetting plastics will eventually end up in landfills. Even recyclable plastics face challenges. The different chemical compositions and additives of these plastics make recycling difficult. Mixing and melting PE and LDHE together for recycling purposes, for example, will not result in high-quality material. These challenges are discussed further in Chapter 9.

B The Growth of an Industry

Baekeland's success prompted oil and chemical companies like DuPont, Dow, Monsanto, and Standard Oil to invest in the research and development of new polymers. In 1926, a researcher at the Goodrich Company in the United States invented plasticized polyvinyl chloride (PVC), which was used for golf balls and shoe heels. In 1931, DuPont invented Lucite (also known as acrylic glass or Plexiglass), a clear, water-resistant, and UV-resistant plastic derived from petroleum (polymethyl methacrylate). In 1933, Saran (polyvinylidene chloride [PVDC]), a product that was sprayed on upholstery of cars, was accidently discovered by a Dow employee. By 1937, a powerful industry and lobbying group, the Society of the Plastic Industry, was formed, bolstering the growth of the plastic industry.

While scientists were busy in laboratories discovering different types of plastics, inventors were busy experimenting with different ways to manufacture plastic. For example, injection molding – an assembly-line process whereby liquid plastic is poured into a closed mold, cooled, and ejected – was critical to the expansion of the plastic industry. This manufacturing process, which has been called the "holy grail of mass production,"[18] allowed the same plastic product to be mass-produced, transforming the volume of plastic products made.

The demand for plastics increased during World War II, and the plastic industry expanded by 300 percent, with plastics comprising many military supplies. Lucite was used as aircraft windshields, and Saran was sprayed on planes to protect against natural elements. Manufacturers of nylon, which was first synthesized by DuPont in 1935, switched production from stockings to parachutes and mosquito nets. And, in 1941, a Dow chemist mixed styrene (a monomer) with isobutene to make polystyrene, which, because of its high strength-to-weight ratio, quickly replaced balsawood as a material for airplanes. The war effort is credited with spurring the development of new plastics.

After the war, however, companies needed to find new markets for plastic. A 1947 article in *Scientific American* touted the "range of … possibilities" for the "civilian market," including such "diverse items as boat hulls, decks, and bulkheads, toys, luggage, gift packages, ornaments, refrigerators, shipping containers, partitions, prefabricated housing panels, aircraft components, buoys and floats, all types of

[18] www.sciencehistory.org/distillations/plastic-town (last accessed October 31, 2021).

sandwich structures with core materials, and thermal, electrical, and sound insulation."[19] At the same time, the development of screw injection machines transformed plastic manufacturing, allowing for the mixing of recycled and plastic material before injection into molds. Today, screw injection machines account for over 90 percent of all injection machines, and the injection molding process dominates the plastics industry; the global market of injected plastics is expected to reach $233 billion by 2023.

With new markets and new machinery, the plastic industry continued to expand. Plastic freed manufacturers from the need to use more expensive and scarce materials such as glass, metal, wood, and ivory. A vast number of new products were created, and because plastic was inexpensive, it furthered the development of a new class of consumers: the middle class. "[N]ewly flush Americans had a never-ending smorgasbord of affordable [and disposable] goods to choose from."[20]

After the war, Dow developed Styrofoam from polystyrene to use as an insulation material. Dow also created Saran wrap, the first cling wrap designed for commercial and household works. A DuPont worker was credited for discovering Tupperware from polyethylene slag in 1946, though Tupperware parties did not become popular until the 1950s. In his book *American Plastic: A Cultural History*, historian Jeffrey Meikle writes that "Tupperware's popularity signaled an overall acceptance of plastic."[21]

During the 1950s and 1960s, plastic continued to be "domesticated," making its way into the hands of consumers in various forms: Hula-Hoops, milk jugs, fiberglass chairs, and clothing. In 1951, DuPont introduced a polyester fabric that was 100 percent synthetic (from the polymer PET), called Dacron. It was publicized to the American public in the *New York Times* as a miracle fabric – wrinkle

[19] Charles A. Breskin, Expanding fields for expanded plastics, *Scientific American* 177, no. 3 (1947): 119–21 (available at www.jstor.org/stable/24945678) (last accessed October 31, 2021).

[20] Susan Freinkel, A brief history of plastic's conquest of the world, *Scientific American* (May 2011).

[21] Jeffrey Meikle, *American Plastic: A Cultural History* (Rutgers University Press, New Brunswick, NJ, 1997).

resistant, damage resistant, economical, cool, and comfortable.[22] One of Dacron's selling points was the fact that it could be worn for sixty-eight days straight without ironing or care and still look fresh.[23] Through the 1960s, 1970s, and early 1980s, the production of polyester for apparel continued to grow. From World War II and the frugality that accompanied that time, "[t]he mindset of the typical consumer was longevity and good wear performance, so [polyester] really had a rapid acceptance."[24]

Global plastic production increased by 400 percent during the 1960s and new companies joined in. Mobil Chemical (now ExxonMobil), for example, pursued an aggressive policy on polyethylene packaging between 1960 and 2000, and patented approximately 500 inventions dealing with plastic bags and packaging.[25] Plastic was just beginning to make its way into landfills and was less than 1 percent by mass of the 88.1 million tons of municipal solid waste generated in the United States. Recycling was essentially nonexistent.

The 1970s saw growth in plastic used for packaging (e.g., Styrofoam peanuts, food packaging, plastic bags) and other one-time uses (e.g., utensils, straws, and Styrofoam cups). Unlike plastic toys, fiberglass furniture, or polyester clothing – products made popular because of their durability – single-use plastics were intended to be used only once. In 1970, the Spork (a hybrid fork and spoon) was patented and the plastic picnic tray, which had the knife, spoon, and fork built into it, further spurred the growth of the single-use plastic industry. Plastic bags made their way into consumer's hands in the late 1970s, and by 1985 plastic bags could be found in over 75 percent of US supermarkets. PET plastic bottles were patented in 1973; their ability to withstand pressure from carbonated drinks made them the bottle of choice with soft drink manufacturers. By the late 1980s,

[22] Stephen Demeo, Dacron polyester: The fall from grace of a miracle fabric, *Science as Culture* (2013).

[23] www.lawrencehuntfashion.com/blogs/news/history-of-polyester-fabrics (last accessed October 31, 2021).

[24] Demeo, Dacron polyester.

[25] Arnaud Gasnier, *The Patenting Paradox: A Game-Based Approach to Patent Management* (Eburon, Delft, 2008), p. 53.

almost all refillable glass soda and milk bottles were replaced with plastic bottles intended to be thrown away.

C Emerging Concerns

While plastic's characteristics had made it the raw material of choice, exceeding aluminum and steel production by volume in 1989, concerns about plastic waste were emerging. A growing throwaway culture escalated a plastic waste management problem and the widespread accumulation of plastic debris in the natural environment. In 1987, insufficient landfill space led to a barge full of waste wandering in the Atlantic with nowhere to deposit its cargo. Some credit this event with creating an interest in recycling and by 1990 2 percent of plastic waste was recycled.[26] Businesses were also starting to become aware of plastics' harms and, in 1990, McDonald's replaced foam-based packaging used for the BigMac, Egg McMuffin, and Chicken McNuggets with paper-based packaging.

Cultural acceptance of plastic was also waning. In the 1960s plastic had become a "cultural metaphor for superficiality and excess," as illustrated in the conversation between Benjamin and Mr. McGuire that took place in *The Graduate.*[27] By the 1980s, wearing polyester was considered cheap and in bad taste.[28]

In addition to aesthetic and cultural concerns, alarming information about the ecological and health impacts of chemicals, including those chemicals found in plastic, were emerging. Toxicologists discovered that a whole host of commonly used man-made products – lead paint, cigarettes, pesticides, artificial sweeteners – could harm or potentially harm humans and wildlife. Recognizing that humans and the environment were exposed to a large number of chemicals, Congress enacted the Toxic Substances Control Act in 1976 (15 U.S.C. § 2601 et. seq.) and authorized the Environmental Protection Agency (EPA) to regulate certain chemicals. Under this Act, the EPA can require companies

[26] www.epa.gov/facts-and-figures-about-materials-waste-and-recycling/national-overview-facts-and-figures-materials#Trends1960-Today (last accessed October 31, 2021).

[27] www.csmonitor.com/1996/0523/052396.feat.books.4.html (last accessed October 31, 2021).

[28] Demeo, Dacron polyester.

to test and report on hazardous chemicals. As a result, some chemicals such as PCBs, which could be found in plastics, and DDT were banned by the EPA.

A period of environmental awareness and activism, however, did not dramatically impact plastic's standing in the marketplace. Manufacturing of the most common kinds of plastic polymers swelled from 2 million metric tons in 1950 to 380 million metric tons in 2015. And as global demand for oil and gas declines, the fossil fuel industry is looking at plastic as an alternative market for fossil fuels. Today, 14 percent of oil and 8 percent of gas is used for the manufacture of petrochemicals, the essential feedstock of plastic production. In September 2018, The American Chemistry Council reported that since 2010, 333 new chemical-manufacturing projects have been announced in the United States, representing more than $200 billion in capital investments, half of which is complete. By May 2019, ExxonMobil, Dow, and companies from France, South Africa, and Saudi Arabia built or announced at least $40 billion in new petrochemical facilities in Texas and Louisiana. Similar plans are underway in the Rustbelt region of the United States, with project funding coming primarily from foreign investors. In November 2017, the China Energy Investment Corp. signed a "memorandum of understanding" with West Virginia for 83.7 billion dollars' worth of plastic and petrochemical projects over the next twenty years. One analyst predicts that the petrochemical industry's focus on producing the raw materials for plastic will have "greater influence on the future of oil demand than cars, trucks and aviation."[29]

Plastic continues to be the popular choice for consumers as well. In the past six months, nearly 80 million Americans have used the equivalent of at least one roll of plastic wrap.[30] Worldwide, a million plastic bottles are bought every minute – a number that will only increase.[31] Unfortunately, only 9 percent of the plastic generated is recycled, 12 percent is incinerated, and 79 percent accumulates in landfills or

[29] Sharon Kelly, Plans to turn America's rust belt into a new plastics belt are bad news for the climate, *The Revelator* (November 2018).

[30] www.nationalgeographic.com/environment/2019/07/story-of-plastic-sticky-problem-of-plastic-wrap/ (last accessed October 31, 2021).

[31] www.theguardian.com/environment/2017/jun/28/a-million-a-minute-worlds-plastic-bottle-binge-as-dangerous-as-climate-change (last accessed October 31, 2021).

in the natural environment.[32] Of that 79 percent, a significant amount of plastic is mismanaged either through littering or inadequate disposal. As described in Chapter 2, mismanaged and incinerated plastic enters our oceans through inland waterways, wastewater outflows, and transport by wind or tides. And because it never fully decomposes, plastic ends up on islands, in ocean trenches, and deposited on mountain tops.

The remaining chapters describe how public concern over the impacts of plastic has intensified and offers solutions that can be used by a variety of stakeholders.

[32] Ronald Geyer, Jenna R. Jambeck, and Kara Lavendar Law, Production, use, and fate of all plastics ever made, *Science Advances* (July 2017).

2 MEASURING PLASTIC

"You Can't Manage What You Don't Measure"

Like the plastic industry, the study of plastic in the environment has evolved. A relatively new area of academic research, recent scientific studies look at the sources and pathways of plastic pollution, the identification of plastic "hotspots," the categorization of plastic pollution, and plastic's impact on habitat and species.[1] One plastic expert noted in 2019 that "[i]n the last five years there has been more published research on plastics than in the previous 50 years."[2] And those who study plastic often have specialties in other areas such as hydrology, ecology, or chemistry. There are no "plastic scientists" yet. Chapter 2 highlights recent studies that have attempted to measure the amount and origins of plastic in our environment.

Quantifying the amount of plastic in the air, on land, and in our oceans is a difficult but important part of solving our plastic problem. This difficulty arises in part because of the numerous types and forms of plastic that exist. Plastic pollution includes discarded Styrofoam containers and fragments of bags, straws, and bottles that float down rivers and into the ocean. Plastic pollution also includes microplastics such as microbeads from cosmetics that are washed down through our drains and plastic resins (nurdles) that spill during manufacturing or transport. Some plastic is dense (e.g., polyester resins) and can quickly sink to the bottom of a riverbed or ocean floor, while other plastic is light (e.g., polypropylene) and is dispersed by water currents.

[1] J. P. G. L. Frais and Roisin Nash, Microplastics: Finding consensus on a definition, *Marine Pollution Bulletin* (January 2019) (last accessed October 16, 2021).

[2] Erica Cirino, Plastic pollution: Could we have solved the problem 50 years ago?, *The Revelator* (March 2019) (available at https://therevelator.org/plastic-pollution-warnings/) (last accessed October 31, 2021).

In addition to having a variety of forms, plastic can also enter the environment in both accidentally and intentionally. In characterizing plastic pollution, researchers consider a variety of factors including the size and origin of the plastic as well as the physical and chemical properties of the plastic.[3] Despite the many forms, compositions, and places in which plastic appears, scientists are attempting to measure plastic in the environment. Quantifying plastic pollution and understanding these classification systems are critical to understanding the problem and is essential to crafting viable and effective solutions.

I PLASTIC DEBRIS BY SIZE

The most common way to characterize plastic is by size. *Meso-* and *macroplastics* are plastic debris with a diameter of 5 mm or more. These plastics are readily visible, making them an obvious concern. Macroplastics including bottles, bags, straws, and larger plastic products, and fragments of these objects are often seen in depictions of plastic pollution. The aesthetic and physical impacts that macroplastics such as fishing nets and plastic bottles have on the environment, are readily apparent, and the harms associated with large plastic debris became a concern in the 1970s and 1980s. The earliest peer-reviewed articles were published in the 1970s and described how plastic packaging was washing up on shore and experienced slow degradation.[4] Other early studies reported that small pieces of plastic were accumulating in seabirds and that plastic was piling up in the ocean in what is now called the Great Pacific Garbage Patch (GPGP).[5]

More recent research has focused on plastics with diameters smaller than 5 mm, called *microplastics*.[6] A search of the word "microplastics"

[3] Frais and Nash, Microplastics.

[4] Cirino, Plastic pollution.

[5] Ibid.

[6] Berit Gewert, Merle M. Plassmann, and Matthew MacLeod, Pathways for degradation of plastic polymers floating in the marine environment, *Environmental Sciences: Processes and Impacts* 17, no. 9 (2015): 1513–21 (available at https://pdfs.semanticscholar.org/1f30/7652fab7d25caf33ff64764d47b594e599a0.pdf) (last accessed October 16, 2021).

in Google Scholar returned only 56 papers published between 1970 and 1980, but over 15,000 papers have been published since 2018 that mention microplastics. Microplastics are further classified into primary and secondary microplastics. Secondary microplastics are created from larger pieces of plastics that break apart during physical and chemical processes that are discussed further in Chapter 3. Primary microplastics, in contrast, are designed to be small. Examples of microplastics include *nurdles* – resin pellets that are melted to make plastic products – and microbeads, tiny, rounded plastic beads that are used in cosmetics.

A third increasingly important category of plastics is *microfibers*. Microfibers are individual plastic filaments that are woven together and found in clothing or other textiles made of polyester, polyester-blend, and acrylic fabrics. They are used in carpet, furniture, fishing nets, and cigarettes. While these products naturally shed microfibers, microfibers also enter the environment through the washing process. The degree to which everyday activities such as washing your clothes discharges plastic in the environment is a newer area of research. But a 2016 study published in *Marine Pollution Bulletin* reported that a 12-pound load of acrylic-fabric laundry could release 700,000 plastic microfibers.[7]

The next section describes studies that evaluate the origins of plastic in our environment and studies that attempt to quantify plastic in our environment.

II PLASTIC DEBRIS BY ORIGIN

The variety of sizes and characteristics of plastic enable it to enter the environment in a number of ways, some of which are unexpected. Multiple studies have calculated that about 80 percent of the plastic that is in the environment comes from land-based sources, while the

[7] Imogen E. Napper and Richard C. Thompson, Release of synthetic microplastic plastic fibres from domestic washing machines: Effects of fabric type and washing, *Marine Pollution Bulletin* 112, nos. 1–2 (November 2016): 39–45 (available at www.sciencedirect.com/science/article/pii/S0025326X16307639?via%3Dihub) (last accessed October 16, 2021).

remainder comes from sources at sea, such as boats and ships. Plastic's lightweight nature allows for easy dispersal by air, which moves plastic waste into neighborhoods, farms, and other terrestrial areas. Most land-based plastic debris, however, ends up at sea, migrating to our oceans through the globe's vast river network, which has been identified as a "major pathway for plastic transport to the sea."[8]

Studies report that plastic makes up 60–80 percent of all marine debris and 90 percent of floating debris is plastic.[9] 5 Gyres, Surfrider Foundation, and other nonprofits focused on plastic debris have published what they call a BAN list: an "analysis and call-to-action to phase out the most harmful plastic products used in California." That list identifies wrappers/containers, bottle/container caps, plastic bags, stirrers and straws, beverage bottles, and containers as the most common contaminants of beaches.[10]

A separate study on the Great Pacific Garbage Patch reported that about 80 percent of the debris in the Great Pacific Garbage Patch comes from land-based activities in North America and Asia, while the remaining 20 percent of the debris comes from boaters, offshore oil rigs, and large cargo ships that dump or spill debris into the water.

Plastic in freshwater systems is also a concern. Plastic debris makes up 80 percent of the debris along the coastline of the Great Lakes in the United States.[11] Plastic that enters the lake follows lake currents and can potentially migrate to other states. A recent study found that

[8] Christian Schmidt, Export of plastic debris by rivers into the sea, *Environmental Science & Technology* (2017) (available at www.gwern.net/docs/economics/2017-schmidt.pdf).

[9] Kenneth R. Weiss, Altered oceans: Part four: Plague of plastic chokes the seas, *LA Times* (August 2, 2006) (available at www.latimes.com/world/la-me-ocean2aug02-story.html) (last accessed October 31, 2021).

[10] Marcus Eriksen, Matt Prindiville, Beverly Thorpe et al., The Plastic Ban List (2016) (available at https://static1.squarespace.com/static/5522e85be4b0b65a7c78ac96/t/581cd66 3d2b857d18a7db3fd/1478284911437/PlasticsBANList2016–11-4.pdf) (last accessed October 31, 2021).

[11] Tony Briscoe, 22 million pounds of plastics enter the Great Lakes each year. Most of the pollution pours into Lake Michigan. *Chicago Tribune* (September 04, 2019) (available at www.chicagotribune.com/news/environment/ct-met-lake-michigan-plastic-pollution-20190904-2xf3qogqv5bpfco2plndapak2q-story.html#:~:text=Nearly%2022%20mil lion%20pounds%20enter,to%20sunlight%20and%20abrasive%20waves) (last accessed October 16, 2021).

22 million pounds of plastic enter the Great Lakes, the largest freshwater system on the planet, annually.[12]

How does all this plastic debris end up in our lakes and oceans? As explained in the next section, plastic can enter the environment (and eventually the ocean) both intentionally and accidentally.

A Intentional Releases

Plastic enters the environment intentionally through littering and illegal dumping. While regulations often prohibit littering, one item – cigarettes – is particularly pervasive in the environment, despite this prohibition. Four-and-a-half trillion cigarettes make their way into the environment each year, making them the most littered item on Earth. Most cigarette butts are not disposed of properly; rather, they are simply tossed aside onto the ground. In addition, cigarette butts cannot be recycled due to filters made of a plastic fiber called cellulose acetate, a polymer that is not recyclable.

During the 1990s, the tobacco industry encouraged proper disposal by selling portable ashtrays and sponsoring ad campaigns, but those efforts were unsuccessful at curbing cigarette litter, and cigarettes continue to persist in our environment. In 2017, the International Coastal Cleanup, an international cleanup composed of over 800,000 volunteers and organized by the Ocean Conservancy, collectively removed more than 20 million pieces of trash from beaches and waterways around the world.[13] At the cleanup, cigarette butts were the number one item of trash found with over 2,412,151 collected, followed by food wrappers, plastic beverage bottles, plastic bottle caps, and plastic grocery bags.

Illegal dumping is another intentional means by which plastic waste enters the environment. Although there are both domestic and international laws that prohibit this behavior, such as the Marine Protection

[12] Ibid.

[13] The Ocean Conservancy Report, *Building a Clean Swell* (2018) (available at https://oceanconservancy.org/wp-content/uploads/2018/07/Building-A-Clean-Swell.pdf) (last accessed October 31, 2021).

Research,[14] and Sanctuaries Act of 1972 and the London Convention of 1975,[15] illegal dumping continues.

Commercial fishing, recreational fishing boats, and cruise lines have long been responsible for marine debris, and both older and recent studies report that a staggering amount of plastic comes from boats. A 1975 study calculated that approximately 135,400 tons of plastic fishing gear and 23,600 tons of synthetic packaging material were dumped into the ocean.[16] Another study from 1982 found that merchant ships dumped 639,000 plastic containers into the ocean each day.[17] A UNESCO study from 1994, found that approximately 52 percent of all waste dumped in US waters comes from recreational fishing boats and cruise lines.[18]

Carnival Cruise Line made headlines in 2019 when it was ordered to pay $20 million in criminal penalties for illegally dumping plastic waste into the ocean. This is not the first violation for the Carnival Corporation and its Princess subsidiary. In 2016, the popular cruise company was fined $40 million, an amount the Department of Justice called "the largest-ever criminal penalty involving deliberate vessel pollution."[19] As part of the 2019 order, the company must change how it uses and disposes of plastic and other nonfood waste, conduct annual audits, and restructure its corporate compliance office.[20]

Companies can also engage in illegal dumping when they exceed the discharge amounts allowed by their state and federal permits. For example, Formosa Plastics, a Texas-based petrochemical company, violated its environmental permits for years, dumping millions of tiny plastic pellets – known as nurdles – into Lavaca Bay in Texas. Nurdles were also illegally released into the coastal waters of Warrnambool, Australia in 2017, after being illegally dumped into a nearby sewage

[14] Discussed further in Chapter 4.

[15] Discussed further in Chapter 5.

[16] Jose G. B. Derraik, The pollution of the marine environment by plastic debris: A review, *Marine Pollution Bulletin* (2002).

[17] Ibid.

[18] Ibid.

[19] Merrit Kennedy and Greg Allen, Carnival cruise lines hit with $20 million penalty for environmental crimes, *NPR* (June 4, 2019).

[20] Becky Pritchard, Cruise ship company pleads guilty to illegal dumping charges, *Mount Desert Islander* (June 13, 2019).

treatment plant. As explained in the next section, nurdle pollution is particularly challenging because nurdles can often enter the environment unbeknownst to producers and manufacturers, and once in the environment, their small size makes removal economically and ecologically unfeasible.

B Unintentional Releases

The unintentional introduction of plastic into the environment can occur through obvious means such as unsecured landfills and accidental spills, but scientists are continuing to discover the many ways plastic "innocently" enters our environment through everyday activities such as showering and laundry.

1 Unsecured Landfills and Inadequate Infrastructure The release of plastic into the environment is often the result of inadequate waste disposal systems. In the United States, plastics are a subset of municipal solid waste (MSW) – waste that is generated by residential, commercial, and institutional (e.g., schools, government offices) sectors.[21] Municipal solid waste is what most people think of as garbage – the discarded stuff found at the curb each week: food scraps, yard clippings, newspapers, junk mail, chairs, lamps, pens, toys, mattresses, diapers, socks, and of course plastic containers, packaging, and products such as milk cartons, plastic bags, and toothbrushes. In 2015, MSW consisted of plastics (13.1 percent), paper (25.9 percent), food waste (15 percent), and metal (9 percent).[22] In the United States, municipal solid waste is distinguished from industrial, hazardous, and construction wastes, which have different handling and disposal rules.

Some municipal solid waste is diverted for recycling or composting. For example, in the United States, 34.7 percent of MSW was

[21] David K. A. Barnes, Francois Galgani, Richard C. Thompson, and Morton Barlaz, Accumulation and fragmentation of plastic debris in global environments, *Philosophical Transactions, The Royal Society of London B Biological Sciences* (2009). In some countries, MSW includes construction and demolition waste, while in others it only includes household waste.

[22] Center for Sustainable Systems, University of Michigan. 2020. "Municipal Solid Waste Factsheet." Pub. No. CSS04–15.

recovered for recycling or composting.[23] Some municipal solid waste is incinerated or burned, in some cases being converted to energy. Unfortunately, however, over the past twenty years, rates of recycling and of burning waste (with its conversion to energy) have not increased dramatically. Recycling, for example, has hovered around 9 percent since 2000. Furthermore, the act of recycling or burning waste is not without environmental costs. Recycling requires resources such as electricity and water, while burning waste can generate harmful air pollutants that contribute to climate change, smog, acidification, asthma, and heart damage.[24] (Recycling is discussed further in Chapter 9).

In developed countries, most municipal solid waste ends up in secure landfills. In 2015, 52.5 percent of MSW generated in the United States was disposed of in 1,738 landfills. Of this amount, 30 percent was packaging and containers.[25] While poor management of plastics in landfills can lead to plastic pollution, the absence of waste management facilities worldwide is a bigger concern. The United Nations Environmental Programme's Global Waste Management Outlook report from 2015 estimates that around 2 billion people worldwide still lack access to "solid waste collection," while 3 billion people lack access to "controlled waste disposal services."[26]

A 2015 study found that the amount of plastic debris released into the environment by a given country is dependent on coastal population size and the quality of the country's waste management systems. A subsequent study found that 90 percent of the global input of plastic into the ocean comes from ten river systems – two in Africa and eight in Asia – where hundreds of millions of people live.[27] As a result, countries in Asia are often cited as the source of plastic debris in our oceans. In July 2019, then-EPA Administrator Andrew Wheeler declared that 60 percent of all marine litter comes from six Asian countries. But, as

[23] Ibid.

[24] Ibid.

[25] Ibid.

[26] United Nations Environmental Program and International Solid Waste Association, Global waste management outcome (2015) (available at www.uncclearn.org/sites/default/files/inventory/unep23092015.pdf) (last accessed October 31, 2021).

[27] Schmidt et al., Export of plastic debris by rivers into the sea.

explained later, this is not the complete picture. A significant amount of the marine litter in these Asian and African countries originated in the United States, where the practice has been to ship over half of its MSW to these countries. Because of the recipient countries' inadequate waste management systems, waste from the United States ends up in the ocean through these ten African and Asian river systems.

Plastic that is collected but not disposed of in a landfill is often burned. In the poorest countries, about 93 percent of waste is burned or discarded in roads, open land, or waterways.[28] The health and environmental implications of this kind of disposal are discussed in Chapter 3.

2 Accidental Spills While most (80 percent) ocean plastic originates on land, accidental spills at sea also contribute to plastic pollution. As an illustrative example, in 1992 a shipping crate with over 28,000 bath toys fell overboard while in transit from Hong Kong to the United States. Almost two decades later, in 2011, rubber ducks allegedly from the lost crate were washing ashore in Hawaii, Alaska, and Canada, as per a 2011 article in the *Independent*.[29] This story is not unique. In March 2019, the *New York Times* published an article on the mystery of "[b]right orange novelty phones shaped like . . . Garfield" that kept washing up on the rocky Atlantic shoreline of Brittany, France.[30] The mystery was solved earlier in the month when the shipping container that was lost at sea in the early 1980s was discovered in a sea cave.[31] This same article reports that between 2006 and 2016, on average 1,500 shipping containers were lost each year.[32] Many, though not all, contain plastic.

[28] Tearfund Report, No time to waste (2019) (available at https://opendocs.ids.ac.uk/opendocs/bitstream/handle/20.500.12413/14490/J32121_No_time_to_waste_web.pdf?sequence=1&isAllowed=y) (last accessed October 31, 2021).

[29] Guy Adams, Lost at sea: On the trail of Moby Dick, *The Independent* (February 2011) (available at www.independent.co.uk/environment/nature/lost-at-sea-on-the-trail-of-moby-duck-2226788.html) (last accessed October 31, 2021).

[30] Palko Karasz, Solving the mystery if a sleepy, bright orange coastline hazard, *The New York Times* (March 30, 2019), A4.

[31] Ibid.

[32] Ibid.

Nurdles are a more likely source of plastic pollution in the ocean; in fact, it is estimated that these plastic pellets are the second-largest direct source of microplastic pollution in the ocean by weight. One study of the Tokyo Bay determined that plastic pellets made up 80–85 percent of the seabed debris.[33]

Nurdle spills happen when these tiny pellets undergo transport, storage, loading, and cleaning, and it is estimated that over 250,000 tons of nurdles enter the ocean annually. Billions and billions of nurdles are shipped around the globe by cargo ships. Nurdles' small size makes them almost impossible to clean up when they enter the ocean. In 2017, 49 tons of nurdles went overboard off the coast of South Africa. A few days later, nurdles were washing up over thousands of kilometers of coastline. More than four months later, only 11 tons (or 23 percent) had been recovered, with experts predicting that it will be several years before all the nurdles are recovered.[34]

Nurdle accumulation is of concern in the Gulf Coast of Mexico on the shores of Texas because of the high concentration of pellet producing companies and the currents that flow in the Gulf. One study showed that cumulation rates of plastic pollution were ten times higher in Texas than other Gulf Coast states sampled over a year-and-a-half period.[35] Some residents successfully sued Formosa Plastics, a known nurdle polluter, for violating state and federal permits.[36]

3 Bathing and Washing Clothes Personal activities such as bathing and washing clothes also contribute to microscopic plastics that enter our environment. Before a federal ban in 2017, some soaps and facial scrubs contained microbeads that could be rinsed down the drain and into waterways. Although microbeads have been removed from most

[33] H. Kanehiro, T. Tokai, and K. Matuda, Marine litter composition and distribution on the sea-bed of Tokyo Bay. *Fisheries Engineering* 31 (1995): 195–9.

[34] https://news.sky.com/story/south-africas-ecological-nightmare-after-plastic-pellets-spill-11264554 (last accessed October 31, 2021).

[35] Julissa Trevino, The relentless (and growing) problem of plastic 'nurdle' pollution, *Undark* (July 3, 2019) (available at https://undark.org/2019/07/03/nurdle-plastic-pollution/) (last accessed October 31, 2021).

[36] The outcome of this lawsuit is discussed more in Part II.

products, the microbeads that escaped into the environment are still there. Microfibers are also a growing concern. Most clothing today is made of synthetic fibers that are released because of the mechanical and chemical stresses the fabric undergoes while in a washing machine. The microfibers can detach from the fabric, and because of their size, pass through wastewater treatment plants and flow into the oceans. A 2021 study of seventy-one seawater stations across the European and North American Artic found that polyester comprised 73 percent of total synthetic fibers and noted the "pervasive spread of synthetic fibers throughout the waters of the Arctic Ocean."[37]

C Conclusion

Plastic comes in a variety of sizes and new sources and locations of plastic pollution are continuously being discovered. As a result, outcomes of studies quantifying the amount of plastic in our environment are regularly superseded by subsequent studies. Below are two recent and influential studies that provide early markers in quantifying plastic waste, and as a result, have been especially helpful in educating the public about the magnitude of our plastic problem.

III QUANTIFYING PLASTIC DEBRIS

One widely cited study, published in 2015 in *Science*, quantified for the first time the amount of plastic waste making its way from land to ocean.[38] In the study, a team of engineers from the University of Georgia used data on solid waste, population density, and economic status to calculate the mass of plastic waste entering the ocean. The

[37] Peter Ross, Stephen Chastain, Ekaterina Vassilenko et al., Pervasive distribution of polyester fibres in the Arctic Ocean is driven by Atlantic inputs, *Nature Communications* (2021) (available at www.nature.com/articles/s41467-020-20347-1) (last accessed October 31, 2021).

[38] Jenna R. Jambeck, Plastic waste inputs from land into the ocean, *Science* (February 2015) (available at https://science.sciencemag.org/content/347/6223/768); *see also* www.nytimes.com/2015/02/13/science/earth/plastic-ocean-waste-levels-going-up-study-says.html (last accessed October 31, 2021).

authors note that while "[p]lastic debris in the marine environment is widely documented . . . the quantity of plastic entering the ocean from waste generated on land is unknown."[39] Looking at 2010 data from 192 countries, the scientists (1) estimated the mass of plastic waste entering the ocean from each country; (2) used population growth data to project the increase in mass to 2025; and (3) predicted growth in the percentage of waste that is plastic. They concluded that 275 million metric tons of plastic waste was generated from these countries in 2010, with 4.8 to 12.7 million metric tons entering the ocean.

This seminal study has been widely discussed, making its way into the *Washington Post*, *New York Times*, and other news outlets. In an interview with NPR, lead researcher Jenna Jambeck explained the importance of data-keeping in shaping public opinion about this issue, and discussed an app she developed for citizen-scientists to track plastic pollution called the Marine Debris Tracker.[40] In 2016, Professor Jambeck testified before Congress about plastic pollution, and is currently co-leading an all-female National Geographic Expedition to study plastic pollution in one of the world's most iconic (and polluted) waterways – the Ganges River – to better understand and document how plastic waste travels form source to sea. Professor Jambeck followed up her 2010 study with a 2016 study which concluded that the United States generates around 42 metric tons of plastic waste each year, and that the amount entering the costal environment in 2016 was five times larger than what was estimated in 2010.[41]

Another study that garnered significant attention measured garbage in the Great Pacific Garbage Patch. The earth houses five large gyres, whirlpool-like rotating ocean currents: one in the Indian Ocean, two in the Atlantic Ocean, and two in the Pacific Ocean. Each gyre contains some garbage, but the largest of the gyre garbage patches is the Great

[39] Jambeck, Plastic waste inputs from land into the ocean.

[40] Christopher Joyce, We're drowning in plastic trash. Jenna Jambeck wants to save us, *NPR* (July 24, 2018).

[41] Kara Lavendar Law, Natalia Starr, Theodore R. Siegler et al., The United States' contribution of plastic waste to land and ocean, *Science Advances* (2020) (available at https://advances.sciencemag.org/content/6/44/eabd0288) (last accessed October 31, 2021).

Pacific Garbage Patch. Located between California and Hawaii, the Great Pacific Garbage Patch is larger than Texas. Although the GPGP was first discovered in 1997, it is believed to have existed at least twenty years prior to its discovery.

A March 2018 study in *Scientific Reports* evaluated the load and composition of buoyant ocean plastics inside the GPGP.[42] The study found that in 2015, the GPGP consisted of nearly 2 trillion pieces of plastic, weighing nearly 80,000 metric tons. Microplastics accounted for 94 percent of the estimated 1.8 trillion pieces of plastics analyzed. However, microplastics only accounted for only 8 percent of the total mass. Discarded fishing nets, weighing as much as 2 tons, accounted for over half of the plastic mass in the gyre. This is consistent with an earlier study that found that 70 percent, by weight, of floating macroplastic debris in the open ocean is fishing related.[43]

The composition of the plastic was also analyzed, and polyethylene (PE) and polypropylene (PP) pieces dominated the samples. Plastic objects and fragments that were identifiable included: containers, bottles, lids, bottle caps, packaging straps, eel trap cones, oyster spacers, ropes, and fishing nets. Some fragments included information about the age and geographical origin of the fragment. Fifty items had identifiable production dates: one in 1977, seven in the 1980s, seventeen in the 1990s, twenty-four in the 2000s, and one from 2010. Around 386 objects had recognizable words or sentences written on them. In total, nine different languages were found.

Unlike Professor Jambeck, the lead researcher of the GPGP study published in *Nature* is not a scholar, but a twenty-something Dutch entrepreneur named Boyan Slat, whose inventions for removing plastic from the Garbage Patch are discussed in Chapter 9. But like Professor Jambeck's article in *Science*, Slat's article in *Nature* made its rounds in the popular press, appearing in the *Washington Post*, NPR, *National Geographic*, and *Teen Vogue*.

[42] L. Lebreton, B. Slat, F. Ferrari et al., Evidence that the Great Pacific Garbage Patch is rapidly accumulating plastic, *Scientific Reports* (March 22, 2018).

[43] M. Eriksen, Laurent C. M. Lebreton, Henry S. Carson et al., Plastic pollution in the world's oceans: More than 5 trillion plastic pieces weighing over 250,000 tons afloat at sea. *Plos One* (2014).

These oft-cited studies are just the tip of the iceberg in terms of providing what needs to be known to understand the amount of plastic in our environment. In a recent *New Yorker* article, Judith Enck, a senior official at the Environmental Protection Agency under President Obama, stated: "Where we are on plastics is where we were fifteen years ago on climate change. We're just beginning to get the picture."[44]

Chapter 3 describes the impacts of plastic in our environment.

[44] Carolyn Korman, A grand plan to clean the Great Pacific Garbage Patch, *The New Yorker* (January 28, 2019) (available at www.newyorker.com/magazine/2019/02/04/a-grand-plan-to-clean-the-great-pacific-garbage-patch) (last accessed October 31, 2021).

3 PLASTIC AS A POLLUTANT

A Revolutionary Material Becomes a Global Threat

Plastic's aesthetic harm – to beaches, waterways, and roadsides, for example – is apparent. Less apparent – and less studied – is the harm that results from plastic's persistence in our environment. Because the mass-production of plastic has only been around for sixty years or so, no one really knows how long it will remain in the environment. That said, there is agreement that plastic has the potential to persist for a very long time in the environment. One study found, for example, that PET-plastic bottles, while recyclable, would take 400 years to naturally decompose. Most plastics, however, are not biodegradable, and one study estimates that 60 percent of the 8,300 million metric tons (Mt) of virgin plastics that have been produced to date are on the planet somewhere.[1]

Coastal area residents feel like they are drowning in plastic, while marine organisms are actually drowning in plastic. Nearly 90 percent of floating marine litter is plastic – polyethylene and polypropylene, Styrofoam, nylon, and saran.[2] Birds, fish, and mammals can become entangled in and choke on plastic debris. As plastic slowly break down, smaller toxic pieces leach into the soil, water, and air. These tiny pieces of plastic harm aquatic ecosystems, damage coral reefs, and contaminate water. When consumed by fish and animals, microplastics can enter the human food chain. One study found that swallowing fourteen pieces of plastic significantly increases the risk of death in turtles, while

[1] Roland Geyer, Jenna R. Jambeck, and Kara Lavendar Law, Production, use, and fate of all plastics ever made, *Science Advances* 3 (July 2017) (available at https://advances.sciencemag.org/content/3/7/e1700782) (last accessed October 16, 2021).

[2] United Nations, Marine litter: An analytical overview, *Web* (February 14, 2011) (available at https://wedocs.unep.org/bitstream/handle/20.500.11822/8348/-Marine%20Litter%2c%20an%20analytical%20overview-20053634.pdf?sequence=3&isAllowed=y) (last accessed October 31, 2021).

another found that by the year 2050, 99 percent of all seabirds will have ingested plastic. Humans are not immune to plastic's touch. Microplastics have been found in table salt and human stools. More recently, plastic has been tied to climate change. A 2019 study published in *Nature Climate Change* found that if plastic production continues at its current rate, the greenhouse gas emissions from plastics would reach 15 percent of the total carbon emissions by 2050.[3]

These visible and invisible harms are the focus of Chapter 3.

I THE PLASTIC DEGRADATION PROCESS AS A POTENTIAL CHEMICAL HAZARD

If plastic is not recovered from the environment, it will remain there for some time – albeit in a different form. Plastic polymers are extremely stable and durable, making them resistant to complete degradation. Some estimates predict that certain plastics will persist in the environment for 400 years. A 2006 article in the *Los Angeles Times* described an albatross that had eaten a piece of plastic with WWII markings.[4] Elsewhere, scientists explained that the "[d]urability of plastic ensures that wherever it is, it does not 'go-away.'"[5]

Nevertheless, to say that plastic is not biodegradable is somewhat of a misstatement. Like most things, plastic will eventually break down if exposed to the natural elements – wind, water, sun. Sunlight, oxidants, and physical stress are all sources of energy that gradually weaken the polymer bonds. More specifically, degradation occurs by four processes: photodegradation, thermooxidative degradation,

[3] Jiajia Zheng and Sangwon Suh, Strategies to reduce the global carbon footprint of plastics, *Nature Climate Change* (April 2019) (available at www.nature.com/articles/s41558-019-0459-z) (last accessed October 31, 2021).

[4] Kenneth R. Weiss, Altered oceans: Part four: Plague of plastic chokes the seas, *LA Times* (August 2, 2006) (available at www.latimes.com/world/la-me-ocean2aug02-story.html) (last accessed October 31, 2021).

[5] David K. A. Barnes, Francois Galgani, Richard C. Thompson, and Morton Barlaz, Accumulation and fragmentation of plastic debris in global environments, *Philosophical Transactions, The Royal Society of London B Biological Sciences* (2009) (available at www.ncbi.nlm.nih.gov/pmc/articles/PMC2873009/) (last accessed October 31, 2021).

hydrolytic degradation, and biodegradation by microorganisms.[6] *Photodegradation* is the process by which the energy from the sun's UV rays "initiate[s] the incorporation of oxygen atoms into the polymer" causing the plastic to become brittle and to gradually break down into smaller and smaller pieces.[7] In *thermooxidative degradation*, heat and oxygen cause the physical properties of plastic to change. *Hydrolytic degradation* is degradation by water, with wave action and river and ocean currents whittling away at plastic. *Biodegradation* by microorganisms occurs when polymers of plastic are small enough to be metabolized by microorganisms.[8] The speed of these processes is often reduced in sea water where the temperatures are cooler and there is less oxygen available.[9]

The degree to which plastic will break down also depends on the polymers of which it is made. Polymers vary depending on the chemical composition, molecular weight, crosslink density, morphology (i.e., degree of crystallinity), and concentration of impurities, all of which impact the degradation process.

Chemical additives are frequently incorporated during the production process to improve plastic characteristics such as durability or color. Some additives are used to make the plastic more stable and to forestall degradation. While other additives are not strongly bonded to the plastic and, therefore, can leach into the environment as the plastic degrades. These additives include catalysts, solvents, plasticizers, metals, dyes, flame-retardants, UV stabilizers, antioxidants, and antimicrobials.[10] For example, when nylon experiences thermal degradation, "carbon monoxide, ammonia, aliphatic amines, ketones, nitriles, and hydrogen cyanide, which may be flammable, toxic and/or

[6] Hayden K. Webb, Plastic degradation and its environmental implications with special reference to poly(ethylene terephthalate), *Polymers* (2013) (available at www.mdpi.com/2073-4360/5/1/1) (last accessed October 31, 2021).

[7] Ibid.

[8] Ibid.

[9] Ibid.

[10] J. N. Hahladakis, Costas A. Velis, Roland Weber, Eleni Iacovidou, and Phil Purnell, An overview of chemical additives present in plastics: Migration, release, fate and environmental impact during their use, disposal and recycling, *Journal of Hazardous Materials* 344 (2018): 179–99.

irritating" may be released.[11] In addition to the additive or colorant used, the amount and rate of leaching depend on temperature, time of exposure, and other immediate environmental factors.

In addition to leaching chemicals, plastics, particularly microplastics, can absorb (or sorb) persistent organic pollutants (POPs) that are already in the environment. Well-known POPs include DDT, PCBs, and dioxins. As their name suggests, POPs can persist for long periods in the environment and their concentration increases as they move through the food chain. A 2017 study that took plastic samples from the North Pacific Subtropical Gyre found that 84 percent of the samples had at least one chemical with concentrations exceeding the threshold effect levels. As a result, the authors conclude that plastics in this region "may pose a chemical risk to organisms that ingest them."[12] Another study found that in 2015, 190 tons of chemical additives entered the ocean from seven common plastic debris items: bottles, bottle caps, expanded polystyrene (EPS) containers, cutlery, grocery bags, food wrappers, and straws or stirrers.[13]

Plastic in the environment is an aesthetic injury that also causes harm to whales, seals, and seabirds. Research shows that plastic breaks down through wind, wave, and sun action, but that this process often lasts centuries. Research also shows that POPs sorb to plastic and chemical additives leached from plastic. What is less clear are the chemical harms posed by these processes. Some have declared the ocean toxic soup,[14] while others call plastic a potential chemical hazard[15] or

[11] http://skipper.physics.sunysb.edu/HBD/MSDS/NylonMSDS.pdf

[12] Qiqing Chen, Julia Reisser, Serena Cunsolo et al., Pollutants in plastics within the North Pacific Subtropical Gyre, *Environmental Science and Technology* (2017) (available at https://pubs.acs.org/doi/10.1021/acs.est.7b04682) (last accessed October 31, 2021).

[13] Hannah L. De Frond, Estimating the mass of chemicals associated with ocean plastic pollution to inform mitigation efforts, *Integrated Environmental Assessment and Management* (March 2019) (available at https://setac.onlinelibrary.wiley.com/doi/pdf/10.1002/ieam.4147) (last accessed October 31, 2021).

[14] Jazmine Mejia-Muñoz, The Great Pacific Garbage Patch is a toxic soup, *Science* (2019) (available at www.kqed.org/science/1946988/a-toxic-soup-the-great-pacific-garbage-patch) (last accessed October 31, 2021).

[15] Berit Gewert, Merle M. Plassmann, and Matthew MacLeod, Pathways for degradation of plastic polymers floating in the marine environment, *Environmental Sciences: Processes and Impacts* (2015). https://pdfs.semanticscholar.org/1f30/7652fab7d25caf33ff64764d47b594e599a0.pdf (last accessed October 31, 2021).

"pollutant."[16] But some still question whether the amount of chemicals released is significant considering the vast size of the ocean.[17] The known and potential harms to sea, land, and humans, are explored next.

II HARM TO SEA AND LAND

There are many ways plastic impacts the environment. Plastic debris can become the new habitat for a species, such as a plastic cap becoming the shell for a hermit crab. Plastic debris can also transport species through "rafting" to new environments creating an invasive species. Perhaps most alarming, however, are the harms to fish, birds, and mammals from entanglement, ingestion,[18] and the resulting harm to the food web, and therefore, us.

A Entanglement and Ingestion

Most readers have seen an image of a bird or seal caught in a piece of plastic. Entanglement of marine life in plastic is well-documented and has been associated with plastic pollution since the 1970s and 1980s when the first International Coastal Cleanup was held and *A Citizen's Guide to Plastics in the Ocean: More Than a Litter Problem* was published. Seals, sea turtles, albatrosses, and other animals at the top of the food chain are easy victims to stray fishing nets and the plastic rings that hold six-pack drinks together. These encounters with plastic can gradually kill larger animals as their mobility is impacted. Decreased mobility, in turn, makes it harder for species to capture food, escape prey, migrate, and reproduce.

[16] J. L. Lavers, L. Dicks, M. R. Dicks, and A. Finger, Significant plastic accumulation on the Cocos (Keeling) Islands, Australia, *Scientific Reports* (May 2019) (available at www.nature.com/articles/s41598-019-43375-4.pdf) (last accessed October 31, 2021).

[17] Hadley Leggett, Toxic soup: Plastics could be leaching chemicals into ocean, *Wired* (August 2009) (available at www.wired.com/2009/08/plasticoceans/) (last accessed October 31, 2021).

[18] C. Wilcox, Threat of plastic pollution to seabirds is global, pervasive, and increasing, *Environmental Science* (2015) (available at https://pdfs.semanticscholar.org/810f/aa730722495ad9b745578f82c0f6f72b2db3.pdf?_ga=2.158136506.1450254424.1567178737-1156281880.1566583859) (last accessed October 31, 2021).

1 Documented Harms Ingestion of plastic is often linked to entanglement. A study published in 2015 compared data from 1997 and found the total number of marine species with documented records of either entanglement and/or ingestion had doubled with an increase from 267 species in 1997 to 557 species in 2014. The documented impact for marine mammals increased from 43 to 66 percent of species (now 81 of 123 species) and for seabirds from 44 to 50 percent of species (now 203 of 406 species).[19] Plastic ingestion has been reported in all species of marine turtle.[20] Death can occur quickly if vital organs are impaled or intestines are blocked, but death can also be gradual. Like entanglement, ingestion of plastic can have numerous secondary impacts including the ability of organisms to digest food and feel hungry.[21] "An estimated one million seabirds choke on or get tangled in plastic nets or other debris every year. About 100,000 seals, sea lions, whales, dolphins, other marine mammals, and sea turtles suffer the same fate."[22]

The popular press has reported extensively on the deaths associated with plastic ingestion. In 2018, at least three whale deaths were tied to plastic pollution. In February 2018, a sperm whale with 64 pounds of plastic in its stomach washed up on the shores of Spain. In May, a pilot whale discovered in a Thai canal near the Malaysian border had 17 pounds of plastic, including 80 plastic bags, in its stomach. In November, a dead sperm whale washed up on the shores of Indonesia with 13 pounds of plastic in its stomach, including 115 drinking cups, 4 plastic bottles, 25 plastic bags, and 2 flip-flops.

In September 2019, an orphaned dugong, a marine mammal related to the manatee, died because of plastic ingestion. The dugong had received widespread attention due to her unusual attachment to

[19] Suzanne Kuhn, Elisa L. Bravo Rebolledo, and Jan A. van Franeker, Deleterious effects of litter on marine life. In: M. Bergmann, L. Gutow, and M. Klages (eds.), *Marine Anthropogenic Litter* (Springer, Cham, 2015) (available at https://link.springer.com/chapter/10.1007/978-3-319-16510-3_4#citeas) (last accessed October 31, 2021).

[20] Emily M. Duncan, Jessica A. Arrowsmith, Charlotte E. Bain et al., Diet-related selectivity of macroplastic ingestion in green turtles (Chelonia mydas) in the eastern Mediterranean, *Scientific Reports* (2019) (available at www.nature.com/articles/s41598-019-48086-4) (last accessed October 31, 2021).

[21] Ibid.

[22] Weiss, Altered oceans: Part four.

humans. Videos posted on social media showed the dugong snuggling with her caretakers and quickly went viral. The autopsy of this animal, which was performed by Thailand's Department of National Parks, Wildlife and Plant Conservation, revealed tiny plastic pieces in the animal's intestines.

Seabirds are also frequent victims of plastic pollution. Photographer Chris Jordan first traveled to the Midway Atoll, home to the largest Layan albatross (*Diomedea immutabilis*) colony in the world, in 2009 to document the toll plastic is taking on the albatross population. Photographs in his exhibit, which opened in 2017, document brightly colored pieces of plastics such as bottle caps, lighters, and plastic fragments in the exposed bellies of decaying albatross corpses. Plastic is often included in the regurgitated matter the adult albatrosses feed their chicks. Chicks, however, cannot regurgitate plastic, which then accumulates in the chicks' bellies, becoming a significant source of chick mortality. One study of albatross chicks in Hawaii found that 90 percent of the chicks had plastic debris of some kind in the GI tract.[23] Chris Jordan's images, which serve as the basis for the 2018 film *The Albatross*, illustrate the casualties associated with plastic debris.

The albatross is not alone. A 2015 study found that over 90 percent of seabirds have plastic in their stomachs.[24] This same study found that "seabird ingestion rates scale with plastic exposure" – that is, the more plastic that is introduced into the ocean, the more plastic is ingested. Plastics ingestion is increasing in seabirds, and it is expected that by 2050, 99 percent of all seabirds will have ingested plastic.[25] Plastic pieces can puncture a bird's stomach, creating life-threatening injuries. Other times, the birds die of dehydration, starvation, or poisonous toxicity.

Although marine life is often the focus of plastic-related deaths, land animals also ingest plastic. In summer 2019, a Cape buffalo died

[23] D. Michael Fry, Stewart I. Fefer, and Louis Sileo, Ingestion of plastic debris by Laysan Albatrosses and Wedge-tailed Shearwaters in the Hawaiian Islands, *Marine Pollution Bulletin* (June 1987) (available at www.sciencedirect.com/science/article/abs/pii/S0025326X8780022X) (last accessed October 31, 2021).

[24] Wilcox, Threat of plastic pollution to seabirds is global, pervasive, and increasing.

[25] Ibid.

at the National Zoological Park in Delhi, India, after eating a plastic bag that was believed to be discarded by a zoo visitor. Ranchers in Texas supported local bans on plastic bags (which were eventually overturned by the State Supreme Court) because of the harm they cause to livestock. And scientists are now studying the impact of plastic bags on cattle health.

Microplastics have the potential to cause harm, though the studies involving microplastic are fewer and less certain. One study that evaluated the impact of ingested microplastics on beach hoppers (*Platorchestia smithi*) (an amphipod) found that exposure to microplastics can affect beach hopper survival. Individuals also displayed a reduced jump height and an increase in weight.[26] Laboratory studies have shown exposure to microplastics has a number of adverse impacts on the beach hoppers including mortality, reduced feeding rate, body mass, and metabolic rate, reduced allocation of energy for growth, decreased predatory performance, changed behavioral response and reduced swimming performance, decreased fertilization, and larval abnormalities.[27]

This research suggests that in areas with high concentrations of plastic debris (e.g., heavily industrialized and urbanized areas and oceanic gyres), populations may be negatively affected. Scientists agree, however, that more research on the long-term effects of microplastic exposure is needed.[28]

2 ***Drivers*** While there are numerous instances of plastic ingestion resulting in harm, the specific drivers behind plastic ingestion are still poorly understood. Studies have shown that the ingestion of plastic

[26] Louise Tosetto, Microplastics on beaches: Ingestion and behavioural consequences for beachhoppers, *Marine Biology* (2016) (available at https://link.springer.com/article/10.1007/s00227–016-2973-0) (last accessed October 31, 2021).

[27] Luís Gabriel Antão Barboza, A. Dick Vethaak, Beatriz R. B. O. Lavorante, Anne-Katrine Lundebye, and Lúcia Guilhermino, Marine microplastic debris: An emerging issue for food security, food safety and human health, *Marine Pollution Bulletin* (August 2018) (available at www.sciencedirect.com/science/article/pii/S0025326X1830376X) (last accessed October 31, 2021).

[28] Ibid.

varies among marine life and such differences can be based on diet and foraging strategies as well as the size of the plastic.

Some organisms such as turtles, for example, are "actively selecting" to ingest plastic because it resembles a food source.[29] As "visual feeders" sea turtles do not discriminate among colors and shapes.[30] To Leatherback turtles (*Dermochelys coriacea*), plastic bags resemble their jellyfish prey. Loggerhead sea turtles (*Caretta caretta*) are thought to ingest plastic bottle lids because their round shape and presence near the surface resemble organisms that are normally preyed upon.[31]

Turtles are not the only organism that ingest plastic based on appearance. Planktivores – marine organisms that forage on plankton – are more likely to confuse plastic pellets with their prey than piscivores – marine organisms that feed on fish.[32] As a result, planktivores have a higher incidence of ingested plastics.

While some organisms are actively selecting plastic because it looks like a meal, for other organisms, ingestion is unintentional. Many seabirds do not discriminate between their prey and colored pieces of plastic. The albatross, for example, feeds on crustaceans that swarm near the surface of the ocean. These birds fly overhead and skim the water with their beaks open, indiscriminately scooping up everything in their path – food and plastic.

Seabirds might also be responding to the smell of plastic breaking down. Dimethyl sulfide (DMS) is produced by the enzymatic break down of marine phytoplankton as they are being consumed by zooplankton. Birds and other marine organisms have evolved to respond to the odor and use it as a cue to locate prey. But a similar smell to DMS is also produced when certain plastics break down. As a result, species that have adapted to locate prey by tracking DMS might be especially predisposed to consume plastic debris.

Size also factors into the ingestion of plastic. Unlike plastic bags and bottle caps (i.e., macroplastics), microplastics are ingested by

[29] Duncan et al., Diet-related selectivity of macroplastic ingestion in green turtles (Chelonia mydas) in the eastern Mediterranean.

[30] Ibid.

[31] Ibid.

[32] Suzanne Kuhn et al., Deleterious effects of litter on marine life.

organisms at all levels of the food chain. Because these plastic particles are similar in size to the food of many marine organisms and because they appear at all depths within the ocean, they can easily be ingested by smaller marine organisms such as zooplankton, crabs, and shellfish. Ingestion of microplastics through passive water filtration and deposit-feeding activity has also been observed.[33]

B Ecosystem Impacts

Plastic ingestion is a growing concern because chemicals that are ingested can be absorbed and distributed through an organism's circulatory system. The chemicals can then enter different tissues and cells and can potentially cause several types of adverse effect.[34]

In addition, chemicals can be passed onto a predator up the food chain. A recent study found microfibers in all of the amphipods collected from six ocean trenches in the Pacific Rim.[35] This discovery is of concern because the amphipods become vectors for introducing plastic into the food web. Lab and field studies have demonstrated the trophic transfer of microplastics in amphipods such as beach hoppers, as well as zooplankton, gobies and other ray-finned fish, mussels, and crabs.[36] These organisms are prey for larger fish which in turn become prey for larger predators, including fish that humans consume.

As the plastic moves through the food web, chemicals bioaccumulate along the way. Numerous studies have revealed that the intestines of these larger predators are lined with microfibers.[37] As a result, the scientific community agrees that plastics threaten aquatic

[33] Barboza et al., Marine microplastic debris.

[34] Ibid.

[35] A. J. Jamieson, L. S. R. Brooks, W. D. K. Reid et al., Microplastics and synthetic particles ingested by deep-sea amphipods in six of the deepest marine ecosystems on Earth, *Royal Society Open Science* (2019) (available at https://royalsocietypublishing.org/doi/pdf/10.1098/rsos.180667) (last accessed October 31, 2021).

[36] Inneke Hantoro, Ansje J. Löhr, Frank G. A. J. Van Belleghem, Budi Widianarko, and Ad M. J. Ragas, Microplastics in coastal areas and seafood: Implications for food safety, *Food Additives & Contaminants: Part A*, 36, no. 5 (2019): 674–711 (available at www.tandfonline.com/doi/pdf/10.1080/19440049.2019.1585581?needAccess=true& and X) (last accessed October 31, 2021).

[37] www.nationalgeographic.com/environment/2019/02/deep-sea-creatures-mariana-trench-eat-plastic/

food webs because they are ingested at multiple trophic levels and may bioaccumulate.

In addition to causing harmful bioaccumulation, plastic might also impact other natural processes such as photosynthesis, the process by which plants convert carbon dioxide and water into carbohydrates – food – using sun energy. A recent study looked at how plastic affected photosynthesis in bacteria, an area of study where "virtually nothing is known."[38] The 2019 study concluded exposure to leachate from two common plastic items, HDPE bags and PVC matting, significantly impaired the *in vitro* growth and photosynthetic capacity of *Prochlorococcus* in a laboratory setting. Marine *Prochlorococcus* is "the most abundant photosynthetic organism on Earth and [a] vital contributor to global primary production and carbon cycling."[39]

While plastic's effect on photosynthesis in the wild is unknown, this lab study suggests that plastic has the potential to disrupt important ecosystem processes such as the exchange of oxygen and the regulation of temperatures. For example, a study from the 1990s found that plastic accumulation can inhibit the gas exchange between the overlying waters and the pore waters of the sediments, and the resulting depletion of oxygen can interfere with the normal ecosystem functioning and alter the makeup of life on the seafloor.[40] A study of Hawaii's beaches found that beach sediment containing plastic bits warmed more slowly and reached lower maximum temperatures. These changes have a variety of potential effects on beach organisms, including those with temperature-dependent sex determination such as sea turtle eggs.[41]

Through ingestion, sorption, and leaching, plastic and its associated chemicals have the potential to impact organisms throughout the

[38] Sasha Tetu, Indrani Sarker, Verena Schrameyer et al., Plastic leachates impair growth and oxygen production in Prochlorococcus, the ocean's most abundant photosynthetic bacteria, *Communications Biology* (2019) (available at www.nature.com/articles/s42003-019-0410-x) (last accessed October 31, 2021).

[39] Ibid.

[40] E. D. Goldberg, Diamonds and plastics are forever?, *Marine Pollution Bulletin*, 28, no. 8 (1994): 466.

[41] Henry Carson, Small plastic debris changes water movement and heat transfer through beach sediments, *Marine Pollution Bulletin* (2011).

food chain, including humans, and can influence important ecosystem processes.

C Harm to Humans

Humans are not immune to plastic ingestion or the subsequent exposure to the chemicals plastics contain. One study found that humans are ingesting around 5 g of plastic – the equivalent of a credit card – a week.[42] Humans consume plastic through seafood, bottled water, beer, honey, and salt. There is also concern that humans are inhaling plastic.[43] While there is strong evidence that humans consume plastic, the science surrounding the associated harms is less settled.

Seafood consumption is probably the most documented method of human ingestion of plastic. Studies have found microplastics in a variety of seafood including shellfish and fish. The abundance of microplastics is generally higher in shellfish than in fish.[44] And seafood species that are eaten whole (e.g., mollusks, crustaceans, and small or juvenile phases of fish) pose a greater threat of plastic ingestion than gutted fish or peeled shrimp.[45]

Microplastics in seafood is of particular concern in areas where seafood is frequently eaten. One study found that in European countries with high shellfish consumption, people ingest up to 11,000 microplastic particles per year, whereas in countries with low shellfish consumption, people ingest an average of 1,800 microplastic particles per year.[46]

Ingestion of plastic through drinking water is a newer area of study. Scientists at SUNY-Fredonia in the United States have studied both

[42] Kala Senathirajah and Thava Palanisami, How much microplastics are we ingesting?: Estimation of the mass of microplastics ingested, University of New Castle (2019) (available at www.newcastle.edu.au/newsroom/featured/plastic-ingestion-by-people-could-be-equating-to-a-credit-card-a-week/how-much-microplastics-are-we-ingesting-estimation-of-the-mass-of-microplastics-ingested) (last accessed October 31, 2021).

[43] Stephanie L. Wright and Frank J. Kelly, Plastic and human health: A micro issue?, *Environmental Science and Technology* (June 20, 2017) (available at www.ncbi.nlm.nih.gov/pubmed/28531345) (last accessed October 31, 2021).

[44] Hantoro et al., Microplastics in coastal areas and seafood: implications for food safety.

[45] Barboza et al., Marine microplastic debris.

[46] Ibid.

drinking and tap water. In 2018, the lab conducted the first-ever investigation of plastic pollution within globally sourced tap water, which included a total of 159 samples from 7 geographical regions spanning 5 continents). The same lab tested bottle water in 259 bottles from 11 brands purchased from 19 locations in 9 countries.[47] The results, which were not peer reviewed, found that 93 percent of the bottles tested showed signs of microplastic contamination. The study also revealed twice as many plastic particles within bottled water as compared to tap water on average. While microfibers made up 97 percent of the microplastics within the tap water study, they only composed 13 percent of the particles within bottled water.[48] Polypropylene was the most common polymer in bottled water leading scientists to believe the contamination could be coming from the industrial process of bottling the water or from the simple act of opening the bottle.[49]

While industry executives admit to plastic particles in bottled water, they dispute the amounts. Another point of contention is the degree to which very small amounts of plastic can harm humans.

While evidence supports the conclusion that humans ingest plastics, research on the effects of microplastics on humans is new, and evidence on the specific harms of plastic to humans is inconclusive. That said, some scientists argue that "'there cannot be no effect'" since ingesting plastics further exposes humans to harmful chemicals.[50]

One concern is the accumulation of toxic chemicals in our bodies. Chronic exposure to the chemicals either leached by or absorbed to plastic could disrupt immune and endocrine systems.[51] Of concern is the leaching of bisphenol A (BPA) and phthalates, known hormone (endocrine) disrupting chemicals. PVC (polyvinyl chloride), a solid plastic used to make pipes, siding, raincoats, and cling wrap, is just one

[47] Sherri A. Mason, Victoria G. Welch, and Joseph Neratko, Synthetic polymer contamination in bottle water, State University of New York-Fredonia (available at http://news.bbc.co.uk/2/shared/bsp/hi/pdfs/14_03_13_finalbottled.pdf) (last accessed October 31, 2021).

[48] Ibid.

[49] Ibid.

[50] Kevin Loria, How to eat least plastic, *Consumer Reports* (available at www.consumerreports.org/health-wellness/how-to-eat-less-plastic-microplastics-in-food-water/ (last updated April 30, 2020).

[51] www.haaretz.com/science-and-health/.premium.MAGAZINE-you-re-eating-a-hamburger-s-worth-of-plastic-every-year-1.7365420 (last accessed October 31, 2021).

example of a plastic polymer that might release or attract bisphenol A, phthalates, and dioxins. Studies have linked phthalates, which are used to soften plastic, to reduced testosterone and fertility in laboratory animals, and prenatal exposure to lower testosterone in males. Exposure to another additive, bisphenol A, used to make lightweight, heat-resistant baby bottles and microwave cookware, has been linked to reduced fertility in males and females.[52] Sorbing of chemicals is also a concern. Polychlorinated biphenyl (PCB), a chemical that sorbs to microplastics, has been linked to various cancers, compromised immune systems, and reproductive problems.[53]

Inhalation of pollutants is another concern for humans that exists at both the production and disposal stage. The impacts from plastic refineries are particularly apparent in an 85-mile stretch between Baton Rouge and New Orleans, Louisiana, dubbed Cancer Alley. This area, which is home to more than 150 plants and refineries, is also home to some of the highest cancer rates in the country. In early 2020, federal and state officials granted environmental permits to Formosa Plastics for a new $9.4 billion plastic complex made up of fourteen plants on 2,300 acres in the St. James Parish section of Cancer Alley. Shortly thereafter, the Center for Biological Diversity (CBD), and local organizations including Healthy Gulf, Louisiana Bucket Brigade, and Rise St. James filed a suit against the US Army Corps of Engineers (Corps) in the U.S. District Court for the District of Columbia arguing that Formosa's permit violates the Clean Water Act, the National Environmental Protection Act, the Rivers and Harbors Act, and the National Historic Preservation Act.[54] Before the court could rule on the merits of the case or any motion, the Corps suspended the permit.

Although the specific reasons for the Corps decision are unknown, there was significant opposition to this project from the local community of St. James Parish. While the governor of Louisiana promoted the

[52] Weiss, Altered oceans: Part four.

[53] Loria, How to eat least plastic.

[54] Complaint at 4-5, *Ctr. for Biological Diversity* v. *U.S. Army Corps of Engineers*, No. 20-103, 2021 WL 14929 (D.D.C. 2021).

project as one of economic development and job creation, the plaintiffs raised environmental justice concerns. The complex would be in a community that is 90 percent Black, according to the CBD. The complex is expected to double the release of toxic chemicals from 1.6 million pounds to 3.2 million pounds per year, making the plastic complex the state's second-largest emitter of benzene and ethylene oxide, two cancer-causing chemicals.

Burning plastic is also a concern, especially in developing countries that lack facilities to manage waste. Burning is a way to get rid of the plastic waste, but burning plastic can also serve as a heat or energy source. For example, in Indonesia, plastic is burned to fuel the kitchen broilers used in making tofu. When plastic is burned, toxic chemicals such as polychlorinated biphenyls, polycyclic aromatic hydrocarbons (PAHs), dioxins, and furans are released, and chronic exposures to these chemicals cause cancer and interfere with hormone functions.[55] Children who live in areas with uncollected waste are more likely to suffer from acute respiratory infections than those living where there were regular waste collections. Unfortunately, many developing countries lack the resources and infrastructure to put waste management systems into place, leaving burning of waste as the only option.

While the direct impact of plastic on human health is less apparent, it is known that the effects of the exposure to any pollutant depend on the nature of the toxic chemical, the extent of the exposure, and the individual's susceptibility.[56] Thus, living in areas close to where plastic is produced or disposed of is likely to have an impact on human health. It is safe to say that because of the uncertainty surrounding the potential harms, research into the effects of microplastics that are ingested and inhaled by humans will be an area of intense research over the next decade.

[55] Rinku Verma, Toxic pollutants from plastic waste – A review, *Procedia Environmental Sciences* (2016) (available at www.sciencedirect.com/science/article/pii/S187802961630158X) (last accessed October 31, 2021).

[56] Madeline Smith, David C. Love, Chelsea M. Rochman, and Roni A. Neff, Microplastics in seafood and the implications for human health, *Current Environmental Health Reports* (2018) (available at www.ncbi.nlm.nih.gov/pmc/articles/PMC6132564/) (last accessed October 31, 2021).

D Harm to the Economy

Plastic debris has been estimated to cause more than $13 billion (US) in economic damage. In 2014, the United Nations Environment Programme released the first study to apply "natural capital valuation" to the impacts of plastic on the marine environment. The "natural capital valuation" methodology converts impacts into monetary terms, reflecting the scale of damage caused. In essence, it puts a "price on pollution."[57] The overall value or "natural capital cost" gives an indication of the financial cost to companies were they to internalize impacts associated with their current practices. These costs can also be factored into business and investment decision-making.

This estimate, calculated by the United Nations Environment Programme in 2014, was derived by estimating what it would cost companies that produce consumer goods to "internalize" the costs associated with their current practices (e.g., pay for cleanup of plastic waste).[58] This amount is considered to be on the low end because there is so little information on the impacts of plastic waste (e.g., for micro-plastics) and it does not include costs such as the transport of invasive marine species attached to plastics in the ocean.

E Harm to the Climate

Finally, plastic production and incineration generates carbon dioxide. Plastics originate as fossil fuels and release greenhouse gases when burned and are therefore considered a climate issue as well. A 2019 report found that in 2019, the production and incineration of plastic will add more than 850 million metric tons of greenhouse gases to the atmosphere.[59] A report released by the Center for International Environmental Law called *Plastic & Climate: The Hidden Costs of a Plastic Planet* contains data with respect to plastic and greenhouse

[57] UNEP, Valuing plastics: The business case for measuring, managing and disclosing plastic use in the consumer goods industry (2014).

[58] Ibid.

[59] Center for International Law, Plastic and climate: The hidden cost of a plastic planet (May 2019) (available at www.ciel.org/plasticandclimate) (last accessed October 31, 2021).

gases. The 2019 report, which looked across the life cycle of plastic, reported the following for 2015. In the United States, the extraction and production of plastic resulted in at least 9.5–10.5 million metric tons of carbon dioxide equivalents (CO_2-eq) per year. With respect to refining and manufacturing, twenty-four ethylene facilities in the United States produced 17.5 million metric tons of CO_2-eq. Globally, emissions from ethylene production were 184.3–213.0 million metric tons of CO_2-eq. Plastic incineration resulted in 5.9 million metric tons of CO_2-eq. Carbon dioxide emissions from ethylene production are projected to expand by 34 percent between 2015 and 2030.[60] While these emissions are significant, as discussed later, some of plastic's proposed replacements have even larger carbon footprints.

III CONCLUSION

Understanding the harms associated with plastic is a critical part of crafting effective solutions. While some harms are well-documented, others are less studied. Harms exist on land, in the ocean, and in the air. And harms extend across the life cycle of plastic from production to disposal. Harms are aesthetic, economic, and health related. Also important is the close association between the plastic and oil and gas industries and their promotion of self-regulation and recycling over government intervention. Industry's sway, coupled with plastic's harm, compels a multimodal approach to solving our plastic problem.

[60] Brooke Bauman, How plastics contribute to climate change, *Yale Climate Connections* (August 20, 2019) (available at https://yaleclimateconnections.org/2019/08/how-plastics-contribute-to-climate-change/) (last accessed October 31, 2021).

PART II

Multimodal Approaches to Solving Our Plastic Problem

Environmental law scholars agree that we have entered a new era for solving environmental problems such as plastic pollution – a era where solutions are multimodal.[1] Solving our plastic problem will require a concerted effort from governments, businesses, and the general public. Gone are the days where environmental harms could simply be legislated away.

In the 1970s, US environmental law transitioned quickly from a body of common law principles developed through judicial decisions to a series of federal laws enacted by Congress and designed to be carried out and enforced by federal agencies. Within the span of a few years, the Clean Air Act, Clean Water Act, Endangered Species Act, and other comprehensive environmental laws were enacted or significantly strengthened. As Robert V. Percival observed, this "burst" of federal legislation was in response to "perceived inadequacies in the common law" and had "overwhelming, bipartisan support."[2] The legislation mandated a reduction in emissions from industrial polluters and forced companies to implement new pollution control technologies. Laws imposed heightened liability standards and authorized citizen suits, opening the door for individual citizens, not just the government, to sue and seek redress for environmental harm.

1 Craig Anthony (Tony) Arnold, Fourth-generation environmental law: Integrationist and multimodal, *William & Mary Environmental Law and Policy Review* 35 (2011): 771, 792 (defining multimodal as "the use of multiple modes or methods of protecting the environment.")

2 Robert V. Percival, Regulatory evolution and the future of environmental policy, *The University of Chicago Legal Forum* 1997 (1997): 159.

In the 1990s, in response to claims of over-regulation, new and amended legislation incorporated more flexible approaches, such as information disclosures and market mechanisms, to the existing "command and control" laws of the 1970s. Today, traditional means of curbing environmental harm through enacting federal legislation have become increasingly difficult to implement as political discourse has polarized and courts have shown less deference to environmental agencies. As a result, alternatives to historical approaches have become correspondingly popular as opposition to government regulation grows and partisanship intensifies.

Part II demonstrates the multimodal nature of plastic pollution solutions. Multimodal solutions reimagine existing approaches in terms of what is regulated and how regulation occurs.

I CONSIDERATIONS: WHAT, WHERE, WHO, AND HOW

The scope and structure of the solutions discussed in the chapters that follow are influenced by a number of factors discussed in Part I including the type of plastic, the size of the plastic, the origin of the plastic waste, and where in the life cycle of plastic, from production to disposal, the waste occurs. For example, a ban on single-use plastics would be an upstream solution (i.e., it would seek to prevent plastic from entering the environment by reducing the amount of plastic produced), while beach cleanup efforts would be a downstream solution (i.e., it would seek to remove plastic that has already entered the environment). Likewise, a law focused on illegal dumping from ocean vessels addresses water-based sources of plastic pollution and requires international cooperation, while a regulation focused on discharges from plastic producers addresses land-based sources and invokes federal law. Finally, the smallest kind of plastic pollution – microfibers released from vehicular tire wear and clothes washing – might not fall within current regulations at all, thus making design and innovation even more important to solving plastic pollution.

The polluter is also an important consideration. The plastic industry has many sectors: pellet producers, who create the polymers and extrude the pellets; pellet transporters and packagers, who move the pellets from producer to processor; and pellet processors, who turn pellets into plastic products. But businesses that use plastic, such as bottling companies, and consumers who purchase plastic items can also be polluters. Regulators must also decide whether to employ mandatory or voluntary methods to prevent plastic pollution.

Although solutions to environmental harms have become increasingly diverse and extend beyond formal regulation, the first chapter, Chapter 4, in Part II starts by describing the ways in which the federal government can act to address environmental harm through enacting new laws and strengthening existing ones such as the Clean Water Act. States and local governments also have been enacting laws, like bans on single-use plastic, to address plastic's harm. These and other state efforts are described in Chapter 5. International efforts, such as the use of global treaties and campaigns, are discussed in Chapter 6. In addition to public regulation, lawmakers increasingly are looking to private entities – businesses, nonprofits, and institutions – to curb environmental harm. Private regulation offers solutions to these problems through voluntary reductions, education campaigns, and certification programs. This, and plastic pollution solutions led by individuals, are addressed in Chapter 7.

These chapters are grounded in theories of environmental policy and regulation. Some scholars categorize environmental policy into three instruments: regulative, economic, and persuasive.[3] These measures can range from "hard" to "soft" depending on how strict, as well as from "direct" to "indirect" depending on how much influence is asserted over the actor. An example of an instrument that is both strict and direct would be plastic bag bans. This regulatory instrument would be deemed strict and direct because it prohibits the product's manufacture and use, effectively eliminating choice. An example of a

[3] N. Brennholt, Maren Hess, and Georg Reifferscheid, Freshwater microplastics: Challenges for regulation and management. In: M. Wagner and S. Lambert (eds.), *Freshwater Microplastics. The Handbook of Environmental Chemistry*, vol. 58 (Springer, Cham, 2018) pp. 239–72, 260 (available at https://doi.org/10.1007/978-3-319-61615-5_12) (last accessed October 31, 2021).

soft and indirect instrument would be educational programming on plastic pollution. This persuasive instrument would be deemed soft and indirect because it does not directly regulate the plastic industry and consumer behavior is influenced solely by information on plastic pollution. Subsidies and taxes are economic instruments, with subsidies being less direct than taxes. Subsidies might encourage businesses to invest in certain technological advances to improve recycling, while taxes might discourage certain behaviors such as using single-use plastic products. Businesses that agree to reduce their plastic use through voluntary commitments would be an example of a soft, regulative instrument, while research funding for technical improvements would be an example of a hard, persuasive instrument.

Legal scholar Lawrence Lessig has advanced a taxonomy based on similar reasoning. Professor Lessig maintains that regulatory tools fall into one of four modalities: laws or mandates, markets, social norms, and architecture.[4] Lessig explains that the law can modify behavior directly through regulations and indirectly through social norms, markets, and architecture. Social norms, markets, and architecture, however, do not exist separate or operate independently from the law. A change in one modality could end up affecting one or all the other modalities. Therefore, the question for the regulator is never "law or something else." While Lessig identifies the government as the regulator, other scholars such as Michael Vandenbergh,[5] Sarah Light, and Eric Orts[6] have noted that businesses and NGOs have similar instruments available for use in regulating behavior. Ultimately, by the end of Part II, the reader will better recognize the various actors involved and mechanisms available in solving our plastic problem.

[4] Lawrence Lessig, The law of the horse: What cyberlaw might teach, *Harvard Law Review* 113 (1999): 501.

[5] Michael P. Vandenbergh, Private environmental governance, *Cornell Law Review* 99 (2013): 129.

[6] Sarah E. Light and Eric W. Orts, Parallels in public and private environmental governance, *Michigan Journal of Environmental & Administrative Law* 5 (2015): 1.

4 FEDERAL EFFORTS

News of plastic's harm has made its way to Washington, DC. In October 2018, President Donald Trump signed the Save Our Seas Act of 2018 into law.[1] The Act, which is not specifically aimed at plastics, reauthorizes the Marine Debris Program and "require[s] the National Oceanic and Atmospheric Administration (NOAA) to work with: (1) other agencies to address both land-and sea-based sources of marine debris, and (2) the Department of State and other agencies to promote international action to reduce the incidence of marine debris."[2] Advocates consider this a "modest, but important piece of legislation" because of the bipartisan effort to address the problem of global marine debris.[3]

Individual members of Congress are taking an approach that specifically targets plastic pollution. In June 2019, Senator Tom Udall (D-NM) and Representative Alan Lowenthal (D-CA) wrote a letter to President Trump stating that there was "unified concern and a call to action from both parties in both chambers [of Congress] regarding the global plastic pollution problem."[4] While the lawmakers recognized the usefulness of plastics, they also reported many of the alarming statistics and numbers already mentioned in this book. The

[1] Public Law No: 115–265; 132 Stat. 3742 (2018).

[2] Congress.gov, Summary: S. 576, Sec. 2, as Passed Senate amended (August 3, 2017) (available at www.congress.gov/bill/115th-congress/senate-bill/756) (last accessed October 31, 2021).

[3] Ocean Conservancy, Save our Seas signed into law (October 11, 2018) (available at https://oceanconservancy.org/blog/2018/10/11/save-seas-act-signed-law/) (last accessed October 31, 2021).

[4] Tom Udall and Alan Rosenthal Letter to President Trump (June 5, 2019) (available at www.documentcloud.org/documents/6152103-Plastic-Pollution-Letter-to-Potus-Udall-Lowenthal.html) (last accessed October 31, 2021).

letter recommended that "departments and agencies across the federal government develop a coordinated interagency research and response plan to address th[e] growing problem [of plastic pollution]."[5] Continuing with their efforts, on October 31, 2019, Udall and Lowenthal posted a draft of a proposed bill to address plastic pollution, which includes phasing out plastic. The bill was formally introduced in February 2020.

At the same time the draft proposal was being considered, over 100 environmental groups sent a petition to the Environmental Protection Agency, requesting that it strengthen the Clean Water Act (CWA) effluent limitations on facilities that convert fossil fuels to plastic.

This chapter addresses these recent actions as well as other ways in which the federal government can work to solve our plastic problem.

Apart from the Microbead-Free Waters Act (MFWA), there is currently no federal law whose sole purpose is to regulate the production, control, and cleanup of plastic waste. Most environmental regulations are the product of a series of independently established statutes enacted in the 1970s that focus on different environmental media (i.e., air, water, and soil) rather than on a particular pollutant. Furthermore, regulators of the 1970s were more focused on pollution control and cleanup rather than on pollution prevention. As this chapter explains, this patchwork of existing laws and regulations can and has been used to address plastics' downstream harms. But relying on multiple laws to address plastic after it has entered the environment has limitations. And as plastic continues to accumulate in the environment, the need to do more (or to do something different) has increased.

This chapter describes these distinct laws and how they might be used to address plastic pollution. It evaluates proposals to amend existing federal laws and to enact new ones, and it considers nonregulatory efforts by the federal government, including grants and educational campaigns. By the end of the chapter, the reader should understand the shortcomings of existing federal law and understand the need for a multimodal approach to solve our plastic problem.

[5] Ibid.

I FEDERAL AGENCY INVOLVEMENT

Discussions of federal environmental laws naturally include the Environmental Protection Agency (EPA) and the National Oceanic Atmospheric Agency (NOAA). Less obvious federal agencies include the Food and Drug Administration (FDA) and the State Department. Through enabling legislation and statutes, these agencies promulgate regulations which might limit, prohibit, or require certain actions. The strictness of these regulations, as well as the degree to which the regulations are enforced, can reflect the priorities of the administration at any given time. Administrators can also demonstrate support for federal environmental laws through funding grants that often fund efforts organized or led by states or nonprofits.

Because an environmental problem such as plastic pollution can transcend boundaries, discussions of federal law can invoke state, international, and individual interests. Some federal laws, such as the Clean Water Act, include some form of *cooperative federalism* – that is, the state and the federal agency work together to address the problem. Many environmental statutes have a mechanism – *citizen suits* – that allows individuals to sue when violations of federal law occur, thus allowing for an additional layer of enforcement. Finally, some laws that concern global resources, such as our oceans, are enacted in furtherance of *international agreements*. While this chapter will identify situations where cooperative federalism, citizen suits, and international law are at play, detailed discussions of state, individual, and international actions occur in later chapters.

Table 4.1 includes the federal laws discussed in this chapter that could be used to address plastic's harms. The table identifies whether the law expressly includes "plastic" in its text, whether the law focuses on land-based sources or water-based sources of plastic pollution, and whether the law is regulatory in that it prohibits or requires certain conduct.

II A BRIEF HISTORY

Plastic pollution is not a new issue for the federal government. But, because plastic continues to flow into the environment, the

Table 4.1 *Summary of US laws that involve plastic pollution*

Statute (original and reauthorized)	Expressly names plastic/ marine debris	Land-based sources	Water-based sources	Regulatory
Microbead-Free Waters Act	Yes	Yes	No	Yes
Save our Seas Act 2018 and 2020 (reauthorization Marine Debris Research, Prevention, and Reduction Act of 2006)	Yes	No	Yes	No
Break Free from Plastic Pollution Act (amends Solid Waste Disposal Act/RCRA)	Yes	Yes	No	Yes
Clean Water Act	No	Yes	No	Yes
Clean Air Act	No	Yes	No	Yes
The Pollution Prevention Act of 1990	No	Yes	No	Yes
Toxic Substances Control Act (TSCA)	No	Yes	No	Yes
Resource Conservation and Recovery Act (RCRA)	No	Yes	No	Yes
Marine Protection, Research, and Sanctuaries Act (1972) (Ocean Dumping Act) → London Convention	Yes	No	Yes	Yes
Marine Plastic Pollution Research and Control Act (1987) (Act to Prevent Pollution from Ships) → MARPOL	Yes	No	Yes	Yes

government's response can be characterized as inadequate. For the most part, source reduction, or reducing the amount of plastic that is produced, has not been a priority. This is somewhat paradoxical given that the EPA identifies source reduction as the preferred method of waste management for a material such as plastic.

Instead, and despite knowing about land-based sources of pollution, the United States has relied on existing legislation to address plastic pollution, after it is found in the environment. And legislation that has been enacted has been in response to international laws that have focused on water-based sources of pollution. The US approach to plastic pollution can be described as reactive rather than proactive, stymied by unreliable funding sources, overreliance on nonregulatory approaches such as education campaigns, and ineffective coordination at the federal level.

Agencies have been aware of the problem of marine debris, including plastics, for decades. A 1986 *New York Times* editorial encouraged the United States to ratify Annex V of the MARPOL Convention – an international treaty focused on regulating garbage generated on ships.[6] A year later, this agreement was implemented through the passage of the Marine Plastic Pollution Research and Control Act of 1987, which specifically prohibits discharge into the ocean of plastics, synthetic ropes, fishing gear, plastic garbage bags, lining and packing materials, bottles and similar refuse.[7]

A 1992 EPA report, *Plastic Pellets in the Aquatic Environment: Sources and Recommendations*,[8] shows that the EPA was not just concerned with ocean dumping but was also aware of a specific kind of land-based source of pollution – plastic pellets. The report, which was part of the EPA's "new" national policy on pollution prevention[9] as authorized under the Pollution Prevention Act of 1990 (discussed later), was the "first [U.S.] comprehensive assembly of information regarding the presence and ecological effects of pellets in the aquatic environment."[10] The hope was that this report would "become a basic reference for EPA and industry."[11] It discovered what studies continue to show, namely, that there are two primary ways in which plastic

6 Opinion, The oceans are choking on plastic debris, *The New York Times* (March 1, 1986) (available at www.nytimes.com/1986/03/01/opinion/l-the-oceans-are-choking-on-plastic-debris-539786.html) (last accessed October 31, 2021).

7 33 U.S.C. §§ 1901 (West 2018).

8 EPA, Plastic pellets in the aquatic environment: Sources and recommendations final report, EPA842-B-92–010 (1992) (available at www.globalgarbage.org/13%20EPA%20Plastic%20Pellets.pdf) (last accessed October 31, 2021).

9 EPA, An analysis of pollution prevention as an environmental policy (1991) (available at https://nepis.epa.gov/Exe/ZyPDF.cgi/200060C6.PDF?Dockey=200060C6.PDF) (last accessed October 31, 2021).

10 Davis Truslow, Microbeads and the toxics use reduction act: Preventing pollution at its source, *Boston College Environmental Affairs Law Review* 44 (2017): 149 (available at https://lawdigitalcommons.bc.edu/cgi/viewcontent.cgi?referer=&httpsredir=1&article=2219&context=ealr) (last accessed October 31, 2021).

11 EPA, Plastic pellets in the aquatic environment.

pellets are released into aquatic environments: discharges through combined sewage systems (CSS) and stormwater drains, and direct spills during the handling or transport of pellets.

The report, however, did not spur prompt enactment of new legislation. Instead it recommended that industry follow "voluntary control measures" and that existing federal laws, discussed in more detail below, be enforced to prevent and control the release of pellets into aquatic environments. Similar recommendations were articulated in the 1994 EPA report titled *Status of Efforts to Control Aquatic Debris*.[12] This report offered recommendations that fell into five categories: continued federal leadership, public awareness and educational campaigns, vigorous implementation of laws, continued research and monitoring; and beach cleanups.

The United States, however, was prepared to act on water-based sources of plastic pollution, and in 2006, the Marine Debris Research, Prevention, and Reduction Act (Marine Debris Act) became law, establishing NOAA's Marine Debris Program (MDP). According to NOAA, the MDP achieves its mission through five program "pillars": prevention, removal, research, regional coordination, and emergency response. The statute defines marine debris as "any persistent solid material, manufactured or processed and directly or indirectly, intentionally or unintentionally, disposed of or abandoned into the marine environment or Great Lakes"[13] and therefore includes plastic. The Act also codified the Interagency Marine Debris Coordinating Committee (IMDCC), led by NOAA, which has seen various configurations since the Marine Plastic Pollution Research and Control Act of 1987. The IMDCC coordinates federal agency activities and, through a biennial report, makes recommendations on research priorities, monitoring, and regulatory action. Although the committee's goal was to improve coordination among agencies, a 2008 report from the National Research Council found that leadership and governance of the IMDCC "remain diffuse and ineffective, and current mitigation efforts

[12] EPA, State efforts to control aquatic debris (1994) (available at https://nepis.epa.gov/Exe/ZyPDF.cgi/200050JJ.PDF?Dockey=200050JJ.PDF) (last accessed October 31, 2021).

[13] 33 U.S. Code § 1956 (3).

are episodic and crisis driven."[14] This report also found "a need for a reliable, dedicated funding stream to support mitigation efforts and a national strategy and framework for identifying priorities for addressing marine debris."[15]

Despite this criticism, the IMDCC did publish its first set of recommendations in 2008. The twenty-five recommendations were divided into five groups: (1) education and outreach; (2) legislation, regulation, and policy; (3) cleanup; (4) research and technology development; and (5) coordination. The legislation, regulation, and policy recommendations included: strengthening and enhancing federal agencies' "ability to fulfill both regulatory and nonregulatory mandates for marine debris prevention" and referring "violations of federal law, such as the Act to Prevent Pollution from Ships, Clean Water Act, and Ocean Dumping Act, to the Environment and Natural Resources Division of the U.S. Department of Justice for civil or criminal enforcement action."[16]

The Marine Debris Act has been amended several times, including in 2012, and most recently in 2018 through Title I of the Save Our Seas (SOS) Act of 2018.

With the reauthorization of the Marine Debris Program through the Save our Seas Act in 2018, the federal government continues to suggest a policy where existing laws are enforced and nonregulatory approaches are emphasized. This approach focuses on studying the problem and educating others about it and on providing funds and other support to others to address the problem. Finally, the emphasis on "marine debris" seems to paint this problem as a problem "at sea" rather than on land. While there is some enforcement of existing laws, as explained later, the effectiveness of existing laws depends on significant human and monetary resources.

[14] National Academies of Science, Tackling marine debris in the 21st century (2008) (available at www.nap.edu/resource/12486/marine_debris_brief_final.pdf) (last accessed October 31, 2021).

[15] Ibid.

[16] Government Accountability Office, Marine debris: Interagency committee members are taking action, but additional steps could enhance the federal response (2019) (available at www.gao.gov/assets/710/701694.pdf) (last accessed October 31, 2021).

The only Act targeting *plastic production*, the Microbead-Free Waters Act, was enacted in 2015 and effectively banned microbeads from certain products, such as cosmetics. This law demonstrates how broad coalitions can help spur legislation to deal with upstream plastic pollution control. This Act, however, is an anomaly when considering the overall federal approach to plastic, which has been to rely on existing laws and to address plastic pollution after it enters the environment.

III RECENT AND PROPOSED LAWS AND REGULATIONS

Given that the federal government's approach to plastic pollution has been to encourage the use of existing laws, which focus on education and cleanup efforts, the enactment of the Microbead-Free Waters Act is a small victory.

A A New Law: Microbead-Free Waters Act

One way to eliminate plastic from the environment is to ban its production altogether: If plastic is no longer made, the possibility of it entering the environment no longer exists. The federal government took this step in 2015 when, through the Microbead-Free Waters Act, it banned the manufacturing and sale of microbeads: tiny bits of plastic added to face washes, toothpastes, and other rinse-off personal care products.[17] According to the statute, plastic microbeads are "any solid plastic particle that is less than five millimeters in size and is intended to be used to exfoliate or cleanse the body."[18] Because of microbeads' small size, they were not being caught by sewers' water filters, and microbeads were being flushed out into open waters.

The MFWA amended the Federal Food, Drug, and Cosmetic Act, a federal law that gives the Food and Drug Administration authority to

[17] 21 U.S.C. § 331(ddd)(1) (2015) (prohibiting "[t]he manufacture or the introduction or delivery for introduction into interstate commerce of a rinse-off cosmetic that contains intentionally-added plastic microbeads.")

[18] 21 U.S.C. § 331(ddd)(2)(A).

regulate the safety of food, drugs, medical devices, and cosmetics. The FDA notes on its website that the new law addresses "concerns about microbeads in the water supply" . . .. However, "[t]he new law does not address consumer safety, and [the FDA does] not have evidence suggesting that plastic microbeads, as used in cosmetics, pose a human health concern."[19] The law provided deadlines for both the manufacture of plastic microbeads and the introduction of plastic microbeads into the marketplace, and as of July 1, 2019, microbeads are no longer made or included in cosmetics manufactured and sold in the United States.

One legal scholar notes that "the confluence of growing scientific understanding, broad stakeholder support from the grassroots and from industry, and the growing number of state bans all likely contributed" to the easy passage of this Act.[20] As public awareness of the harms of microbeads grew in early 2010, consumers put pressure on businesses such as Unilever, Johnson & Johnson, and the Body Shop, and these businesses announced their intent to stop using microbeads in their products prior to the passage of MFWA. In addition, several states, including New York, Wisconsin, and Illinois, had enacted statewide bans, prompting federal intervention – in the form of MFWA – to prevent a patchwork regulatory scheme.

While the Microbead-Free Waters Act is viewed as a positive step, it is not expected to have a dramatic impact on our plastic problem. First, the Act applies only to the manufacture of microbeads in rinse-off cosmetics and is silent on removing cosmetic-based microbeads already in the environment, and on eliminating microbeads used in cleaning products, industrial abrasives, and medical applications.[21] Furthermore, microbeads in cosmetics represent only a small fraction of all microplastics in the environment. Studies looking at microbeads

[19] FDA, The Microbead-Free Waters Act: FAQs (August 2020) (available at www.fda.gov/cosmetics/cosmetics-laws-regulations/microbead-free-waters-act-faqs) (last accessed October 31, 2021).

[20] David Strifling, The Microbead-Free Waters Act of 2015: Model for future environmental legislation, or black swan?, *Journal of Land Use & Environmental Law* 32 (2017): 151, 161.

[21] Riley E. J. Schnurr, Vanessa Alboiu, Meenakshi Chaudhary et al., Reducing marine pollution from single-use plastics (SUPs): A review, *Marine Pollution Bulletin* 137 (2018): 162.

in Europe have calculated that 0.1–4.1 percent of marine microplastic pollution come from cosmetic product sources.[22] Finally, microbead bans for cosmetics are limited to only a few countries, including the United States, Canada, United Kingdom, and France. Many countries still manufacture microbeads and sell products that contain them.

However, as the next chapter explains, in some US states and cities, bans have been applied to other kinds of single-use plastics (e.g., straws and bags).

B Reauthorized Laws: The Marine Debris Research, Prevention, and Reduction Act and the Save Our Seas Acts

Like the Microbead-Free Waters Act, the Save Our Seas Act had bipartisan support. The Save Our Seas Act was unanimously passed by Congress and signed into law by President Trump in October 2018. SOS is not an entirely new statute; rather, it reauthorizes and amends the Marine Debris Research, Prevention, and Reduction Act (MDRPRA or Marine Debris Act), 33 U.S.C. § 1951 et seq., whose purpose is to "address the adverse impacts of marine debris on the United States economy, the marine environment, and navigation safety through the identification, determination of sources, assessment, prevention, reduction, and removal of marine debris."[23]

1 The Marine Debris Research, Prevention, and Reduction Act (MDRPRA or The Marine Debris Act) The Marine Debris Act was enacted in 2006[24] and focuses on nonregulatory measures such as research, education, and outreach, and coordination and support for state and international efforts.[25] A major purpose of the Act was to

[22] David Hirst and Oliver Bennett, Microbeads and microplastics in cosmetic and personal care products, House of Commons Briefing Paper (2017) (available at https://researchbriefings.parliament.uk/ResearchBriefing/Summary/CBP-7510) (last accessed October 31, 2021).

[23] 33 U.S.C. § 1951.

[24] 33 U.S.C. § 1951–1958.

[25] 33 U.S.C. 1952(b). "work with other Federal agencies to develop outreach and education strategies to address both land- and sea-based sources of marine debris; and (7) work with the Department of State and other Federal agencies to promote international action to reduce the incidence of marine debris."

establish the Marine Debris Program – a program run by NOAA and the US Coast Guard that would help identify, assess, reduce, and prevent marine debris and its adverse impacts on the marine environment and navigation safety. The Marine Debris Act called for the development of the "[f]ederal marine debris information clearinghouse"[26] and reactivated and codified the duties of the Interagency Marine Debris Coordinating Committee to facilitate international collaboration and advise Congress. The IMDCC comprised of senior officials from NOAA, the EPA, the US Coast Guard, and the US Navy. The IMDCC was instructed to coordinate with federal agencies, nongovernmental organizations, universities, industries, states, Indian tribes, and other nations researching marine debris and to report within one year about sources of debris and the ecological, economic, and social impacts of such debris. The inaugural report, *Interagency Report on Marine Debris Sources, Impacts, Strategies & Recommendations*, published in 2008, resulted in a number of recommendations including the following: education and outreach, incentive programs, enforcement of existing laws, support of cleanup efforts, research to reduce, prevent, and control pollution prevention, and improved coordination. Five additional reports have since been published, most recently in 2017. Each report provides status updates on "the IMDCC federal agency partner activities to implement the 2008 report recommendations and an analysis of their effectiveness."[27]

These reports, which are typically between sixty and seventy pages, reflect the federal government's growing understanding of plastic pollution. For example, the inaugural report does not mention microplastics, while the most recent report mentions the term seventy-five times. The term "microfiber" is first mentioned in the most recent report. Use of the words "international" and "emergency" has also increased over time. These reports have helped inform the recent reauthorization of statutory provisions and programs included in the Marine Debris Act. For example, the composition and mandates of the IMDCC have

[26] 33 U.S.C. § 1951(2)-(3) (2006).

[27] Interagency Marine Debris Coordinating Committee, 2014–2015 progress report on the implementation of the Marine Debris Act (December 2016) (available at https://marinedebris.noaa.gov/sites/default/files/2014–2015_IMDCC_Report_0.pdf) (last accessed October 31, 2021).

broadened to include members from the Department of State and Department of the Interior and studies and reports on the consumption rates and environmental harms of plastics waste.

2 Save Our Seas Act In 2018, the Marine Debris Act was reauthorized through the Save Our Seas Act. The Act reauthorized the Marine Debris Program, 33 U.S.C. § 1952, and allocated $10 million to the program through 2022. New to the Act is a provision which directs the NOAA administrator to "promote international action" – and, notably, not just research – to address the growing effects of marine debris.[28] Also new to the Act is the inclusion of federal assistance and funding for "severe marine debris events."[29] The bill allows the NOAA administrator, in coordination with governors of affected states, to declare severe marine debris events, and to authorize funding to assist with cleanup and response.[30] Nonprofit advocacy organization such as the Ocean Conservancy has shown some approval for this Act because of the bipartisan effort to address the problem of global marine debris.

Save Our Seas Act 2.0, 33 U.S.C § 4201 et seq., another bipartisan piece of legislation, takes a deeper look at plastic marine pollution. The bill, which was introduced by Senators Dan Sullivan (R-AK), Sheldon Whitehouse (D-R.I.), and Robert Menendez (D-N.J.) in June 2019 and passed by the Senate in January 2020, builds on the 2018 law. The Act has three provisions: combatting marine debris, enhancing global engagement to combat marine debris, and improving domestic infrastructure to prevent marine debris.

The first provision creates a Marine Debris Foundation and adds additional resources to strengthen the US Marine Debris Program. It also establishes a "genius prize" to "encourage technological innovation with the potential to reduce plastic waste, and associated and potential pollution, and thereby prevent marine debris" and a pilot program to assess the feasibility of providing incentives to fishermen who incidentally capture marine debris while out at sea.[31] Finally, this

[28] 33 U.S.C. 1952(b)(7).
[29] 33 U.S.C. 1953(c).
[30] Ibid.
[31] Public Law No: 116–224; U.S.C. 4232.

provision calls on the IMDCC[32] to bring together other agencies to study specific aspects of plastic pollution including the following: pollution from microfibers, pollution from fishing gear, innovative uses of plastic waste, and the certification of (or creation of certain criteria for) circular polymers (i.e., polymers that can be reused multiple times or converted into a new, higher-quality product).

The second provision makes it the policy of the United States to work with foreign governments and international organizations to: increase awareness about causes and harms of plastic waste, support waste reduction efforts and access to information, and work cooperatively to set waste reduction targets. This title also requires the secretary of state to assess "the potential for negotiating new international agreements or creating a new international forum to reduce land-based sources of marine debris and derelict fishing gear" and requires the president to consider marine debris in negotiating international agreements.[33]

The final provision focuses on improving domestic infrastructure to prevent marine debris and requires the EPA administrator to "develop a strategy to improve post-consumer materials management and infrastructure for the purpose of reducing plastic waste and other post-consumer materials in waterways and oceans."[34] These efforts will focus on improving the collection, sorting, and processing of recycled materials. This provision also provides grants to states to address plastic pollution and authorizes the EPA – together with the National Academies of Sciences, Engineering, and Medicine – to study emerging areas of interest such as repurposing plastic for infrastructure uses and microplastics in food and drinking water. The Act also calls on the EPA to work with the IMDCC to produce reports on the barriers to increasing collection, processing, and use of recyclable materials; economic incentives to spur the development of additional new end-use markets for recyclable plastics; and minimizing the creation of new plastic waste.[35]

[32] 33 U.S.C. 1954 (a) & (B).
[33] Public Law No: 116–224; 33 U.S.C. 4251.
[34] 33 U.S.C. 4281.
[35] www.congress.gov/bill/116th-congress/senate-bill/1982/text#toc-id09282AD819FF4CC09E00F93B61F66F6C (last accessed October 31, 2021).

In addition to the Ocean Conservancy, which has again voiced its support of this bill, industry also supports these federal efforts. The Plastic Industry Association and the American Chemistry Council, for example, support this legislation because of its focus on plastic recovery and recycling.

But SOS 2.0 is not without its critics. In November 2019, several environmental groups, including the Center for Biological Diversity, Waterkeeper Alliance, and The 5 Gyres Institute, sent the Senate a letter opposing the legislation. The letter criticized the government's focus on removing plastic from the environment, rather than on reducing the amount of plastic waste generated. While these environmental groups appreciated Congress' attention to plastic pollution, they argued that the legislation does not do enough to "reduce[] the generation of plastic, particularly single-use plastic packaging."[36] Instead, the letter advocated for the policies in the legislation introduced by Senator Udall and Representative Lowenthal discussed below. One former EPA official echoed these concerns: "The Save Our Seas 2.0 Act does virtually nothing to require a reduction in the production of plastics while propping up an anemic approach to recycling." The official said "Congress can and must do much better on this urgent matter."[37]

C Proposed Law: Break Free from Plastic Pollution Act

Senators Udall and Lowenthal have taken a more preventative and comprehensive approach in their bill – the Break Free from Plastic Pollution Act. These representatives, who unveiled a draft of their bill in October 2019, focus on amending the Solid Waste Disposal Act, an Act better known as the Resource Conservation and Recovery Act (RCRA) that regulates the disposal of solid and hazardous waste.[38]

[36] Opposition letter to Save Our Seas Act 2.0 (November 8, 2019) (available at www.breakfreefromplastic.org/2019/11/08/opposition-to-save-our-seas-2-0-senate-bills-1982-2260-2364-and-2372/) (last accessed October 31, 2021).

[37] Steve Toloken, Save Our Seas 2.0 bill moves in Congress but faces rough waters, *Plastic News* (September 27, 2019) (available at www.plasticsnews.com/news/save-our-seas-20-bill-moves-congress-faces-rough-waters) (last accessed October 31, 2021).

[38] 42 U.S.C.§ 6901et. seq.

The goals of the amendments are to reduce production of certain single-use plastic products, to improve the responsibilities of plastic producers in terms of collection and disposal, and to prevent plastic pollution from entering animal and human food chains and waterways.

This bill is expansive in that it focuses on producer, consumer, and government conduct. For example, the bill incorporates extended producer responsibility (EPR) principles, which would require plastic manufactures to design, manage, and finance for the end-of-life management of their products before the time of sale. Additionally, the bill incorporates "polluter pays" principles where the producer pays for the harm caused by its product and is responsible for the cleanup and recycling of the material. Major beverage manufacturers would be required to operate "reverse" vending systems, whereby consumers could return empty beverage containers at a machine for recycling in exchange for a refund dispensed by the machine.

The bill also addresses consumer behavior by imposing a national 10-cent container deposit or "federal bottle bill." Revenue from the bottle tax would go toward improving recycling infrastructure and supporting litter cleanup efforts. Consumers would also incur a fee for using carryout bags.

The bill calls for banning certain types of plastic including Styrofoam used in food and shipping packaging, as well as labeling plastics to tell consumers how much plastic an item contains and how the plastic could be disposed of.

Finally, the bill calls on revising regulations already in place under the Clean Water Act and Clean Air Act (CAA), including revising effluent limitations guidelines for organic chemical plastics and the synthetic fiber industries – a call that has also been made by nonprofit and advocacy groups as discussed later in this chapter. A moratorium on the issuance of new permits for "covered facilities" as required under the Clean Air Act and Clean Water Act would be imposed. Under the moratorium, no new permits would be issued to a facility that transforms natural gas liquids into ethylene and propylene and later plastic polymers or a facility that polymerizes plastic or produces polymers. This would give environmental agencies more time to consider the impacts on air, water, and climate at those sites.

With respect to "covered facilities," the Act also requires the EPA administrator to conduct a study with the National Academy of Sciences and the National Institutes of Health on the following: the entire supply chain, end uses, disposal fate, and life cycle impacts; the environmental justice – or inequitable pollution – impacts; the standard practices with respect to the discharge and emission of pollutants into the environment; and the best available technologies and practices that reduce or eliminate the environmental justice and pollution impacts.

Unlike its response to the Save Our Seas Act, the plastic industry has pushed back against the Break Free from Plastic Pollution Act because of its focus on the plastic industry itself. Recycling groups also came out against the proposed legislation. The National Waste and Recycling Association released a statement in "strong opposition" to the proposed law stating that "many aspects of the bill [such as a federal bottle-bill] remain counterproductive to the overall goal of cleaning up plastic waste."[39]

The Break Free from Plastic Pollution Act was introduced in February 2020 and has not yet been taken up by Congress. While Senator Udall retired in November 2020, this legislation continues to receive attention from legislators interested in stopping plastic pollution at its source.

IV EXISTING LAWS AND REGULATIONS

A Land-Based Sources: The Clean Water Act

Because discharges and spills of plastic from land-based sources often make their way into streams, rivers, and harbors, provisions of the Clean Water Act can be used to offer redress. The Clean Water Act and its accompanying regulations can provide remedies for plastic pollution because the CWA requires permits for discharges of

[39] Press release, National Waste and Recycling Association, NWRA announces opposition to proposed Udall-Lowenthal Bill (November 22, 2019) (available at https://wasterecycling.org/press_releases/nwra-announces-opposition-to-proposed-udall-lowenthal-bill/) (last accessed October 31, 2021).

pollutants, sets effluent limitations for certain industries, authorizes citizen suits when violations occur as well as authorizes the EPA to take enforcement action, and provides funding for research. Yet even though there are many ways in which the CWA can be invoked, and the penalties for CWA violations can be significant, there are many reasons why the Act has proved ineffective at preventing pollution. First, the statute was not designed to address plastic pollution in all its forms; it was meant to prevent all kinds of pollution from entering waters. Second, permit violators are often difficult to identify or are municipalities that do not have the resources to remedy violations. Third, the enforcement often used by the EPA is voluntary and administrative rather than criminal. That is, the EPA tends to want to work with violators to bring them into compliance rather than to penalize and further deter such behavior.

1 An Overview The Clean Water Act is an example of a piece of federal legislation that does not explicitly mention plastic, but that could be used to address plastic discharged from a land-based source. It is one of several environmental statutes that were amended or enacted during the burst of federal environmental action in the 1970s. Many associate the enactment of the CWA with the burning of Ohio's Cuyahoga River in 1969, but the CWA is actually an amendment to the Federal Water Pollution Control Act of 1948. The 1948 Act provided funding for states to research and regulate water pollution. This Act proved ineffective, and in 1972, the Federal Water Pollution Control Act was overhauled. Federal water quality standards were established, and states were placed in charge of meeting these standards. One way to approach plastic pollution today is to consider the ways in which plastic "impairs" these water quality standards and then to regulate sources of pollution as part of a broader effort to achieve these standards.

Like the Clean Air Act, the Clean Water Act is an example of cooperative federalism, whereby the federal government sets national standards to be implemented by the states. The 1972 Act charged the EPA, together with state agencies and municipalities, to "prepare or develop comprehensive programs for preventing, reducing, or eliminating the pollution of the navigable waters ..."

of the United States.[40] Additionally, states have the authority, with the federal government's approval, to implement and enforce key provisions of the Act.[41]

The CWA categorizes pollution in terms of its source – point or nonpoint – and regulates point sources through a permitting system. Point sources include ditches, pipes, tunnels, and other defined structures from which pollutants are or may be discharged. Pollution from diffuse sources such as runoff is a nonpoint source of pollution. Discharges from point sources into navigable waters require a permit while those from nonpoint sources do not.

The EPA determines limits on how much of a particular pollutant can be discharged from a point source. These *effluent standards* are met using the CWA discharge permitting system. Title IV of the CWA requires a National Pollutant Discharge Elimination System (NPDES) permit (or a comparable state permit) before any discharge of a pollutant from a point source occurs. This means that point source discharges are allowed, if done in compliance with a permit. The permit ensures "compliance with effluent limitations – limits on how much of a particular pollutant may be discharged at one time – as determined by the EPA." Permits must be updated every five years and violations can result in monetary penalties. Compliance with a NPDES permit is compliance with the CWA. Although penalties alone will not completely control the release of plastic, they can encourage industries and municipalities that require permits to implement control measures.

2 Who Needs a Permit? A NPDES permit is required for a number of different point sources. The most relevant to plastic pollution include stormwater discharges from both industrial and municipal sources; municipal wastewater, including combined sewer overflows (CSOs); and industrial wastewater. Because all three sources are point sources, the CWA regulations permit for all three.[42]

Stormwater system is a system designed to carry runoff from rain events. In more developed areas, surface runoff moves over the ground

[40] 33 U.S.C.A. § 1252 (West 2019).

[41] Some states have left enforcement to the federal government.

[42] 40 CFR 122.26(b)(14)(i)–(xi).

and into drains in curbs and other low-lying areas. These drains connect to a system of underground storm sewer pipes and lead ultimately to local streams, rivers, and waterbodies. Because stormwater flows over hard surfaces directly into storm drains, there is no opportunity for soil, plants, or a water treatment facility to filter out pollutants. Any solid – such as plastic debris – or chemical dissolved in storm water runoff has the potential to be released into the waterbodies. As a result, pollutants, including plastic and materials used during its production, can make their way into lakes and rivers.

Wastewater system is a system designed to carry water from toilets, sinks, and other drains in homes and businesses and is treated before it is discharged into surface water. Primary treatment removes large debris items with screen mesh sizes of 6 mm or larger, while secondary treatment removes suspended and dissolved organic material and nutrients. There are also settling tanks to encourage the separation of sewage sludge from the effluent that is further treated, before being discharged into a nearby waterbody. A recent study found that municipal waste water treatments were effective at removing most microplastics but still found plastic microfibers and microfilaments in effluent samples from seventeen different facilities in the United States.[43] This most likely comes from clothing, but given that wastewater systems are fairly good at removing larger microplastics, wastewater systems in and of themselves are not a concern in terms of failure to mitigate plastic pollution.

In some cities, when the volume of water is larger than the amount the wastewater treatment facilities were designed to handle, as, for example, during a heavy rain event, the overflow is sent directly to the river without any treatment – hence the name *combined sewer overflows*. These events can cause plastics to enter the waterway directly since plastics bypass the treatment process.

Industrial wastewater is another potential source of plastic pollution. By-products from plastic production, particularly pellets, may become

[43] Sherri A. Mason, Daniella Garneau, Rebecca Sutton et al., Microplastic pollution is widely detected in US municipal wastewater treatment plant effluent, *Environmental Pollution* (2016) (available at www.sherrimason.com/uploads/WWTP_EnvironPollution2016.pdf) (last accessed October 31, 2021).

marine debris when dropped, washed, or blown away during transport to or from the factory or during production. The NPDES permitting program establishes discharge limits and conditions for industrial and commercial sources with specific limitations based on the type of facility and activity generating the discharge.

With respect to plastic, the EPA has the authority to regulate wastewater discharges from industries that manufacture organic chemicals, plastics, and synthetic fibers (OCPSF). 40 C.F.R. 414.11. Specifically, the OCPSF regulations apply to wastewater discharges resulting from the manufacture of the products or product groups identified in the following subcategories: rayon fibers, other fibers, thermoplastic resins, thermosetting resins, commodity organic chemicals, bulk organic chemicals, and specialty organic chemicals. These regulations were promulgated in the 1980s and 1990s.

In July 2019, the EPA was asked to review these effluent standards as well as the petroleum refining industry.[44] The petitioners, over 100 advocacy groups, noted that the "EPA has not revised or updated the Effluent Limitation Guidelines and Standards for Petroleum Refining (Cracking and Petrochemical subcategories) in any way since 1985 or the Organic Chemicals, Plastics, and Synthetic Fibers ('Plastics') industries in any way since 1993."[45] Petitioners argued that updates were necessary given the fact that plastic production is a much larger industry than it was twenty-five years ago and that continued reliance on outdated, and hence, lax regulations and the resulting weak enforcement could lead to greater environmental harm.

Under the Administrative Procedures Act, the EPA is required to respond to this petition in a timely manner, requiring that "[w]ith due regard for the convenience and necessity of the parties or their

[44] Under the Administrative Procedure Act (APA), citizens have the right to petition for the "issuance, amendment, or repeal" of any federal rule.

[45] Petition to revise the Clean Water Act effluent limitations and guidelines and standards for the petro-plastic industry under the 40 C.RF.R. Part 419 petroleum refining industrial category (cracking and petrochemical subparts) and Part 414 organic chemicals, plastics, and synthetic fibers industrial category, 280 *Environmental, Public Health, Indigenous, and Community Non-Governmental Organizations* v. *Andrew Wheeler, Administrator, United States Environmental Protection Agency* (July 23, 2019) (available at http://waterkeeper.org/wp-content/uploads/2019/07/CWA-Petro-Plastics-Petition-to-EPA-6–23-19.pdf) (last accessed October 31, 2021).

representatives and within a reasonable time, each agency shall proceed to conclude a matter presented to it." In the event EPA seeks to deny the petition in whole or in part, it must provide "[p]rompt notice" to the petitioners.[46] While petitions do not initiate the rulemaking or litigation process, they can prod the government to act. The EPA has not yet acted on this petition.

3 Enforcement of CWA: EPA While a discharge without a permit or a discharge that exceeds permit limits is a violation of the CWA, ultimately the effectiveness of the statute depends on the degree to which it is enforced. Scholars note that the EPA "could never hire a sufficient number of inspectors to regularly inspect each of the thousands of facilities regulated under the various pollution control laws."[47] As a result much regulatory enforcement relies on voluntary compliance and self-monitoring.[48]

When the government does detect a violation, the CWA provides the EPA with the authority to enforce the CWA and resolve NPDES permit violations in two ways: administrative and judicial. (States can also enforce the CWA if authorized by the EPA). With administrative enforcement, the EPA can issue an administrative compliance order requiring a violator to stop any ongoing illegal discharge activity and, where appropriate, to remove the illegal discharge and restore the area. A fine can also be imposed. With judicial enforcement, the EPA, together with the Army Corps of Engineers, has the authority to bring civil or criminal judicial enforcement actions which could result in injunctions and fines.[49]

4 Enforcement of CWA: Citizen Suits Permit violations can also be enforced through the citizen suit provision of the CWA, 33 U.S.C. § 1365a(1). The citizen suit provision authorizes "any citizen" to file a civil suit "against any person" who is alleged to be in violation of an effluent standard or limitation or in violation of an order issued by the

[46] Ibid.

[47] David M. Driesen and Robert W. Adler, *Environmental Law: A Conceptual and Pragmatic Approach*, 3rd ed. (Wolters Kluwer, New York, January 29, 2016).

[48] Ibid.

[49] Sections 309 and 404 of the Clean Water Act.

EPA or a state with respect to the standard or limitation. While citizens can sue municipalities for permit violations at combined sewage overflows and wastewater treatment plants, such efforts might not lead to the desired results because the ability of the municipalities to achieve the goals of any judgment depends on the financial resources available to the city.[50]

Unlike citizen suits against municipalities, which drain resources that would otherwise be available to municipalities to achieve compliance, citizen suits against private industrial permittees can apply industry wide pressure. Although infrequently used against the plastic industry, a recent case illustrates the potential use of CWA citizen suits to address plastic pollution. In July 2017, Diane Wilson, a Texas shrimper, sued plastic manufacturer Formosa for illegal discharges of plastic pellets from its plastic facility in Point Comfort, Texas, in violation of its NPDES permit. Several years earlier, Diane, a resident of the area, began finding nurdles in Lavaca Bay, located between Corpus Christi and Houston, Texas, and began to see an impact on the ecosystem and her shrimping business. She began taking daily samples, videos, and photographs of the plastic pellets she found around Lavaca Bay, building her case against the petrochemical manufacturer.

Formosa's original CWA permit was issued by the Texas Department of Environmental Quality in 1993 and allowed Formosa to treat and discharge wastewater and stormwater into Lavaca Bay. Formosa's permit, however, which was renewed most recently in 2016, prohibited the "discharge of floating solids or visible foam in other than trace amounts."[51]

Using the citizen suit provision of the CWA, Diane, along with the San Antonio Bay Estuarine Waterkeepers, filed a suit in federal court in 2017 and alleged that Formosa was in violation of its permit and thereby violating the CWA. The plaintiffs were represented pro bono

[50] Peter Crane Anderson, The CSO sleeping giant: Combined sewer overflow or congressional stalling objective, *Virginia Environmental Law Journal* 10 (1991): 371, 396.

[51] *San Antonia Estuarine Waterkeeper* v. *Formosa Plastic Corps.*, Civil Action No. 6:17-CV-0047 (S.D. Tex. June 27, 2019) (available at https://static.texastribune.org/media/files/193f5484368b30dcdd2e6dd1b30a1eec/Formosa.pdf?_ga=2.230896537.707500406.1573009504–816833637.1572574364) (last accessed October 31, 2021).

by Texas Rio Grande Legal Aid. At a bench trial or nonjury trial in March 2019, a federal judge reviewed "30 containers containing 2,428 samples of plastics"[52] and "at least 110 videos and 44 photos" from Lavaca Bay.[53] After reviewing the evidence and hearing from multiple witnesses including several expert witnesses, the court issued its order in plaintiffs' favor.

In its June 2019 order, the court found that "Formosa's discharges at its outfalls have consistently exceeded trace amounts . . . ." and labeled Formosa a "serial offender"[54] for "violating its Permit concerning discharge of floating solids, in other than trace amounts . . . [s]ome 1,149 days . . . ."[55] The court also recognized the harm these discharges caused the community noting that the plastic pellets and PVC powder discharged by Formosa "caused or contributed to the damages suffered by the recreational, aesthetic, and economic value"[56] of the area and harmed the shrimp population.

After the court's ruling, the parties entered into settlement negotiations. Formosa agreed to pay $50 million over five years for mitigation efforts to "provide environmental benefits to affected areas."[57] Formosa also agreed to engage engineers to design a system to "halt" the discharge of plastics[58] and to pay more than $3 million in attorneys' fees.[59] Experts are hailing it as a historic settlement that has the potential to change both the way the US plastics industry handles its pollution problem and how advocates approach plastic pollution.

Inspired by the Formosa decision, a similar suit was filed in 2020 by the Charleston Waterkeeper – an environmental nonprofit located in South Carolina – and the Southern Environmental Law Center – an environmental law group. The plaintiffs sued plastic resin packaging

[52] Ibid. at 8.
[53] Ibid. at 10.
[54] Ibid. at 17.
[55] Ibid. at 17.
[56] Ibid. at 19.
[57] Final consent decree, *San Antonia Estuarine Waterkeeper* v. *Formosa Plastic Corp.*, Civil Action No. 6:17-CV-47, (S.D. Tex. November 27, 2019) (available at https://drive.google.com/file/d/1LobihPcOEutp44a2PmTQjTxbJ09i5zE4/view) at 15 (last accessed October 31, 2021).
[58] Ibid. at 7.
[59] Ibid. at 21.

company Frontier Logistics using the citizen suit provisions of the Resources Conservation and Recovery Act and the Clean Water Act.[60] The plaintiffs claimed Frontier violated these laws by releasing plastic pellets into the Cooper River, Charleston Harbor, and other Charleston waterways; since July 2019, the Waterkeeper had collected over 14,000 nurdles.[61] In March 2021, Frontier settled with the plaintiffs for $1.2 million.

Citizen suits are a central, but often overlooked, component of environmental laws.[62] More citizen suit actions have been brought under the CWA than any other environmental statute because of the relative ease of proving a CWA violation.[63] In an era of decreased regulation and under-enforcement, citizen suits offer a promising way to ensure compliance with federal law and to reduce plastic pollution. The hope is that exposure to liability will lead to improved self-regulation by plastic manufacturers and will prompt these businesses to avoid harms by taking adequate precautions, such as complying with CWA permits.

*5 **CWA: Trash Free Water Grants*** Grants are a nonregulatory way to address plastic pollution, and one which the EPA has enthusiastically embraced. In July 2019 and September 2019, the EPA announced two opportunities to submit grant applications for Trash Free Water Grants: one targeting pollution in the Great Lakes and the other targeting the Gulf of Mexico. In announcing the Great Lakes grant, then-EPA Administrator Anthony Wheeler explained that the grants were intended to fund efforts by communities and organizations to cleanup beaches and waterways in the Great Lakes watershed. The EPA estimates that $2 million in total funding will be available for the Great Lakes grants and $5 million for the Gulf of Mexico grants, with the maximum amount being capped at $500,000. Types of eligible

[60] Complaint for Injunctive and Declaratory Relief, *Charleston Waterkeeper* v. *Frontier Logistics, L.P.*, 20-cv-01089-DCN (D.S.C. March 18, 2020).

[61] Ibid. ¶ 2.

[62] Jonathan H. Adler, Stand or deliver: Citizen suits, standing, and environmental protection, *Duke Environmental Law & Policy Forum* 12 (2001): 39, 42.

[63] Karl S. Coplan, Citizen litigants citizen regulators: Four cases where citizen suits drove development of clean water law, *Colorado Natural Resources, Energy, & Environmental Law Review* 25 (2014): 61, 85.

projects include trash prevention, trash removal, and outreach/education. Applications are accepted from state agencies, federally recognized tribes, local governments, nonprofit organizations, interstate agencies, and colleges and universities. Funds for the Gulf of Mexico project are authorized under Section 104(b)(3) of the Clean Water Act, which authorizes grants to reduce pollution generally, while funds for the Great Lake Projects are authorized as part of the Great Lakes Restoration Initiative, Section 118(c)(7) of the Clean Water Act.

B Land-Based Sources: The Clean Air Act

Under the Clean Air Act, the EPA has the authority to regulate the air pollution emitted by stationary sources including the foam, fiber, plastic, and rubber products industries. These industries often emit pollutants deemed hazardous by the EPA. For example, reinforced plastic composite production facilities release styrene, methyl methacrylate, and methylene chloride (dichloromethane), while facilities fabricating flexible polyurethane foam release hydrochloric acid, 2,4-toluene diisocyanate, and hydrogen cyanide. These emissions trigger EPA's regulatory authority.

Under the national emission standards for hazardous air pollutants (NESHAP) set through the Clean Air Act, 42 U.S.C. § 7401, the EPA can regulate the hazardous pollutants emitted by foam and plastic industries.[64] Section 112(d) of the Clean Air Act requires major sources of flexible polyurethane foam fabrication to meet hazardous air pollutant emission standards that reflect the application of maximum achievable control technology (MACT).[65] These standards and regulations have not been updated in almost thirty years, and as was done with the CWA effluent standards, hundreds of nonprofits have petitioned the EPA to revise standards applicable to plastics production facilities under Sections 111 and 112 of the Clean Air Act. Specifically, the petition argues that "[e]thylene, propylene,

[64] www.epa.gov/stationary-sources-air-pollution/clean-air-act-standards-and-guidelines-foam-fiber-plastic-and (last accessed October 31, 2021).

[65] www.epa.gov/stationary-sources-air-pollution/flexible-polyurethane-foam-fabrication-operations-national-emission (last accessed October 31, 2021).

polyethylene, and polypropylene production facilities are stationary sources that emit air pollution that endangers public health and welfare and therefore must be listed as a source category under CAA Section 111."[66] The EPA has yet to take action on this petition.

While requiring more stringent air pollution standards for plastic production would address some of the harms generated during the production of plastic, it would not address the harms associated with finished plastic products. That said, use of the CAA by environmental advocates illustrates a growing recognition that a life cycle approach is necessary to address plastic pollution in a holistic way from production to disposal.

C Land-Based Sources: Other Laws

Pollution control statutes, such as the Clean Water Act and the Clean Air Act, focus on controlling or limiting the amount of pollution released into the environment, usually seeking to achieve the controls or limits by means of technology. In contrast, *pollution prevention* statutes focus on generating less pollution in the first instance by encouraging facilities to operate in ways that generate less pollution.

The *Pollution Prevention Act* (PPA) of 1990 established a national policy that pollution "should be prevented or reduced at the source whenever feasible," and that "disposal or other releases into the environment should be employed only as a last resort and should be conducted in an environmentally safe manner."[67] This Act defines pollution prevention as "the preferred means of waste management for the country by putting the hierarchy into national law," with source reduction at the top and disposal the least optimal choice.[68]

[66] Petition to the US Environmental Protection Agency to revise the Clean Air Act Section 111 and Section 112 standards applicable to petro-plastics production facilities, 364 *Environmental, Public Health, Indigenous, Labor, and Community Non-Governmental Organizations* v. *Anthony Wheeler*, Administrator, United States Environmental Protection Agency (available at www.biologicaldiversity.org/campaigns/plastic-production/pdfs/19-12-3-NSPS-Petition.pdf) (last accessed October 31, 2021).

[67] 42 U.S.C. §§ 13101–13109.

[68] Joel S. Hirschhorn, Pollution prevention comes of age, *Georgia Law Review* 29 (1995): 325.

The pollution prevention approach was adopted in the *Toxic Release Inventory* (TRI) program established with the enactment of the Emergency Planning and Community Right to Know Act of 1986. This program requires all US facilities that meet TRI reporting criteria to submit TRI data to the EPA and the relevant state or tribe by July 1 of each year. The chemicals included in the TRI program are those that cause cancer or other chronic or adverse acute human health effects as well as chemicals that cause significant adverse environmental effects. There are currently 755 individually listed chemicals and 33 chemical categories.[69] Facilities required to report a TRI are typically larger facilities involved in manufacturing, metal mining, electric power generation, chemical manufacturing, and hazardous waste treatment, and could potentially include different sectors of the plastic industry. Plastic manufacturers that use chemicals requiring a Toxic Release Inventory must file a toxic chemical source reduction and recycling report.

For example, 51 percent of all styrene (or ethylbenzene) releases reported to the EPA's TRI program came from what the EPA has termed the Plastics Product Manufacturing sector.[70] The EPA reports that since 2006 this industry sector has reduced its styrene emissions by 40 percent.[71] Source reduction techniques include using substitute chemicals, upgrading equipment, and improving work practices.[72] Failure to report releases, such as the release of styrene, can result in fines. For example, in 1999, Associated Plastics Corp.[73] was fined by the EPA for failing to report styrene releases between 1994 and 1997 as part of its TRI.[74]

[69] www.epa.gov/toxics-release-inventory-tri-program/tri-listed-chemicals (last accessed October 31, 2021).

[70] Environmental Protection Agency, Reducing styrene waste in the plastics product manufacturing sector (2018) (available at www.epa.gov/sites/production/files/2018-04/documents/tri_p2_spotlight_styrene_25apr2018.pdf) (last accessed October 31, 2021).

[71] Ibid.

[72] Environmental Protection Agency, TRI P2 Industry Profile (available at www.epa.gov/toxics-release-inventory-tri-program/tri-p2-industry-profile) (last accessed October 16, 2021).

[73] https://archive.epa.gov/epapages/newsroom_archive/newsreleases/2e950dfb938d1f5f852570d8005e1324.html (last accessed October 31, 2021).

[74] 12 No. 23 Cal. Envtl. Insider 3 (available at https://archive.epa.gov/epapages/newsroom_archive/newsreleases/2e950dfb938d1f5f852570d8005e1324.html) (last accessed October 31, 2021).

Although the mandatory information disclosure method used by the TRI has been successful in reducing chemicals in our environment, it only addresses some of the chemicals used by the plastic industry. Consequently, adding more chemicals used in plastic production to the TRI might be one way to address some aspects of plastic pollution. Scholar Jodi Short notes that TRI has been deemed a "success not because it prompted neighbors of polluting factories to move, but rather because it changed the way that those factories measured and managed toxic releases, resulting in significant emissions declines."[75]

The *Toxic Substances Control Act* of 1976 authorized the EPA to require the testing of new and existing chemical substances entering the environment and the contingent authority to regulate the substance.[76] The standard established by the statute is that "the chemical presents or will present an unreasonable risk of injury to health or the environment."[77] If unreasonable risk is determined, the EPA can ban or limit the production of the chemical. Because the EPA's focus is on the toxicity of the chemicals and not on the effects of the products in which the chemicals are used, the EPA has historically applied its authority to substances deemed more acutely toxic than plastic materials.[78] For example, the EPA banned polychlorinated biphenyl (PCB) in 1979 after it was determined to be a human carcinogen. While PCBs are no longer manufactured, they persist in the environment and are absorbed by plastic polymers. Given that the EPA released its first update to Toxic Substances Control Act (TSCA) in forty years in 2019, working to add chemicals used in plastic to TSCA might not be the most effective means to address plastic's harms.

Finally, the *Resource Conservation and Recovery Act* (RCRA) and the *Comprehensive Environmental Response, Compensation, and Liability Act* (CERCLA or Superfund) could be invoked when dealing with plastic pollution.[79] RCRA deals with the current waste disposal of solid and hazardous wastes, while CERCLA deals with problems from prior

[75] Jodi L. Short, The political turn in American Administrative Law: Power, rationality, and reasons, *Duke Law Journal* 61 (2012): 1811, 1851.

[76] 15 U.S.C. § 2601 et seq.

[77] 15 U.S.C. § 2605(a).

[78] EPA, Plastic pellets in the aquatic environment.

[79] 42 U.S.C. § 6901 et seg (RCRA) and 42 U.S.C. § 9601 et seq. (CERCA).

waste disposal practices and imposes liability to ensure cleanup of contaminated sites. States play the lead role in implementing nonhazardous waste programs of RCRA. Under the RCRA, the EPA has the authority to regulate "waste" that falls within the statute from its creation to its disposal or "cradle-to-grave." As the agency in charge of developing regulations and policies surrounding solid and hazardous waste, the EPA must ensure the safe management and cleanup of these materials and encourage their reduction and beneficial reuse.

Currently, plastic is treated as solid waste, but recently scientists have called for the reclassification of plastic from solid waste to hazardous waste.[80] Doing so would invoke stricter regulations. The international community also encouraged this reclassification in summer of 2019 with amendments to the Basel Convention as is discussed in Chapter 6.

D Water-Based Sources: Marine Protection, Research, and Sanctuaries Act (Ocean Dumping Act)

In addition to federal laws focused on pollution generated on land, federal laws, such as the Marine Protection, Research, and Sanctuaries Act (MPRSA), can focus on water-based sources of pollution.[81] Like other water, air, and marine protection laws, MPRSA does not target plastic pollution per se and instead regulates "all types of materials" that could "adversely affect human health, welfare … or the marine environment, ecological systems, or economic potentialities"[82] when dumped in the ocean. Enacted in 1972, the MPRSA, also known as the Ocean Dumping Act, has two purposes: to regulate intentional ocean disposal of materials and to authorize related research.[83] The EPA and NOAA, together with the US Army Corps of Engineers and the Coast Guard are responsible for implementing MPRSA. Like the CWA,

[80] Chelsea M. Rochman, Mark Anthony Browne, Benjamin S. Halpern et al., Classify plastic waste as hazardous, *Nature* (February 14, 2013) (available at www.nature.com/articles/494169a.pdf) (last accessed October 31, 2021).

[81] 33 U.S.C. §§ 1401–1445.

[82] 33 U.S.C. § 1401(b).

[83] Claudia Copland, Ocean Dumping Act: A summary of the law, Congressional Research Service (October 18, 2016) (available at https://aquadoc.typepad.com/files/crs_ocean_dumping_18oct2016.pdf) (last accessed October 31, 2021).

MPRSA prohibits ocean dumping except in the limited circumstances when a permit has been obtained.

The primary concern today appears to be dredged materials – sediments removed from the bottom of waterbodies that are later transported out to the ocean for disposal. Other materials of concern are vessels themselves, fish wastes, and human remains. Under the Act, the EPA can impose civil penalties of not more than $50,000 for each violation of a permit or permit requirement, and can consider the gravity of the violation, prior violations, and demonstrations of good faith when assessing the penalty.

While the author could not find recent applications of MPRSA to plastic pollution, an EPA report from 1992 notes that "[u]nder the MPRSA, no US vessel may transport any material, including plastic, for the purpose of dumping the material into the ocean unless the vessel has a permit to dump from EPA; EPA does not grant permits for the dumping of plastics into the ocean and regulations implementing the MPRSA also prohibit such dumping."[84]

MPRSA was enacted to comply with the obligations of Article VI of the London Convention of 1972, which provided a framework for the "global control of the deliberate disposal of all wastes in the oceans."[85] This international treaty is discussed in Chapter 6.

E Water-Based Sources: The Marine Plastic Pollution Research and Control Act (Act to Prevent Pollution from Ships)

The Marine Plastic Pollution Research and Control Act (MPPRCA), passed in 1987, also focuses on ocean-based sources from ships including merchant and military vessels, recreational and commercial fishermen, and cruise lines.[86] The MPPRCA was an amendment to the Act to Prevent Pollution from Ships (APPS), whose goal was to

[84] EPA, Plastic pellets in the aquatic environment.

[85] Susan L. Dautel, Transoceanic Trash: International and United States strategies for the Great Pacific Garbage Patch, *Golden Gate University Environmental Law Journal* 3 (2009): 181, 190.

[86] 33 U.S.C. § 1952.

implement the 1973 International Convention for the Prevention of Pollution from Ships (MARPOL 73/78) – an international effort to curb marine pollution. The MPPRCA implements provisions of MARPOL Annex V (discussed in Chapter 6), which specifically prohibits the discharge of plastics in the oceans. MPPRCA gives enforcement of the Act to the Coast Guard, with NOAA, the EPA, and other federal agencies being responsible for monitoring and public education duties. The Act also authorizes rewards for information leading to a conviction or the assessment of a civil penalty for the unlawful disposal of pollution.[87] MPPRCA requires ships to keep record books and waste management plans, and ports and terminals to provide reception facilities for waste generated at sea.[88]

Under the Act, the US Coast Guard is required "to cost-effectively monitor and enforce compliance with MARPOL Annex V and the Act to Prevent Pollution from Ships (APPS) (33 U.S.C. § 1901 et seq.), including through cooperation and coordination with other Federal and State enforcement programs."[89] As an example, in 2017 the Department of Justice prosecuted two shipping companies for, among other things, falsifying records regarding disposal of garbage from a ship, in violation of the Act to Prevent Pollution from Ships. Specifically, the company discharged bilge water into the ocean without it first passing through its pollution prevention equipment.[90] Crew members were also instructed to throw plastic garbage bags filled with metal and incinerator ash into the sea. The ship did not record the discharge of bilge water and of plastic garbage into the ocean in violation of APPS.[91] The shipping company entered into a plea agreement and the settlement included a $1.9 million penalty.[92] Part of the criminal fine assessed went to a crew member "whistleblower" who provided the information that initiated the government's investigation into the shipping company.

[87] 33 U.S.C. § 1908.
[88] 33 U.S.C. § 1905(a)(2); 33 U.S.C. § 1903(b)(2)(A).
[89] 33 U.S.C. § 1953(a)(2).
[90] Press release from the US Attorney's Office, Eastern District of Texas, Two international shipping companies pay $1.9 million for covering up vessel pollution (June 20, 2017).
[91] Ibid.
[92] Ibid.

This case highlights an important challenge when addressing water-based sources of plastic pollution: detection. As a 2015 *New York Times* article explained, there are "few places on the planet that are as lawless as the high seas, where egregious crimes are routinely committed with impunity."[93] This includes environmental crimes such as illegal dumping of waste. The investigative report by the newspaper found that while "[c]ountries have signed dozens of maritime pacts, the shipping industry has published reams of guidelines and the United Nations maritime agency has written hundreds of rules, all aimed at regulating ships, crews and safety … [these] … laws are also often weak, contradictory and easily skirted by criminals. National and international agencies usually have neither the inclination nor resources to enforce them."[94] In the article, Mark Young, a retired US Coast Guard commander and former chief of enforcement for the Pacific Ocean, remarks that the oceans are "like the Wild West. Weak rules, few sheriffs, lots of outlaws."[95]

Because of this, tips from citizens about violations are extremely important. In April 2019, the Environmental Law Institute (ELI), hosted a webinar with panelists from ELI, DOJ, the US Coast Guard, and the National Whistleblower Center on Citizens Enforcement of Maritime Laws: the Role of Private Citizens. The webinar explained how citizens can be the eyes and ears of ocean pollution violations including violations of the Act to Prevent Pollution from Ships. While it is important to continue to enforce these laws focused on water-based sources of plastic, it is also important to recognize that most plastic pollution originates from land-based sources.

F Other Statutes

Finally, several statutes focus narrowly on small contributors of plastic waste. For example, the Magnuson Fishery Conservation and

[93] Ian Urbina, Stowaways and crimes aboard a scofflaw ship, *The New York Times* (July 19, 2015) (available at www.nytimes.com/2015/07/19/world/stowaway-crime-scofflaw-ship.html) (last accessed October 31, 2021).

[94] Ibid.

[95] Ibid.

Management Act, was amended in 1987 and 1990, 16 U.S.C. §§ 1801–1861, to implement the moratorium called for by the United Nations General Assembly and outlaw the use of large-scale driftnets. The Medical Waste Tracking Act (MWTA)[96] establishes a cradle-to-grave tracking system for medical waste, and the US Public Vessel Medical Waste Anti-Dumping Act[97] outlaws the dumping of medical waste. Other statutes address handling of waste generally, such as the Shore Protection Act of 1987, which specifies waste-handling practices for loading, receiving, and offloading municipal and commercial waste transported in coastal waters.[98]

V CONCLUSION

Several federal statutes can be used to prevent and respond to plastic pollution. The federal government has been aware of plastic pollution for decades and has consistently identified different ways its federal agencies can fulfill their regulatory and nonregulatory obligations. Yet our plastic problem persists and worsens for several reasons. First, apart from the Microbead-Free Waters Act, no statute specifically regulates the production of plastics. Second, many of the statutes address only marine debris generally and do not directly target plastic producers. Acts such as the Marine Debris Act are focused on important, but nonregulatory methods of addressing marine debris control, such as research and education. Third, those statutes focused on direct regulation of marine debris are focused on pollution from vessels in our ocean and not on plastic generated from land-based sources. And finally, the effectiveness of statutes with regulatory teeth, such as Clean Water Act or the Act to Prevent Pollution from Ships, depends on detection and enforcement, which is particularly challenging for water-based sources of pollution.

From a policy perspective, the federal government has not focused on plastic production or plastic manufacturers, and instead has

[96] 42 U.S.C. § 6992.
[97] 33 U.S.C. § 2501.
[98] 33 U.S.C. § 2601.

embraced the argument that plastic pollution is a waste management problem created by other countries. Former EPA Administrator Anthony Wheeler was quick to point out that nearly 60 percent of marine litter comes from six Asian nations – China, Indonesia, the Philippines, Vietnam, Sri Lanka, and Thailand – overlooking the fact that the United States has been shipping its plastic waste to these countries for decades. The federal government's narrow legislative approach, an approach embraced by the petrochemical and plastic industries, has limited the executive branch's ability to craft solutions that will result in measurable reductions and have global impacts.

At the same time, the United States is fortunate to have waste management and pollution prevention statutes in place. The federal government should adopt a plastic policy that is committed to fully funding existing programs and enforcing violations of federal law.

Unlike the federal government – whose approach has been to embrace nonregulatory approaches and enforce existing laws – states and local governments have sought to enact new laws focused on banning plastic. That approach, and others, is the topic of Chapter 5.

5 STATE AND LOCAL EFFORTS

Almost 100 years ago, Justice Brandeis called states the "laboratories of democracy."[1] The phrase describes how "a state may, if its citizens choose, serve as a laboratory; and try novel social and economic experiments without risk to the rest of the country."[2] Environmental law scholars have argued that states (and cities) are more flexible – and can move faster – and, therefore, offer more opportunity to initiate innovation than does the federal government.[3] And as federal discourse about environmental matters grows more polarized, state and local approaches become more attractive. As Professor Stenzel notes:

> The process of starting on the state or local level seems to work well politically, because the public seems more willing to accept new approaches on a local or state level rather than at the national level. Individual states can choose varying mechanisms as the tools for achieving their goals. Then, those laws can be examined to see which options have proven to be the most effective.[4]

This is particularly true when it comes to plastic.

Because a comprehensive federal legislative solution to plastic pollution is unlikely, many states and local entities are using their legislative powers to reduce plastic pollution. Further, given that the

[1] *New State Ice Co.* v. *Liebmann*, 285 U.S. 262, 311 (1932) (Brandeis, J., dissenting).

[2] Ibid.

[3] David L. Markell, States as innovators: It's time for a new look to our "laboratories of democracy" in the effort to improve our approach to environmental regulation, *Albany Law Review* 58 (1994): 347, 355. ("In sum, innovations at the state level are likely to hold a great deal of promise as potential strategies for addressing concerns about federal approaches to environmental regulation.")

[4] Paulette L. Stenzel, Right to act: Advancing the common interests of labor and environmentalists, *Albany Law Review* 57 (1993): 1, 37.

regulation of solid waste is considered a state and local – as opposed to a federal – issue, it is not surprising that there is considerable state and local activity aimed at reducing plastic pollution. This activity largely centers on regulating consumer use of single-use plastic products – such as bags and straws – as opposed to focusing on regulating the manufacturing of plastic itself. The goal of these regulatory efforts is source reduction rather than cleaning up plastic in the environment.

Chapter 5 discusses three approaches to reducing plastic pollution: bans, taxes, and container deposit laws. While bans and taxes on plastics have similar goals – to reduce the number of straws that wash up on our beaches or the amount of bags that float downstream – container deposit laws, or so-called bottle bills, have the additional waste management goal of encouraging recycling. All three approaches to reducing plastic pollution require different policy instruments. Bans adopt a command and control approach to directly regulate behavior, while taxes are market-based instruments that attempt to indirectly regulate behavior by means of price. Container-deposit laws are a market mechanism called a "deposit-refund system," which combines a tax on plastic consumption with a rebate when the bottle is returned for recycling.

Chapter 5 discusses the occurrence of all three approaches at the state and local levels in the United States. The chapter also discusses attempts to quantify the effectiveness of the different approaches. The chapter discusses the plastic industry's long-standing opposition to local and state efforts to reduce plastic pollution, as well as the more recent phenomenon of state legislatures preempting enactment of local laws, prompting debates between state and local power. The Chapter ends with a discussion of COVID-19's impact on state and local laws and the use of litigation in state courts as a strategy to address plastic pollution.

I PLASTIC BANS AND BOTTLE BILLS

Perhaps the most visible local ban involves plastic straws. Plastic straws became the poster child for the plastic waste movement when, in 2018, a nine-year-old calculated that Americans use an estimated 500 million straws each day. While that number has yet to be confirmed through measurable research, the statistic was circulated in major publication outlets leading many cities and businesses to take up the issue. That same year, the Surfrider Foundation called 2018 the "year we say goodbye to straws." And Eater, a national online publication focused on food and drink, called plastic straw bans the trend of the year.

At the city level, Seattle was the first major metropolitan area to enact a ban on plastic straws and utensils. The law, which went into effect on July 1, 2018, prohibits food establishments, including restaurants, food trucks, and delis, from providing customers with plastic straws and utensils. Recyclable and compostable alternatives may be provided if requested. Other large cities such as Washington, DC, and smaller cities such as Fort Meyers, Florida, followed suit.

While straw bans received media notoriety, other bans have been enacted with less fanfare. Seattle banned polystyrene (or clamshell) containers in 2008 and plastic utensils in 2010. Foam bans were enacted in San Francisco in 2016 and New York City in 2017. Bag bans have been enacted in over 150 cities in the United States, including San Francisco, which is credited with enacting the first bag ban in 2007. Bag bans exist in cities in Alaska, Illinois, Massachusetts, Maryland, New Jersey, New Mexico, Rhode Island, South Carolina, Utah, and Washington.

Statewide action often occurs to create uniformity at the local level. Nine states – California, Hawaii, New York, Connecticut, Delaware, Maine, Oregon, Vermont, and most recently Washington – have enacted statewide bans on single-use plastic bags.[5] While bags seem to be the target of statewide action, states have also explored, but not enacted, bans on plastic straws, utensils, Styrofoam packaging, and plastic bottles for personal care products.

California has been a trailblazing state when it comes to laws aimed at reducing plastic pollution, including plastic bag bans. After more than 100 California cities passed local ordinances outlawing plastic bags, then-Governor Jerry Brown signed into law a statewide ban on plastic bags (Senate Bill 270). In addition to prohibiting single-use

[5] National Conference of State Legislatures, State Plastic Bag Legislation (available at www.ncsl.org/research/environment-and-natural-resources/plastic-bag-legislation.aspx) (last accessed April 11, 2021).

plastic carryout bags, the legislation also created new material content and durability standards for reusable plastic carryout bags and required stores to charge at least 10 cents for any plastic bag it provides to customers.[6] There are exceptions to this law. For example, people who participate in the Supplemental Nutrition Assistance Program (SNAP) program would not be charged the bag fee and plastic bags would still be allowed for prescriptions, produce, and bulk items. The money generated from the plastic bag charge goes toward educational campaigns and offsetting the cost of complying with the law.

Industry groups lobbied against the ban, delaying its implementation, and eventually Proposition 67 was added to the ballot in 2016. Proposition 67 asked voters to decide whether the law should take effect. A yes vote approved the legislation; a no vote rejected it. An additional Proposition, Proposition 65, sought to redirect the income generated by the 10-cent-per-plastic-bag charge to an environmental fund administered by the state Wildlife Conservation Board. Proposition 67 passed, while Proposition 65 failed.

California has also banned the use of plastic straws. In September 2018, Governor Brown signed into law Assembly Bill 1884, which governs the use of plastic straws in full-service restaurants. The law prohibits full-service restaurants, as defined by the law, from providing straws to customers unless requested. This law was enacted after several cities started banning the use of plastic straws at the local level.

California Governor Gavin Newsom, who succeeded Governor Brown, has continued to build on his predecessor's efforts, and in 2019 signed into law Assembly Bill 1162, which prohibits lodging establishments from "providing a small plastic bottle containing a personal care product" to guests. The law, which takes effect in either 2023 or 2024 depending on the lodging establishments' size, imposes a civil penalty (or fine) for those establishments that violate this requirement. While California is the first state to enact such a law, many private hotel chains, including Marriott, are making efforts to eliminate the use of small plastic bottles found in guest rooms. (This and other

[6] Chapter 5.3 sections 42280–42288 et seq. (available at http://leginfo.legislature.ca.gov/faces/codes_displayexpandedbranch.xhtml?tocCode=PRC&division=30.&title=&part=3.&chapter=5.3.&article=) (last accessed August 16, 2021).

efforts such as the voluntary decision of grocery giant Kroger Co. to end the use of plastic bags have been labeled as private environmental governance and are discussed later in Chapter 7).

In 2019, Oregon Governor Kate Brown signed into law HB 2509, which prohibited retailers from providing "single-use checkout bags" to customers. Under this law, single-use checkout bags include any bag "made of paper, plastic or any other material that is provided by a retail establishment to a customer at the time of checkout, and that is not a recycled paper checkout bag, a reusable fabric checkout bag or a reusable plastic checkout bag."[7] At the same time, Governor Kate Brown signed a separate bill, SB 90, which prohibited food and beverage providers and convenience stores from providing single-use straws to consumers unless the consumer specifically asks for it. Both bills went into effect on January 1, 2020.

New York followed California and Oregon's lead and enacted the Plastic Bag Reduction Law in March 2019.[8] Under this state law, shoppers are encouraged to bring a reusable shopping bag when they shop. Retailers will no longer provide plastic bags to customers and consumers will be charged 5 cents for using a paper carry-out bag. Like the California law, the New York law carves out exceptions and allows for the use of plastic bags for items sold in bulk, prescription medication, and uncooked meat products. New York's 2019 law does not impact the 2009 state law that requires larger retailers to collect and recycle plastic bags. The ban, which was scheduled to take effect on March 1, 2020, was delayed due to the COVID-19 outbreak and as of this writing, has not been implemented.

Polystyrene or plastic foam (more commonly known as Styrofoam) used for food packaging has also been banned by state and local authorities. Maine, Vermont, and Maryland, and most recently New York, have enacted bans on expanded polystyrene (EPS) foam often used in food containers such as clamshell cases and egg cartons. While some states have banned EPS foam used as a filler in packages (i.e., packing peanuts), Maine was the first state to enact a statewide ban on

[7] Oregon House Bill 2509.

[8] Title 28 § 27-2801 et seq. (available at www.nysenate.gov/legislation/laws/ENV/A27T28) (last accessed October 31, 2021).

EPS food containers. Enacted in 2019, the Maine law is scheduled to take effect in 2021. The Maryland General Assembly also passed a law in 2019 to "prohibit food service businesses and schools from selling or providing food or beverages in expanded polystyrene food service products."[9] This law went into effect in July 2020.

In addition to bans, some state and local municipalities have adopted policies incorporating financial incentives to curb the use of plastic. With a "bag tax," consumers pay a small fee at checkout for bags they use. Economic theorists have long argued that financial incentives can prompt or "nudge" behavior change. Some policy-makers favor this approach over an outright ban because financial incentives preserve consumer choice while still achieving the goal of reducing plastic use. Financial incentives can take the form of a fee or tax to discourage certain behavior or a reward or refund to encourage certain behavior.

Curbing the use of plastic by means of a tax is an approach that is applied primarily to reducing the use of plastic bags. This bag tax approach has been adopted in several cities. Washington, DC is one of the first locations to have implemented a tax on plastic bags. In 2009, in an effort to cleanup the city's Anacostia River, the District initiated its 5-cent tax on plastic bags. In 2017, Chicago replaced its 2015 bag ban with a 7-cent tax on all paper and plastic checkout bags.

A third and less frequently used policy instrument are container deposit laws or "bottle bills." Bottle bills are a type of deposit-refund program, which combines a tax on the consumption of a beverage with a rebate when the product's packaging is returned. In states with bottle bills, the consumer purchasing the beverage pays the deposit or tax (usually 5 or 10 cents) to the retailer, who has already paid the distributor a deposit. The consumer then receives the deposit back when the empty container is returned to the retailer, and the distributor returns the deposit to the retailer.[10] The retailer, in effect, acts as a middleman. Bottle bills work best when administrative costs are minimized and there is a competitive recycling market.

[9] Maryland House Bill 0109.

[10] https://media.rff.org/documents/RFF-DP-11-47.pdf (last accessed October 31, 2021).

Ten states have bottle bills. Most were enacted in the 1970s and 1980s with the primary goal of reducing litter and the secondary goal of encouraging glass and aluminum recycling. Over the years, these bills have been updated to include plastic bottles for carbonated and noncarbonated beverages. While some states have considered implementing bottle bills, as Colorado did in 2004 and 2010, and six states proposed bottle bills in 2019, no state bottle bills have been enacted in the United States since 2002.

A national bottle bill gained some traction with the US General Accounting Office (GAO) when it studied state beverage container deposit laws in 1977 and 1980. The GAO concluded in 1980 "that if the Congress passed a national law, the beverage container share of litter and post-consumer solid waste would be greatly reduced."[11] While a national law has yet to be enacted, the Break Free from Plastic Pollution Act, which was introduced in 2020, and discussed in Chapter 4, includes a national bottle bill. (Recycling is discussed in more detail in Chapter 9).

A Effectiveness

Empirical studies measuring the effectiveness of bans in reducing plastic waste are limited, but anecdotal evidence and community studies suggest that bans work. One such study conducted by Californians Against Waste (CAW) reported that the number of plastic bags found on California beaches decreased 72 percent between 2010 and 2017, the year that California's statewide ban on the use of plastic bags took effect. The study also concluded that the state's 2017 ban prevented over 13.8 billion grocery bags from entering the landfills or the environment. One economist has written that "bans may be efficient when the marginal benefits of the good are small and the marginal social costs associated with its production/use or improper disposal are high."[12] Another study found that bag bans were effective at

[11] United States General Accounting Office, States' experience with beverage container deposit laws shows positive experience (December 10, 1980) (available at www.gao.gov/assets/pad-81-08.pdf) (last accessed October 31, 2021).

[12] Joshua K. Abbott and U. Rashid Sumaila, Reducing marine plastic pollution: Policy insights from economics, *Review of Environmental Economics and Policy* 13 (Summer

decreasing disposable bag consumption and increasing reusable bag usage, but bans also had the unintended consequence of increasing paper bag demand with its attendant negative environmental impact in terms of air and water pollution, and water and energy use.[13]

This phenomenon is what economists call "leakage." According to economists, "leakage" – or incomplete coverage which causes a problem to persist – occurs when partial regulation of a product (i.e., plastic grocery bags) results in increased consumption of unregulated goods (i.e., paper bags or garbage bags).

An increase in the amount of paper bags used is only one of the unintended consequences of bag bans. Research has also shown that bans lead to an increase in the purchase of larger plastic bags. A researcher at Australia's University of Sydney studied California's plastic bag ban and found the legislation had attained its intended goal of reducing the number of plastic bags used. But people still needed bags to line smaller trash containers and collect dog waste. The study found a significant increase in the purchasing of 4-gallon (120 percent increase) and 8-gallon trash bags[14] after the ban went into place. The study also found that 30 percent of the plastic that was eliminated by the ban was reintroduced into the waste stream in the form of thicker garbage bags; additionally, there was an increase in the use of paper bags. Studies have shown that larger plastic bags and paper bags have a larger carbon footprint than the typical single-use plastic bag; they require more water and energy to produce and take up more landfill space.

Studies on leakage suggest that laws targeting specific plastic *products* rather than their *raw materials* might not be the best approach. These studies suggest further that if a product-specific approach – such as a plastic bag ban – is implemented, it should be paired with a

2019): 327–36 (available at www.journals.uchicago.edu/doi/full/10.1093/reep/rez007#xref_rez007-FN3).

[13] Rebecca L. C. Taylor, Bag leakage: The effect of disposable carryout bag regulations on unregulated bags, *Journal of Environmental Economics and Leakage* 93(C) (2019): 254–71 (available at www.sciencedirect.com/science/article/abs/pii/S0095069618305291?via%3Dihub) (last accessed October 31, 2021).

[14] Ibid.

small fee on the likely replacement products, such as paper bags, to encourage the use of reusable bags.

Unlike bag bans, bag taxes have been more thoroughly studied. Economists agree that "financial incentives aimed at encouraging desirable behaviors or discouraging harmful behaviors will be effective only if the magnitude of the incentive exceeds the costs an individual associates with changing his behavior."[15] NYU Economics Professor, Tatiana A. Homonoff, studied two financial policies implemented in the Washington, DC area that were aimed at reducing disposable bag use: a tax of 5 cents on disposable bag use and a 5-cent bonus for reusable bag use. Her results show that while the tax decreased disposable bag use by over 40 percent, the bonus generated virtually no effect on behavior.[16] The fee was more effective than the reward. Professor Homonoff's results support studies in behavioral economics that suggest "that individuals perceive losses more strongly than gains, i.e., they are 'loss-averse.'"[17]

A 2015 *Washington Post* investigative report was more skeptical in its evaluation of the effectiveness of Washington, DC's tax. Shortly after the tax was imposed, DC officials began claiming an 85 percent decrease in the numbers of plastic bags used each month. *The Washington Post* article states, however, that there was "little evidence" of such a "sudden, drastic reduction." The article was critical of DC officials' reliance on self-reporting by individuals. For example, according to a 2012–2013 municipal survey of DC residents, household consumption of plastic bags decreased by 60 percent, with 74–79 percent of residents surveyed reporting they were now using their own reusable bags.[18] Others, however, dispute the *Post* article's

[15] Tatiana A. Homonoff, Can small incentives have large effects? The impact of taxes versus bonuses on disposable bag use, *American Economic Journal: Economic Policy* 10 (2018): 177–210 (available at www.aeaweb.org/articles?id=10.1257/pol.20150261) (last accessed October 31, 2021).

[16] Ibid.

[17] Ibid.

[18] District Department of the Environment, Bag Law Survey Overview, Government of the District of Columbia (2013) (available at http://doee.dc.gov/sites/default/files/dc/sites/ddoe/documents/0%20BL%20Survey%20Overview%20Fact%20Sheet.pdf) (last accessed April 11, 2021).

"insinuation" that the tax was not working, claiming that the piece relied on data that was mischaracterized or taken out of context.[19]

Studies on the bag taxes in Chicago and San Francisco also show that charging customers a few cents more for plastic bags reduces plastic bag use.[20] A tripartite study by ideas42, a nonprofit group that seeks to apply insights from behavioral science to create lasting positive social impact, the University of Chicago Energy & Environment Lab, and Professor Homonoff evaluated the impact of Chicago's bag tax on consumer behavior by comparing shoppers at stores inside Chicago (subject to the tax) to shoppers at stores outside Chicago (not subject to the tax), from November 2016 through March 2018, before and after the tax went into effect. The study found that during the study period, the proportion of consumers using a disposable bag dropped by 27.7 percent from a baseline of 82.0 percent. The proportion of consumers using a reusable bag more than doubled: reusable bag use increased by 15.5 percent from a baseline of 13.2 percent of consumers. Additionally, the proportion of consumers using no bags at all increased by 12.6 percent from a baseline of 7.8 percent of consumers.[21] The study did, however, show that, over time, the effects of a tax diminish. Another study has shown that Toronto's bag tax affected the behavior of those who already occasionally carried reusable bags and were in a higher social economic tax bracket.[22] While taxes hold promise, policymakers should be aware that the effectiveness of

[19] Julie Lawson, The data proves the DC law is working (May 15, 2015) (available at https://ggwash.org/view/38159/the-data-proves-the-dc-bag-fee-is-working) (last accessed October 31, 2021).

[20] Alex Ruppenthal, Bag tax study: Use of disposable bags down but still above 50 percent (September 2018) (available at https://news.wttw.com/2018/09/07/bag-tax-study-use-disposable-bags-down-still-above-50-percent) (last accessed October 31, 2021).

[21] Tatiana A. Homonoff, Lee-Sien Kao, Doug Palmer, and Christina Seybolt, Skipping the bag: Assessing the impact of Chicago's tax on disposable bags (September 2018) (available at https://urbanlabs.uchicago.edu/attachments/a2bdfd83de8279fa83d9b2ab2d7fd38c926e3ab6/store/3a763ff7774ea3a6547be38d253c958248bcfb0573c436cc5409d4b82f69/I42–1033_BagTaxPaper_final.pdf) (last accessed October 31, 2021).

[22] Nicholas Rivers, Sarah Shenstone-Harris, and Nathan Young, Using nudges to reduce waste? The case of Toronto's plastic bag levy, *Journal of Environmental Management* 188 (March 2017): 153–62 (available at www.sciencedirect.com/science/article/pii/S030147971630980X?casa_token=66CuQrefxyEAAAAA:Bn-krisQj_nCB3qjeEX5t55Ane70jd1cfWh-E8WPITXOsog99XPXcH8Uh-uGx7xP7NKRHBzLY-We) (last accessed October 31, 2021).

economic incentives varies substantially across behavioral and demographic groups, and they should anticipate varying results.

States with bottle bills have some of the highest recycling rates in the country suggesting that bottle bills are effective in keeping plastic bottles out of landfills and our environment. Oregon's redemption rate (or return rate) stands at 90 percent, while Michigan recorded a redemption rate of 89 percent on carbonated beverages. Recycling will be further discussed in Chapter 9.

B Opposition

Bans and taxes have not been without opposition. Addressing concerns that have been raised has resulted in more flexible legislation. For example, straw bans received pushback from disability advocates who feel their needs have been ignored, as well as from retailers who fear the expense associated with replacements for plastic straws. To address these concern, straw ban laws include provisions for straws to be available on request. Arguments that taxes disproportionally harm the poor have led to exemptions from the taxes for those receiving food assistance benefits. This more flexible approach has enabled bans and taxes to gain momentum at the local level.

At the same time, opponents of bag bans began, in some instances, to enlist the help of the legislature and the courts to impede the spread of local bans. For example, in 2012, Brisbee, Arizona, a small artisan community in southeastern Arizona, enacted Ordinance 0-13-14, a bag ban and tax to reduce plastic bag litter, which had become an increasingly common sight in and around town. The Arizona Food Marketing Alliance, representing the state's grocers and food suppliers, opposed the ordinance and lobbied the state legislature to pass legislation that would prevent local entities such as Brisbee from enacting such laws. The Alliance argued that customers should have the option to use plastic bags and that local bag bans would lead to a patchwork of laws that would be difficult for consumers, businesses, and lawmakers to follow.

Finding this argument persuasive, in 2016, the Arizona legislature passed HB 2131. The law goes beyond protecting the use of plastic bags; it prevents towns and cities from imposing taxes on and regulating the sale, use, or disposition of "auxiliary containers."[23] The statute further defines "auxiliary container" to include "reusable bags, disposable bags, boxes, beverage cans, bottles, cups, and containers that are made out of cloth, plastic, extruded polystyrene, glass, aluminum, cardboard or other similar materials and that are used for transporting merchandise or food to or from a business . . ."[24]

The Minneapolis bag ban experienced a similar fate in 2017 when a statewide prohibition on city bag bans was signed into law the day before the city's plastic bag ban was to take effect, Minn. Stat. Ann. § 471.9998 (West). Also, in 2017, North Carolina repealed a 2009 state law that banned plastic bags in the Outer Banks region. Cities in that state are now considering implementing a bag tax.

But local bag taxes, like bag bans, have also been preempted by state law. In Tennessee, for example, both Nashville and Memphis were considering bag taxes when a state law was enacted to preempt such action. The American Progressive Bag Alliance (now called The American Recyclable Plastic Bag Alliance), which represents the US plastic bag manufacturing and recycling industry, opposed a 7-cent bag fee proposed by the Memphis City Council. The Alliance claimed that the tax would exacerbate area food deserts, or locations where people have limited access to healthy food, by causing low-income shoppers to avoid shopping where the fee was in effect. The Tennessee Grocers and Convenience Store Association also opposed the Memphis ordinance, stating it would prefer a statewide law rather than a city-by-city approach. Proponents explained that the city currently spends about $5.6 million annually to bury plastic bags in landfills and cleanup littered bags. They argued that the tax revenue could be used on environmental and drainage projects. The opponents prevailed and in March 2018, the Tennessee State Legislature stepped in to enact a law (SB 0431) to prevent local governments from regulating "the use, disposition, or sale of an auxiliary container, including enacting a fee, charge, or tax on such container."

The Alliance's presence has been felt beyond Tennessee. Recognized as the leader of the movement to oppose plastic bag bans

[23] A.R.S. § 9-500.38(A).
[24] A.R.S. § 9-500.38(D).

and taxes, the Alliance has nearly 25,000 employees in 40 states and is an independent division of the Plastic Industry Association. The Alliance has lobbied heavily against bag bans by arguing that plastic bags are more environmentally friendly than their paper alternatives. The Alliance website notes that plastic bags require less energy and water to make, take up less space than reusable bags in landfills, and are made from a by-product of natural gas, not oil.

The Alliance raised $6.1 million to defeat California's Proposition 67 in 2016 and often foots the bill for legal challenges in court, including the following legal challenge that arose in Texas.

In 2018, the Texas Supreme Court affirmed an appellate court decision invalidating a plastic bag ban enacted by the city of Laredo, Texas.[25] In 2015, the Laredo Merchants Association sued the city of Laredo, arguing that its Checkout Bag Reduction Ordinance was preempted by the state's Solid Waste Disposal Act. The Texas Supreme Court agreed and held that the state statute, which was enacted prior to the local ordinance, barred local governments from prohibiting or restricting, for solid waste management purposes, the sale or use of a container or package in a manner not authorized by state law.[26] The Court acknowledged the environmental harm that plastic bags cause, but concluded that it was the state legislature's duty to "create a specific exception to preemption of local control."[27]

Many argue that preemption laws take away local control and violate home rule provisions that allow local governments to regulate themselves. Scholars are particularly concerned about the preemption of innovative environmental protections that are enacted at the local level. One scholar has warned that "[t]he authority of states to dismantle local environmental policies through targeted prohibitions will have potentially far-reaching [negative] consequences."[28] If Congress were to enact a federal law regulating single-use plastics, such as the Break Free From Plastic Pollution Act, preemption would no longer be an issue. Recognizing this, in early 2020, the American Progressive Bag

[25] *City of Laredo* v. *Laredo Merchants Ass'n*, 550 S.W.3d 586, 590 (Tex. 2018).
[26] Ibid. at 594.
[27] Ibid. at 604.
[28] Sarah J. Fox, Home rule in an era of local environmental innovation, *Ecology Law Quarterly* 44 (2017): 575, 579.

Alliance renamed itself the American Recyclable Plastic Bag Alliance, signaling that its future efforts might focus less on preemption as a strategy to countering bag bans and taxes and more on promoting recycling efforts as a means of forestalling bag bans and taxes.

II COVID-19

While loss of consumer choice and lack inuniformity have long been the primary arguments lodged by opponents of local plastic laws, COVID-19 introduced a new argument: safety. COVID-19 caused many jurisdictions to rescind bag bans because of pandemic-related safety concerns. Many states with bottle bills also suspended enforcement actions against retailers who failed to collect empty bottles during the pandemic. Although there is no evidence connecting COVID-19 to reusable plastic bags or bottles, a widely cited letter written by infectious disease doctors and published in the *New England Journal of Medicine* reported that the virus can remain viable from hours to days depending on the surface.[29] A separate study from 2010, that did not undergo the rigors of peer review and that was underwritten by the American Chemistry Council, found traces of bacteria on reusable bags. Eighty-four bags from Tucson, Arizona; San Francisco and Los Angeles, California were sampled.[30] The Plastics Industry Association seized on these studies and on individual fear about COVID-19 to advocate for a rollback of bans on plastic bags. In March 2020, the Plastic Industry Association sent a letter to the US Department of Health and Human Services requesting that the agency declare that banning single-use plastics during a pandemic was a health risk. Additionally, as many retailers and restaurants moved to curbside pickups, plastic bags were increasingly viewed as a means of

[29] Letter, Aerosol and surface stability of SARS-CoV-2 as compared with SARS-CoV-1, *The New England Journal of Medicine* (August 2020) (available at www.nejm.org/doi/full/10.1056/NEJMc2004973).

[30] David L. Williams, Charles P. Gerba, Sherri Maxwell, and Ryan G. Sinclair, Assessment of the potential for cross contamination of food products by reusable shopping bags (June 9, 2010) (unpublished) (available at http://static1.squarespace.com/static/59bd5150e45a7caf6bee56f8/59bd52c67e2a5fb4e246e29b/59bd52ab7e2a5fb4e246dc4e/1505579691430/study_reusableBagContamination.pdf?format=original) (last accessed October 31, 2021).

minimizing contact between individuals. Thus, despite the low risk of contamination with using reusable bags, many localities and states delayed rolling out plastic bag bans simply because they had "bigger fish to fry."[31]

The long-term impact of COVID-19 on state and local regulation of single-use plastics remains to be seen. Temporary suspensions of existing laws may have little impact. But as of this writing, health concerns have eclipsed concerns over the environmental impacts of plastic. As with most things, COVID-19 has reframed the discussion.

III LITIGATION

In addition to legislative solutions, litigation also offers a potential way to remedy our plastic problem. Claims involving plastic pollution can arise in federal court, as was seen in Chapter 4, but novel claims are being brought under state laws in state court.[32] Many of these claims are claims of first impression as applied to plastic. For example, in 2020, the nonprofit Earth Island Institute sued Crystal Geyser Water Company, the Clorox Company, Coca-Cola Company, PepsiCo, and Proctor & Gamble in California court alleging among other things violations of the California Consumers Legal Remedies Act, public nuisance, negligence, and failure to warn of the harms caused by their plastic.[33] In the complaint, Earth Island Institute contends that the defendants' use of plastic packaging for their products was polluting California's waters and that these companies have spread misinfor-

[31] Peter Passi, Duluth City Council pushes back plastic-bag fee, *Duluth News Tribune* (March 23, 2020) (available at www.duluthnewstribune.com/news/government-and-polit ics/5012551-Duluth-City-Council-pushes-back-plastic-bag-fee) (last accessed October 31, 2021).

[32] Sarah J. Morath, Samantha Hamilton, and Amanda Thompson, Plastic Pollution Litigation (Summer 2021) (available at www.americanbar.org/groups/environment_energy_resources/publications/natural_resources_environment/2021-22/summer/plastic-pollution-litigation/) (last accessed October 16, 2021).

[33] Complaint at 50–60, Earth Island Institute, No. 20-CIV-01213 (Cal. Super. San Mateo Cnty., February 26, 2020).

mation through a "decades long campaign ... to deflect blame for the plastic pollution crisis to consumers."[34]

In suing these companies, Earth Island is seeking to hold corporations responsible for the plastic they push out into the marketplace. In its prayer for relief, Earth Island Institute requested an order from the court requiring the defendants to disburse funds and resources necessary to remediate the harm they have caused to the environment.[35] In addition, it asked that the defendants refrain from marketing their materials as recyclable and implement corrective advertising "to inform consumers that the products do not have the characteristics, uses, benefits, and quality that defendants claim."[36]

This case shows that plaintiffs are becoming more creative and ambitious in their approach, looking beyond existing federal laws. And unlike public nuisance claims involving climate change, which are commonly dismissed for failure to demonstrate causation, the persistent and visible nature of plastic may make it easier for plaintiffs to trace the harm of plastic back to manufacturers.

A success for Earth Island Institute may inspire other plaintiffs to look beyond existing environmental laws and rely on a variety of state tort claims. Fraud, product liability, toxic torts, and property damage claims against plastic producers and manufacturers are no doubt on the horizon. In December 2020, Greenpeace sued Walmart for "unlawful, unfair, and deceptive" practices regarding claims of recyclability on its private-label plastic products.[37] Insurance companies have suggested that microplastics could be the next "toxic tort" and Law.com has speculated about the coming wave of insurance, product liability, and property damage claims involving plastic.[38]

[34] Ibid. at 5.

[35] Ibid. at 60.

[36] Ibid. at 60–1.

[37] Complaint at 1, *Greenpeace, Inc.* v. *Walmart, Inc.* (December 14, 2020) (available at www.greenpeace.org/usa/wp-content/uploads/2020/12/Walmart-Complaintf.pdf) (last accessed October 31, 2021).

[38] Mikaela Whitman, The coming wave of plastic liabilities and insurance coverage, *New York Law Journal* (May 29, 2020) (available at www.law.com/newyorklawjournal/2020/05/29/the-coming-wave-of-plastic-liabilities-and-insurance-coverage/) (last accessed October 31, 2021).

IV CONCLUSION

While activity at the state and local level has been focused on legislative action including plastic bans and taxes, implementation across the country has left a patchwork of laws. Furthermore, COVID-19 has called into question the efficacy of an approach that relies solely on legislation. Because of this realization, the author suspects that plastic litigation, which is in its infancy, will continue, particularly at the state level, as the public seeks to hold plastic companies liable for the harm their products cause.

6 INTERNATIONAL EFFORTS

In the same way that the problem of plastic pollution is not isolated to the United States, so too, solutions to plastic pollution are not – and, in fact, cannot be – limited to remedial action that may be undertaken by the United States. The globalization of our world's economy, the growing consumer demand worldwide for plastic products, and the boundaryless nature of our air and oceans make plastic pollution a global problem requiring worldwide attention. At the same time, the interconnected nature of the world's economy and environment renders the management of plastic pollution at the international level a challenge. Addressing plastic pollution will require the highest levels of goodwill, mutual understanding, and commitment to cooperation demanded of any international undertaking. Yet, despite the difficulties inherent in achieving global agreements, some progress has been made, as Chapter 6 will show.

Chapter 6 discusses international efforts to deal with plastic pollution and highlights successes as well as obstacles to enforcement and implementation. It begins with a discussion of country-specific approaches including bans and taxes, many of which have been implemented to meet the commitments of international law and agreements, the topic of the second part of this chapter. The chapter then examines the international instruments that have spurred action at the national level and points out some weaknesses including the lack of participation by the United States, nonspecific targets and timelines, and insufficient enforcement. The chapter concludes by looking at international efforts to address acid rain, ozone depletion, mercury contamination, and climate change and discusses calls from businesses and nonprofits for a single international treaty to target plastic pollution.

By the end of Chapter 6, readers will understand how non-US domestic laws and international laws have helped to inform the world of – but have proved ineffective at addressing – the dangers of plastic pollution and will recognize the need for a binding international treaty.

I INDIVIDUAL NATION-STATES AND NATION-STATE COLLECTIVES

In many ways, the United States trails other countries in implementing taxes and bans on plastics. Those who study norm theory, a theory that is used to explain collective behavior, note that norm adoption typically begins in the Northern Hemisphere with developed countries and spreads to the Southern Hemisphere to developing countries through "norm entrepreneurs" like international organizations and institutions.[1] This North to South pattern can be seen in the adoption of international norms for a variety of environmental issues: hazardous waste, air pollution, and endangered species.[2]

Surprisingly, however, the North to South pattern has not occurred in the case of bans of single-use plastic bags. In this instance, the first communities to embrace plastic bag bans were countries in the Southern Hemisphere, where the bans are typically called "plastic carrier bans." And the bans have developed, not through "norm entrepreneurs" pursuing environmental change, but rather through government action by nation-states: for example, in such diverse countries as Rwanda and Bangladesh. Since the start of the twenty-first century, simultaneous "ad hoc" bottom-up "plastic carrier ban" events have occurred in different jurisdictional levels around the world.[3]

[1] Jennifer Clapp and Linda Swanston, Doing away with plastic shopping bags: International patterns of norm emergence and policy implementation, *Environmental Politics* 18 (2009): 315–22 (available at www.tandfonline.com/doi/pdf/10.1080/09644010902823717) (last accessed October 2021).

[2] Ibid.

[3] Ibid.

Why this reverse trend from South to North? Most likely, it results from the ability of wealthy countries to distance themselves both physically and psychologically from the environmental harms of plastic pollution, thereby reducing the need to consider plastic bans until recently. On the other hand, developing countries, particularly those in Asia, have been importing plastic waste from North America and Europe since the 1990s. At the same time, these developing countries have been consuming plastic to support their growing economies. Plastic's widespread availability, versatility, and low cost has made it the "workhorse material" of the modern economy. Plastic reduces food waste by increasing shelf life and its lightweight nature reduces fuel consumption for transporting goods. Confronted with this growing, two-pronged waste management problem – imported plastic waste plus domestically generated plastic – developing countries, particularly countries in Asia, were some of the first to implement plastic bans.

Another reason the Northern Hemisphere lags behind developing countries in its adoption of plastic bans is that plastic bans in developed countries would frustrate the growing domestic single-use plastic economy that emerged during the late 1970s. The impact of a growing plastic economy on environmental laws and policy is noticeable in the United States, where lobbying by the petrochemical and plastic industries is particularly strong. In 2018, the Plastic Industry Association reported that the US plastics industry accounted for an estimated $432.3 billion in shipments and 989,000 jobs.[4] And the industry shows no signs of slowing down. Additionally, the practice of sending plastic waste overseas for disposal has added to the argument that plastic bans are both detrimental to the economic interests of the United States and unnecessary. (See more in Chapter 5).

A Southern Hemisphere: Bans

The absence of a strong plastic industry presence in Bangladesh helped this country easily ban plastic bags some two decades ago, in 2002.

[4] Jobs in the U.S. plastic industry increase according to 2018 size and impact report, Plastics Industry Association (January 9, 2019) (available at www.plasticsindustry.org/article/jobs-us-plastics-industry-increase-according-2018-size-and-impact-report) (last accessed October 31, 2021).

The primary incentive for the bag ban was flooding. When it rained, plastic bags clogged drainage systems, exacerbating flooding in a country that is only a few feet above sea level. While there have been several major flooding events in Bangladesh between 1954 and 1998, the 1998 one was the most devastating, lasting more than sixty-five days.[5] Polythene bags that block the drainage system were responsible for causing the floodwater to stay for long. The resulting standing water became a breeding ground for disease-carrying mosquitoes. Shortly after this 1998 flood, the Bangladesh government led campaigns to ban plastic. And on March 1, 2002, the country's Environmental Conservation Act of 1995 was amended to include a national ban on plastic bags. Lack of implementation and enforcement, however, have prevented the full realization of the legislation in halting plastic waste. As a result, environmental activists in the country petitioned the High Court of Bangladesh to strengthen implementation and enforcement. In January 2020, the High Court ordered the government not only to start enforcing the bag ban but also to ban single-use plastic in coastal area hotels and restaurants.

Other Asian countries have also instituted plastic bans encompassing more than plastic bags. In January 2020, the Chinese National Reform and Development Commission ordered that by 2025, restaurants must reduce single-use plastic items by 30 percent and hotels must stop offering single-use plastic items. In 2019, Indian Prime Minister Narendra Modi promised to ban single-use plastics by 2022, but with the 2020 economic slowdown, a state-by-state rather than a national approach has emerged.

It is Africa, however, that is viewed by the international community as a global leader in the implementation of plastic bag bans. In achieving these successes, African nations have taken a legislative approach at the national level. On the African continent, 90 percent of plastics are abandoned at their point of use, which means that plastic waste and its impacts are seen and felt almost immediately.[6] Of particular concern in African countries are the number of plastic bags found in the stomachs

[5] S. U. Ahmed and K. Gotoh, Impact of banning polythene bags on floods of Dhaka City by applying CVM and remote sensing, *Proceedings. 2005 IEEE International Geoscience and Remote Sensing Symposium*, 2005. IGARSS'05, Seoul, Korea (South) (2005) (available at https://ieeexplore.ieee.org/document/1525403) (last accessed October 31, 2021).

[6] Hannah Ritchie and Max Roser, Plastic Pollution (2018), OurWorldInData.org (available at https://ourworldindata.org/plastic-pollution) (last accessed April 12, 2021).

of cows, an important segment of Africa's livestock economy. One study showed that 50 percent of cows near urban areas had plastic bags in their stomachs.[7]

Today, fifteen African countries have enacted plastic bag bans, making Africa the leading continent in terms of number of bans in effect.[8] While most of Africa's bans are relatively recent, some date from earlier in the twenty-first century. Chad, Tanzania, and Rwanda instituted plastic bag bans in 2005, 2006, and 2008, respectively, and today, Rwanda is considered Africa's most litter-free country. Due to the country's plastic bag ban laws, Rwanda's capital, Kigali, is nearly spotless – free from plastic debris.[9]

The African country with the strictest plastic bag bans, however, is Kenya. Kenya's law banning plastic bags, which was enacted in 2017, includes a four-year prison term or fines of $40,000 for anyone producing, selling, or importing a plastic bag. Simply using a plastic bag could result in a fine of more than $500 or a jail term of one year.[10] Kenya's law is largely seen as a success. Streets are cleaner, waterways are less clogged, and the number of plastic bags found in the stomachs of cows has decreased. But the 2017 law is not Kenya's first attempt at banning plastic. The stricter penalties of the 2017 law are in response to the disregard for earlier laws, a problem that is not unique to Kenya.

Kenya and Rwanda are part of the larger East African Community (EAC), an intergovernmental organization created in 1999 that also includes Tanzania, Uganda, Burundi, and South Sudan. Recognizing that plastic pollution was a problem, in 2016 the EAC passed a landmark law called the Polythene Materials Control Bill. This law provides a legal framework for the preservation of a clean and healthy

[7] Has Kenya's plastic bag ban worked?, *BBC News* (August 28, 2019) (available at www.bbc.com/news/world-africa-49421885) (last accessed October 31, 2021).

[8] Richard Kish, Using legislation to reduce one-time plastic bag usage, *Economic Affairs* (June 2018) (available at https://onlinelibrary.wiley.com/doi/epdf/10.1111/ecaf.12287?saml_referrer) (last accessed October 31, 2021).

[9] Kimiko de Freytas-Tamura, Public shaming and even prison for plastic bag use in Rwanda, *The New York Times* (October 28, 2017) (available at www.nytimes.com/2017/10/28/world/africa/rwanda-plastic-bags-banned.html) (last accessed October 31, 2021).

[10] Has Kenya's plastic bag ban worked?

environment through the prohibition of the manufacturing, sale, importation, and use of polyethylene materials such as plastic bags.[11]

While Kenya has been successful at pressuring other EAC countries, such as Tanzania, to adopt plastic bag bans, overall implementation of the 2016 law by EAC countries has been slow. As in other countries, African nations have their share of critics who claim that bans will lead to job loss and that alternative or replacement products are too expensive. Because many street vendors rely on plastic bags, the demand in Africa for plastic bags remains high. In some African countries, including Rwanda, smuggling of plastic across borders has undermined the implementation of plastic bag bans. Plastic bags are like drugs, and authorities are constantly on the lookout for this illegal contraband.

Recent trade negotiations between Kenya and the United States also have the potential to undermine the African continent's success with limiting plastic pollution. Since losing China as a market for its waste, including plastic, the United States has been actively seeking other countries willing to accept its waste and it may have found a willing partner in Kenya. In late August 2020, several news outlets highlighted how a potential trade deal between the United States and Kenya could reverse Kenya's – and Africa's – efforts at curbing plastic pollution.[12] As trade negotiations were transpiring, the American Chemistry Council wrote to the Office of the U.S. Trade Representative seeking "full tariff elimination between the United States and Kenya – without any transition periods or staging of tariff reductions – in order to provide new market access for US-made exports of chemicals and plastics."[13] Many environmentalists in

[11] The East African Community Polythene Materials Control Bill, EALA (2016) (available at www.eala.org/documents/view/the-east-african-community-polythene-materials-control-bill2016) (last accessed October 31, 2021).

[12] Hiroko Tabuchi, Michael Corkery, and Carlos Mureithi, Big oil is in trouble. Its Plan: Flood Africa with plastic, *The New York Times* (August 30, 2020) (available at www.nytimes.com/2020/08/30/climate/oil-kenya-africa-plastics-trade.html) (last accessed October 31, 2021).

[13] Letter to Edward Gresser, Chair of the Trade Policy Staff Committee, Office of the United States Trade Representative, from The American Chemistry Council (April 28, 2020) (available at www.americanchemistry.com/ACC-Public-Comments-on-US-Kenya-Trade-Negotiations_050620.pdf) (last accessed October 31, 2021).

Kenya worry that such trade deals will diminish the strides that have been made in Kenya and turn African countries into the new dumping ground for US plastic waste.

As is often the case anywhere in the world, the success of plastic bans in Africa depends largely on the government's ability to engage stakeholders – from bag manufacturers to community members. In African countries with bans, an increase in tourism and a growing economy has engendered community support for these laws. Further complicating the picture, however, is the fact that economic growth may have a negative effect on plastic bans. A recent paper comparing the bans in Rwanda, Kenya, and Uganda notes that the increased presence of plastic businesses in Kenya and Uganda has made implementing plastic bans more challenging.[14] This conflict lends further support for the circular economy principles addressed in the final chapter – Chapter 10 – of this book.

B Northern Hemisphere: Taxes

While countries in the Southern Hemisphere have approached plastic pollution through the implementation of bans, many countries in the Northern Hemisphere, particularly European countries, have used taxes or levies to address plastic waste. Ireland's bag tax is often cited as a success. In 2002, Ireland implemented a 15-euro cents (22 US cents) levy on plastic bags provided at the point of sale in retail outlets. Revenue from the so-called plas-tax is deposited into a fund operated by the Irish Department of the Environment, Heritage and Local Government and is used to defray the costs of administering the levy and to support and promote various environmental programs. Today cloth bags are the norm in Ireland (a tax on paper bags was also proposed but not passed) and plastic bags are as taboo as fur coats in a country which voted to phase out fur farms, like mink farms, in 2019.

14 Pritish Behuria, The comparative political economy of plastic bag bans in East Africa: Why implementation has varied in Rwanda, Kenya and Uganda, GDI Working Paper 2019-037, Manchester: The University of Manchester (2019) (available at http://hummedia.manchester.ac.uk/institutes/gdi/publications/workingpapers/GDI/gdi-working-paper-2019037-behuria.pdf) (last accessed October 31, 2021).

The "plas-tax," which has been called "the most popular tax in Europe," was primarily passed to address litter concerns.[15] Before the plas-tax, bags accounted for 5 percent of Ireland's litter and had a visible impact on Ireland's countryside and coastline.[16] A few weeks after the plas-tax's passage, the number of plastic bags entering the waste stream was reduced by 94 percent.[17] In its first four months, the plas-tax returned a revenue of 3.5 million euros.[18] A 2014 survey showed that plastic bags constituted 0.13 percent of litter as compared to the 5 percent recorded before the tax went into effect.[19]

Opposition to the tax was minimal, in part because the plastic industry does not have a big presence in Ireland – 80 percent of Ireland's plastic bags are imported – and because a public campaign by the Department of the Environment, Heritage and Local Government successfully conveyed the environmental reasons for the tax, thereby reducing public resistance. As a result, Irish citizens easily adjusted to the tax. In 2007, the tax was increased to 22-euro cents (29 US cents) and it was increased to 29-euro cents in 2019. That same year, Ireland's minister to the environment introduced a similar tax on single-use plastic cups and carry-out packaging.

European countries have also taxed plastic manufacturers. Denmark is credited with the oldest existing bag tax, dating from 1993. Under this tax, bag manufacturers, not consumers, are taxed based on the bag's weight. Stores could either absorb the cost of the tax

[15] Frank Convery, Simon McDonnell, and Susana Ferreira, The most popular tax in Europe? Lessons from the Irish plastic bags levy, *Environmental and Resource Economics* 38 (January 2007): 1–11 (available at https://link.springer.com/article/10.1007/s10640-006-9059-2).

[16] Mauro Anastasio and James Nix, Plastic bag levy in Ireland, Institute for European Environmental Policy (2016) (available at https://ieep.eu/uploads/articles/attachments/0817a609-f2ed-4db0–8ae0–05f1d75fbaa4/IE%20Plastic%20Bag%20Levy%20final.pdf?v=63680923242#:~:text=Paper%20bags%20are%20not%20subject,hygiene%20and%20food%20safety%20purposes) (last accessed October 31, 2021).

[17] Elizabeth Rosenthal, By 'bagging it,' Ireland rids itself of a plastic nuisance, *The New York Times* (January 31, 2008) (available at www.nytimes.com/2008/01/31/world/europe/31iht-bags.4.9650382.html?auth=login-email&login=email) (last accessed October 31, 2021).

[18] Marc Bennrock, Plastic bag levy succeeds spectacularly, *The Irish Times* (August 21, 2002) (available at www.irishtimes.com/news/plastic-bag-levy-succeeds-spectacularly-1.1092623) (last accessed October 31, 2021).

[19] Anastasio and Nix, Plastic bag levy in Ireland.

or pass it along to consumers in the form of a bag charge. The initial effect of Denmark's tax was an impressive 60 percent drop in plastic bag use. More recently, in 2020, Italy introduced a tax covering an even broader range of businesses – manufacturers, sellers of plastic items, and importers of plastic items – and on a broader range of items: plastic products including bottles, bags, and food containers in polyethylene; packaging in expanded polystyrene; and plastic caps.

C European Union Directives

More recent European plastic bans and taxes stem from the European Union's (EU) Directive 2015/720, which in 2015 directed member states to reduce the consumption of plastic bags. The Directive gave member states discretion as to what measures they would implement to achieve this reduction. Some states – such as Portugal – implemented a tax, while other states – such as Italy – banned plastic carrier bags. One study of Portugal's tax found that four months after the tax was implemented, the use of plastic carrier bags had declined by 74 percent, while the use of reusable plastic bags had increased by 61 percent. The study's authors, who published their results in *Waste Management*, concluded that "the change in behavior occurred not only because of the tax, but also because of the alternatives offered by hypermarkets [department store plus grocery store, i.e., big box stores] and supermarkets (i.e., to offer/sell reusable bags instead of taxed plastic bags)."[20]

Building on the EU Directive, the European Parliament in March 2019, voted overwhelmingly in favor of a ban on ten types of single-use plastics for which alternatives exist, including plastic cutlery, plates, straws, and food containers. This Single-Use Plastic Directive also requires member states to achieve a 90 percent recycling rate for plastic bottles by 2029. According to the European Commission, the banned items constitute 70 percent of all marine litter. Finally, the agreement

[20] Garcia Martinho, Natacha Balaia, and Ana Pires, The Portuguese plastic carrier bag tax: The effects on consumers' behavior, *Waste Management* 61 (March 2017): 3–12 (available at www.sciencedirect.com/science/article/pii/S0956053X17300223#t0005) (last accessed October 31, 2021).

holds manufacturers of plastic products such as tobacco filters and fishing gear responsible for environmental costs. European officials remain committed to achieving these goals despite COVID-19 and consequently, unlike states in the United States, have resisted calls from industry asking that the Directive's timeline be modified because of the global pandemic.

II INTERNATIONAL INSTRUMENTS SPUR DOMESTIC ACTION

The action taken by individual nation-states described above is often in response to international treaties (binding) or international agreements (nonbinding). For example, the Act to Prevent Pollution from Ships, discussed in Chapter 4, is the US law enacted to comply with the MARPOL treaty discussed below. Similarly, Kenya's decision to ban plastic bags was in response to joining the Clean Seas campaign, and Canada's commitment to zero plastic waste is an outgrowth of its participation in the Ocean Plastic Charters, both of which are discussed later in this chapter.

In general, international laws can be divided into two categories: soft law and hard law. Hard law, such as treaties, describes legally binding agreements between participating countries. Countries signing the treaty consent to be bound by its terms. Treaties can be further divided into those that are self-executing, such that they are judicially enforceable upon signing, and those that are not "self-executing" and require the adoption of implementing legislation by individual nation-states before they are judicially enforceable. In practice, violations of international law are not usually formally adjudicated.[21] A breach of these agreements generally does not result in the appearance of the offending party before an international tribunal. Instead, violations more often result in "the creation of institutions and compliance

[21] David A. Koplow, Indisputable violations: What happens when the United States unambiguously breaches a treaty, Georgetown University Law Center (2013) (available at https://scholarship.law.georgetown.edu/cgi/viewcontent.cgi?article=2902&context=facpub) (last accessed October 31, 2021).

mechanisms to review state compliance. Such procedures may result in publication of reports that identify failures, adoption of incentives, or other actions aimed at promoting compliance."[22]

The use of soft law – such as charters and campaigns – is a more recent development in international environmental law and describes voluntary and nonbinding agreements between participating countries.[23] Because consensus is easier to reach with nonbinding agreements, soft law agreements allow countries to bypass the long process of negotiating a treaty. Also, NGOs and private businesses can participate in soft law agreements, thus giving these agreements a broader scope than that of treaties.

Because both hard law and soft law are entered into on a voluntary basis, international law has struggled to adequately address plastic pollution. In 2017, the United Nations Environment Assembly described the current efforts to address marine plastic litter as "fragmented and uncoordinated." It therefore suggested putting effort into revising and strengthening existing laws or into developing a new framework.[24] Others have suggested that while it is possible to negotiate a new treaty with measurable targets and timelines that are specific to plastic, individual nation-states' time and energy might be better spent developing state-specific laws for regulating plastic waste.[25] One scholar summed up the causes for the failure of international law to successfully address plastic pollution as follows:

> Governance is fragmented across jurisdictions, sectors, and product lines. There is little policy coordination across states, with

[22] Alex Kiss and Dinah L. Shelton, *Guide to International Environmental Law* (Martinus Nijhoff Publishers, Leiden and Boston, 2007) (available at https://scholarship.law.gwu.edu/cgi/viewcontent.cgi?article=2047&context=faculty_publications) (last accessed October 31, 2021).

[23] Edith Brown Weiss, The evolution of international environmental law, *Japanese Yearbook of International Law* 54 (2011): 1–27 (available at https://scholarship.law.georgetown.edu/cgi/viewcontent.cgi?article=2684&context=facpub) (last accessed October 31, 2021).

[24] Ina Tessnow-von Wysocki and Philippe Le Billon, Plastics at Sea: Treaty design for a global solution to marine plastic pollution, *Environmental Science and Policy* 100 (2019): 94–104 (available at www.sciencedirect.com/science/article/pii/S1462901119301364#sec0020) (last accessed October 31, 2021).

[25] Roger Harrabin, Ocean plastic tide 'violates the law', *BBC News* (February 20, 2018) (available at www.bbc.com/news/science-environment-43115486) (last accessed October 31, 2021).

> international institutions functioning as little more than dialogue forums. National and subnational policies are highly uneven, with loopholes and erratic implementation. Standards are inconsistent and systemic illegalities are common across much of the world.[26]

A Hard Law: Treaties

1 United Nations Convention on the Law of the Sea (UNCLOS) During the mid-twentieth century, many nations became concerned about ocean pollution and the governance of ocean resources. A series of United Nations conferences on the law of the sea, held between the mid-1950s and 1980s, resulted in several treaty agreements, including the 1982 United Nations Convention on the Law of the Sea (UNCLOS). UNCLOS took effect in 1994 upon receiving the necessary number of UN signatories, and although the United States is not a party to UNCLOS, it recognizes that the 1982 Convention reflects customary international law and complies with its provisions.

UNCLOS creates a comprehensive regime governing nations' rights to the world's oceans. The convention addresses several topics, including the economic zones of the sea, navigational rights in territorial and high seas, and the conservation and management of the marine environment. While the convention calls on signatories to protect and preserve the marine environment – for example, Article 194 of UNCLOS provides that states will take "measures to prevent, reduce and control pollution of the marine environment" – the treaty largely leaves it to individual countries to enact legislation to prevent pollution. Plastic is never specifically mentioned, and, thus, the treaty does not provide any framework for addressing plastic pollution. Instead, UNCLOS provisions are to be read in the light of other international

[26] Peter Dauvergne, Why is the global governance of plastic failing the oceans?, *Global Environmental Change* (July 2018) (available at www.sciencedirect.com/science/article/pii/S0959378017314140#:~:text=Global%20governance%20of%20marine%20plastic,uneven%2C%20fragmented%2C%20and%20failing.&text=Durability%20and%20dispersal%20of%20microplastics%20make%20governance%20particularly%20difficult.&text=Globalization%20of%20the%20plastics%20industry%20is%20increasing%20the%20difficulty%20of%20governance) (last accessed October 31, 2021).

conventions, treaties, and standards. As a result, since UNCLOS relates to the management and use of the oceans, in principle it could be used to combat plastic waste at the global level. As described by the World Wildlife Federation, "UNCLOS could be understood as something of a 'constitution' for the oceans, where general rules and principles are enshrined, but without providing a detailed recipe for the fulfilment of its aspirations."[27]

2 London Convention While UNCLOS governs issues of jurisdiction and sovereignty, other treaties have focused on specific practices at sea. For example, the London Convention, also known as the Convention on the Prevention of Marine Pollution by Dumping of Wastes and Other Matter, focuses on all waste. The goal of this 1972 agreement is to prevent waste generated on land from being dumped at sea.[28] Contracting parties agree to

> individually and collectively promote the effective control of all sources of pollution of the marine environment, and pledge themselves especially to take all practicable steps to prevent the pollution of the sea by the dumping of waste and other matter that is liable to create hazards to human health, to harm living resources and marine life, to damage amenities or to interfere with other legitimate uses of the sea.[29]

Dumping means "any deliberate disposal at sea" while waste is defined as "material and substance of any kind, form or description." The Convention permits the dumping of some materials at sea,[30] but plastics are specifically prohibited under Annex 1.[31] While the dumping of plastics at sea is prohibited, the London Convention was

[27] World Wildlife Federation Policy Paper, Tackling Marine Plastic Pollution, WWF (2019) (available at https://d2ouvy59p0dg6k.cloudfront.net/downloads/tackling_marine_plastic_pollution___wwf_2019.pdf) (last accessed October 31, 2021).

[28] Grant A. Harse, Plastic, the great pacific garbage patch, and international misfires at a cure, *UCLA Journal of Environmental Law and Policy* 29 (2011): 331, 345.

[29] Convention on the Prevention of Marine Pollution by Dumping of Wastes and Other Matter (1972) (available at www.epa.gov/sites/production/files/2015-10/documents/lc1972.pdf) (last accessed October 31, 2021).

[30] Ibid. (Annex VI).

[31] Ibid.

not intended to regulate land-based sources of pollution, including plastic.

The London Convention is implemented in the United States by the Marine Protection, Research, and Sanctuaries Act of 1972 (MPRSA), as amended by the Ocean Dumping Ban Act of 1988, both of which are discussed in Chapter 4. The London Convention was modified by the London Protocol in 1996. As of March 2019, there are fifty-three contracting parties to the London Protocol, but the United States is not a contracting party. The United States signed the London Protocol in 1998, and on September 4, 2007 President George W. Bush submitted the Protocol to the Senate for advice and consent, but the Senate did not ratify the treaty.

*3 **MARPOL 73/78*** Another treaty from the 1970s is the International Convention for the Prevention of Pollution from Ships of 1973 (MARPOL 73). The International Maritime Organization (IMO) – the United Nations agency "responsible for developing and adopting measures to improve the safety and security of international shipping and to prevent pollution from ships"[32] – adopted the measure as modified by the Protocol of 1978 (MARPOL 78). Today the treaty is referred to as the MARPOL 73/78. MARPOL 73/78 has been called the most important global treaty for the prevention of pollution from ships. It was signed by the United States in 1978 and implemented through the Act to Prevent Pollution from Ships, as amended by the Marine Plastic Pollution Research and Control Act, discussed in Chapter 4.

MARPOL 73/78 consists of six Annexes that address different types of pollution (e.g., oil, noxious liquids, sewage, etc.). While oil pollution – identified in Annex 1 – was the primary target of this agreement, Annex V of MARPOL 73/78 addresses "garbage" and provides parameters for the disposal of certain kinds of material at sea. This includes a complete ban imposed on the dumping into the sea

[32] Kitack Lim, The role of the International Maritime Organization in preventing the pollution of the world's oceans from ships and shipping, *UN Chronicle*, United Nations (n.d.) (available at www.un.org/en/chronicle/article/role-international-maritime-organization-preventing-pollution-worlds-oceans-ships-and-shipping) (last accessed October 16, 2021).

of all forms of plastic. Additionally, nation-states are required to inspect vessels for compliance with minimum technical standards, to monitor vessel compliance with discharge standards, and to penalize vessels that violate these standards.[33]

Despite this directive, implementing MARPOL 73/78 has been challenging. First, MARPOL does not apply to warships or other ships owned or operated by a state and used on government noncommercial service. Another challenge has been determining which country is responsible for investigating and prosecuting violations – the flag state, the port state, the coastal state, or any combination thereof. Some governments, despite signing the agreement, are unable or unwilling to enforce MARPOL requirements. In the United States, concerns about the MARPOL enforcement were highlighted in a 1995 report to the House Committee on Appropriations. In the report, the United States Coast Guard, the body responsible for enforcing MARPOL in US waters, wrote:

> Although the provisions of MARPOL V became effective on December 31, 1988, the Coast Guard did not begin substantial enforcement efforts until the early 1990s. Following congressional criticism in 1990 and 1992, and aided by additional personnel, the Coast Guard stepped up its enforcement efforts. The number of reported cases involving violations of the MARPOL V regulations has increased steadily from 16 in 1989 to 311 in 1994. Fewer than 10 percent of all cases have resulted in any penalties being assessed on the violator, although a significant number are still being processed.[34]

Despite these enforcement concerns, for the vessels covered by MARPOL's Annex V, the treaty can be used as a governance framework for preventing leakage of plastic waste into the ocean from sea-based sources.

[33] Huang Jie (Jeanne) and Hu Jiaxiang, Can free trade agreements enhance MARPOL 73/78 compliance?, *Tulane Maritime Law Journal* 43 (2018): 59, 66.

[34] GOA Report to Congressional Requesters from the United States Coast Guard, *Enforcement under MARPOL V Convention on Pollution Expanded, although Problems Remain* (May 1995) (available at www.gao.gov/assets/rced-95-143.pdf) (last accessed October 31, 2021).

4 Basel Convention More recently, countries have sought to regulate plastic through the Basel Convention. Adopted in 1989, the Basel Convention on the Control of Transboundary Movements of Hazardous Wastes and their Disposal seeks to protect the health and environment of developing countries that are often the recipient of hazardous waste from wealthy countries. The Basel Convention allows member states to ban the importation of hazardous and other wastes for disposal and requires a written contract before any hazardous waste is imported. The prior informed consent (PIC) procedures are at the heart of the Basel Convention and have strict requirements for: (1) notification; (2) consent and issuance of movement document; (3) transboundary movement; and (4) confirmation of disposal.[35] The Convention also bans the trade of hazardous or other wastes with non-parties and bans the export of such waste to Antarctica.[36]

In May 2019, the Conference of the Parties to the Basel Convention – which includes 187 countries, but does not include the United States – adopted amendments to the agreement to better control the transboundary movements of plastic waste and to clarify the scope of the Convention as it applies to such waste. Of significance, the amendments provide that all plastic waste and mixtures of plastic waste – except plastic waste that can be recycled – will be subject to the PIC requirements of the Basel Convention. Thus, after 2022, plastic waste that is sorted, clean, uncontaminated, and effectively designed for recycling can be traded freely, while other types of plastic will require the consent of importing and transit countries.

While some have hailed the Basel Amendments as "historic" and claim they will lead to better management of plastic waste and transparency of the waste trade, others are not so confident. One concern is that more stringent trade requirements will actually spur continued growth of the illegal trade of plastic waste. Interpol (International Criminal Police Organization), for example, believes that the changes prompted by the Basel Amendments will "result in increased illegal disposal of plastics in source regions, along with illegal imports in

[35] Basel Convention on the Control of Transboundary Movements of Hazardous Wastes and Their Disposal (March 22, 1989). See www.basel.int.

[36] Ibid.

destination regions."[37] Another concern is the lack of punitive measures to which violating countries would be subjected.

This brief overview shows that there are some treaties that could have some effect on reducing plastic pollution at sea. But while these prohibitions are significant, their impact is limited. Only 20 percent of plastic pollution comes from sea disposal (whether intentional or not); the remainder of plastic pollution in oceans comes from land-based sources. Additionally, not all countries are signatories and enforcement will always be a challenge. For these reasons, soft laws are an important component of international solutions.

B Soft Law: Voluntary Agreements and Campaigns

While treaties have primarily focused on ocean-based sources of pollution, voluntary international agreements, charters, and campaigns have a broader scope and often include consideration of land-based sources of plastic pollution. That said, these agreements are voluntary and nonbinding in nature; their impact depends on a country's willingness to achieve the lofty and ambitious goals. Three of the programs discussed here (Global Partnership on Marine Litter (GPML), Clean Seas Campaign, and Honolulu Strategy) were instituted by the United Nations Environment Program (UNEP). The Ocean Plastic Charter was instituted by the G7 countries.

1 Global Partnership on Marine Litter and Clean Seas Campaign The Global Partnership on Marine Litter is a product of the 2012 United Nations Conference on Sustainable Development (Rio+20) and is part of the United Nations 2030 Agenda for Sustainable Development. The GPML is a multistakeholder partnership that seeks to address global marine litter in three ways. First, the partnership provides a platform for "cooperation and coordination, sharing ideas, knowledge and experiences, identifying gaps and emerging issues." Second, the partnership works to

[37] Colin Staub, China ban spurs rise in plastic waste "criminal trends" (September 20, 2020) (available at https://resource-recycling.com/recycling/2020/09/09/china-ban-spurs-rise-in-plastic-waste-criminal-trends/) (last accessed October 31, 2021).

harness the expertise, resources, and enthusiasm of partners. Finally, the partnership aims to make a significant contribution to one of the goals of the 2030 Agenda for Sustainable Development: namely, that by 2025, marine pollution of all kinds, particularly from land-based activities, will be prevented and significantly reduced.

UN leaders of the GPML are eager to engage industry and devise ways in which the private and the public sector can work together to address plastic pollution. As a result, in February 2017, UNEP announced the Clean Seas Campaign as a way to target UN member states, individuals, and industry on the specific issue of plastic pollution. Since its launch, fifty-seven countries have joined the Clean Seas Campaign and have pledged to cut back on single-use plastics, protect national waters, and encourage more recycling. The Clean Seas Campaign now represents the world's largest global alliance for combatting marine plastic pollution, with commitments covering more than 60 percent of the world's coastlines. Notable Clean Seas commitments include Chile's approval of a nationwide ban on single-use plastic bags (South America's first), and Australia's pledge that 100 percent of its packaging would be reusable, compostable, or recyclable by 2025 and that unnecessary single-use packing would be phased out through design, innovation, or introduction of alternatives. Individuals have also joined the Clean Seas Campaign, with over 100,000 people taking the Clean Seas pledge to reduce their plastic footprint. Many use the hashtags #CleanSeas and #BeatPlasticPollution on Twitter and Instagram to urge others to follow their lead and cut single-use plastics from their lives.

2 Honolulu Strategy The Honolulu Strategy is another voluntary framework for addressing plastic pollution. Launched in 2011, the Honolulu Strategy is an outgrowth of the Fifth International Marine Debris Conference and was sponsored by the UNEP and the National Oceanic and Atmospheric Association (NOAA). This strategy sets forth three goals: (1) reduce the impact and amount of land-based litter and solid waste introduced into the marine environment; (2) reduce the impact and amount of sea-based marine debris including abandoned vessels, lost cargo, and solid waste; and (3) reduce the impact and amount of accumulated marine debris in pelagic waters, benthic habitats, and along shorelines.

The Honolulu Strategy expressly declined to incorporate target setting – a strategy seen with greenhouse gas reductions – or extended producer responsibility – which places the burden of plastic disposal on the producer – as methods to reach these goals. The strategy explains that this document was not the place to address or explain these approaches. Instead, the strategy notes that it should be viewed as a companion document to other global, regional, and national efforts that address plastic pollution.[38]

Both the GPML and Honolulu Strategy are nonbinding frameworks that offer planning tools for programs and countries and a common frame of reference for collaboration and sharing best practices. While these campaigns and voluntary agreements have little regulatory muscle, they have helped to make plastic pollution a mainstream issue and have spurred action from businesses, individuals, and NGOs, as discussed in Chapter 7.

3 Ocean Plastic Charter The Ocean Plastic Charter is a final example of a voluntary international agreement. The charter, which was proposed by Canada and initially signed by Canada, France, Germany, Italy, and the United Kingdom, in June 2018, outlines concrete steps to eliminate plastic waste. As of May 2020, the charter had been signed by twenty-six governments and sixty-nine businesses and organizations. The charter identifies sustainable approaches to produce, use, and manage plastic and to reduce plastic pollution in the oceans. It is organized around five topics: (1) sustainable design, production, and after-use markets; (2) collection, management, and other systems and infrastructure; (3) sustainable production and lifestyle; (4) research innovation and new technologies; and (5) coastal and shoreline action.[39] While the charter includes specific targets and

[38] United Nations Environmental Programme and National Oceanic and Atmospheric Association, The Honolulu Strategy (available at https://marinedebris.noaa.gov/sites/default/files/publications-files/Honolulu_Strategy.pdf) (last accessed October 31, 2021).

[39] Government of Canada, Ocean Plastics Charter (June 2018) (available at www.canada.ca/content/dam/eccc/documents/pdf/pollution-waste/ocean-plastics/Ocean%20Plastics%20Charter_EN.pdf) (last accessed October 31, 2021).

dates, it is voluntary and has not been signed by the United States or Japan – the only two G7 countries that have not signed the charter.

The G7 countries have also worked to address plastic in the fashion industry. This effort, also known as the Fashion Pact, is discussed in Chapter 7.

III LOOKING TO OTHER INTERNATIONAL AGREEMENTS

International environmental law scholars agree to the following with respect to existing approaches to addressing plastic pollution. First, current hard law instruments have not been effective at reducing plastic waste primarily because: (1) they do not explicitly focus on plastic pollution, or (2) they focus on ocean-based sources of plastic pollution. Second, while some soft law instruments do address plastic generally and ocean-based plastic pollution specifically, implementation of these instruments is through regional, rather than international, initiatives thereby limiting their effectiveness, given the transboundary nature of plastic pollution. Third, since most plastic pollution is land-based, domestic actions, or actions taken by a specific country, to prevent plastic pollution are a necessary part of any global solution. Therefore, future international legal frameworks should focus on action undertaken by individual countries and should enlist the help of businesses that rely on plastic. These practices are discussed further in Chapter 7.

Given these circumstances, calls for an international treaty that addresses plastic pollution are increasing. In October 2020, the World Wildlife Federation, the Ellen MacArthur Foundation, and several international businesses including Coca-Cola, Starbucks, and Nestlé published "The Business Case for a UN Treaty on Plastic Pollution." The report argues that a global plastic treaty with binding targets would help harmonize policy efforts among signatories, enhance investment planning, stimulate innovation, and coordinate infrastructure development. While there is currently no plastic pollution treaty under consideration, a recent meeting of the United Nations working group on marine litter and microplastics reported that more than two-thirds of member states are interested in a global plastic treaty.

Whatever approach is adopted, government leaders should take cues from successful international policy efforts to address acid rain, ozone depletion, and mercury contamination. With the convention on Long-Range Transboundary Air-Pollution, for example, which was signed in 1973, parties agreed to reduce sulfur emissions to address acid rain. Parties signing the Montreal Protocol, in 1987, agreed to phase out ozone depleting substances such as chlorofluorocarbons (CFCs) and halons. More recently in 2013, the Minamata Convention on Mercury was signed to address the adverse effects of mercury. Parties to the Convention agreed to ban new mercury mines, phaseout of existing ones, and the phase out and phase down of mercury use in a number of products and processes, among other things. These agreements are models of cooperation and consensus to address a global environmental and health problem.

Efforts to tackle climate change can also provide insight into a global approach for addressing plastic pollution.[40] Such policy, as applied to plastic, would establish clearly defined waste reduction targets and would provide nations with the resources necessary to effect local reductions. Measurable reduction targets could be met through a variety of policy instruments including the following: container deposit schemes, legislation to reduce single-use plastics, classification of plastic pollution as a hazardous substance or priority pollutant, and incentives for fishers to collect abandoned fishing gear. While critics are quick to point out the difficulty of enforcing international agreements, the collaboration these agreements require can still have an impact. Working together, countries can monitor a problem, gather robust data, and share best practices, which can lead to the creation of workable solutions.

International agreements should also consider the life cycle of plastic from production to waste management. Fossil fuel subsidies

[40] Stephanie B. Borelle, Chelsea M. Rochman, Max Liboiron et al., Opinion: Why we need an international agreement on marine plastic pollution, *Proceedings of the National Academy of Sciences of the United States of America* (September 19, 2017) (available at www.pnas.org/content/114/38/9994.full) (last accessed October 31, 2021).

should be terminated, and biodegradable materials should replace oil-based synthetic polymers. The goal of these agreements should be to achieve a circular and integrated economy, in which waste is "designed out." These topics of design and innovation are the subject of Part III of this book.

7 BUSINESS, NGO, AND INDIVIDUAL EFFORTS

Many of the efforts to curb plastic pollution discussed in earlier chapters focused on the public sphere and the ways in which governments operating at different levels – local, state, national, and international – can combat plastic pollution. The preceding chapters focused primarily on positive law – the express written commands found in statutes, regulations, judicial decisions, and international agreements – that requires specific action by various actors. Chapter 7 considers the private sphere, exploring governance efforts undertaken by businesses, institutions, nongovernmental organizations (NGOs), and individuals. Although these private efforts might be spurred by a government grant or educational campaign, they are executed outside of Congress and the courts. As such scholars have termed them private governance or, when specific to environmental issues, private environmental governance.

Private efforts to address a perceived shared problem often occur when a collective demand for action by citizens is met with government inaction. These private efforts can be on a large scale, such as Fortune 500 companies agreeing to phase out single-use plastics, as well as on a small scale, such as an individual business or person agreeing to reduce their use of plastic. While these smaller, ad hoc, and individual efforts may seem insignificant, they, in fact, often pave the way for broader, systemic change. Indeed, private environmental governance is premised on individual consumers "voting with their wallets" by selecting products and supporting businesses that reflect their values. Clearly then, private governance and individual action are intertwined and coexistent.

Examples of private – as opposed to public – efforts to prevent plastic pollution are endless. Businesses like Disney, Starbucks, Kroger, and American Airlines have all pledged to eliminate plastic straws or plastic bags. Procter & Gamble, Nestlé, PepsiCo, Unilever, Mars, Petcare, The Clorox Company, The Body Shop, Coca-Cola European Partners, Mondelēz International, and Danone are all participating in a pilot program sponsored by TerraCycle that offers brand-name products in reusable and refillable packaging. In February 2019, Walmart announced a new set of plastic waste reduction commitments, updating earlier commitments made in 2016. In addition to businesses, entities such as zoos, professional sports teams, and universities are announcing plans to reduce their plastic footprint.

Many of these commitments are in response to public pressure. Consumers, investors, and everyday citizens (collectively "stakeholders") are demanding some type of remedial institutional action in the face of the global plastic crisis. The increasing focus of academic scholarship on businesses, institutions, and individual behavior is one signal of the growing role of private efforts in solving environmental problems.

Chapter 7 explains both the benefits and the limitations of these private efforts and provides examples of businesses, nonprofits, and individuals working alone and collaboratively to address plastic pollution – taking actions ranging from gathering data to crafting potential solutions. By the end of the chapter, readers will understand the contours of private environmental governance and the role that private entities and individuals are playing in curbing plastic pollution.

I PRIVATE ENVIRONMENTAL GOVERNANCE: AN OVERVIEW

Private environmental governance is the term used by legal scholars such as Michael Vandenbergh to describe organized, private efforts to address environmental harm.[1] The phenomenon of private

[1] Michael Vandenbergh, Private environmental governance, *Cornell Law Review* 99 (2013): 129.

environmental governance arises when private actors engage in activities typically reserved to public entities (legislatures, courts, agencies, etc.) to achieve an environmental goal. Private entities engaging in standard-setting, implementation, monitoring, enforcement, and adjudication are all examples of private governance. These private–private interactions operate without government involvement and can arise in social settings, the marketplace, or both. In fact, private environmental governance often emerges when there are gaps or dysfunction in public governance.

Private environmental governance includes such governance instruments as third-party certification programs, eco-labels, information disclosure, and private supply chain standards. It also includes corporate social responsibility (CSR) efforts and public reporting undertaken by businesses that are integrating social or environmental concerns into their business practices. Private environmental governance also includes voluntary commitments to change behavior, such as phasing out or reducing the use of a certain product. Private initiatives can encourage industry best practices and spur government action as demonstrated in other environmental contexts.

Advocates of private governance argue that private governance efforts undertaken by businesses signal that these businesses are concerned with their environmental impacts and are willing to take responsibility for their actions. Also, private governance instruments such as information disclosures allow consumer choice to be retained. Additionally, some scholars view private governance as more efficient and effective than public governance because private governance instruments are often tailored to the individual business. Finally, advocates note that private governance is a useful "gap-filler" when public regulation is absent or inadequate to address the problem.

Reservations regarding private governance center on what is termed "greenwashing" – that is, the assumptions that a business is merely making a declaration of, or gestures of, sustainability so as to improve its financial and reputational standing and to forestall imposition of more stringent public regulations. Critics further argue that proponents of private governance (which often includes the business or firm itself) promote this form of governance solely to divert attention away from instituting genuine sustainability or traditional government regulation.[2] Despite these criticisms, however, most legal and policy scholars agree that private efforts are a necessary component in developing solutions to a complex global problem such as plastic pollution; therefore, it is worthwhile to identify private governance tools and to offer examples of these tools as applied to plastic pollution.

A The Marine Stewardship Council: A Pioneering Example

While the Marine Stewardship Council (MSC) does not address plastic pollution, it is a widely cited example of effective private environmental governance and serves as a useful means to understanding the framework of private environmental governance. MSC was developed in the 1990s as a mechanism for regulating global fisheries. Fears of overfishing led Unilever – a multinational corporation – and World Wildlife Federation (WWF) – an NGO – to work together to remedy a problem that was not being addressed through traditional modes of public governance. At the time, Unilever was the world's largest buyer of frozen fish products, while WWF was the largest nonprofit conservation organization in the world. Both had significant interests in preventing the overfishing of marine resources, although their primary motivations differed. WWF sought to protect biodiversity, while Unilever, which was interested in expanding its customer base saw good governance, or being a good corporate steward of the environment, as a way to strengthen customer loyalty.

Working together, Unilever and WWF created a stand-alone, neutral body – the Marine Stewardship Council – to set fishing standards and create a certification and labeling program. Fish caught and processed under these sustainable standards would receive MSC

[2] Peter Dauvergne, Ed., *Handbook of Global Environmental Politics* (Edward Elgar, Cheltenham, 2005). As one scholar surmised, "[i]n the worst case, the hype around [private governance], which has developed since the 1990s with increasing numbers of publications, conferences, professorships, and study programs as well as think-tanks and university centers, is nothing but a red herring, used to prevent rather than foster improvements in the sustainability of the global economy." Ibid. at 299.

certification. Implementation lies with third-party auditors who review fisheries for compliance. Licensing fees paid by the fishing firms adopting these standards include the administrative costs associated with MSC certification.

While overfishing continues to be a problem, some argue that overfishing has in fact been reduced by a factor of three to five for MSC-certified seafood. MSC-certified products are now sold by major retailers such as Walmart and Safeway, and MSC seafood accounted for 15 percent of the global fish catch in 2019.[3] MSC is not without critics. MSC-certification criteria are somewhat narrow in scope and do not address such concerns as the impact of current fishing practices on local marine flora and ongoing greenhouse gas emissions. But for the most part, MSC is widely viewed as a successful private alternative to public governance.

While the MSC is a notable pioneer in private environmental governance, in the context of curbing plastic pollution, private efforts, particularly private environmental governance schemes, are only now emerging and are less developed than private efforts that exist to address other environmental concerns such as climate change. This delay in the establishment of robust private efforts to curb plastic pollution is likely because our understanding of plastic waste as a problem is relatively new. But as our understanding of the harm caused by plastic has grown, businesses, institutions, and individuals have responded with commitments to phase out or reduce the use of plastics. Additionally, nonprofits have contributed to establishing private methods for labeling and identifying plastic-free products. Specific industries have also adopted voluntary measures to quantify and reduce plastic waste, and nonprofits are working to educate and engage the public on this issue. Central to this activity are individuals and organizations whose efforts have pushed into the spotlight the harm

[3] Federic Le Manache, Small is beautiful, but large is certified: A comparison between fisheries the Marine Stewardship Council (MSC) features in its promotional materials and MSC-certified fisheries, *Plos One* 15 (May 4, 2020): 1–12 (available at https://journals.plos.org/plosone/article?id=10.1371/journal.pone.0231073) (last accessed October 31, 2021); 16 (available at https://journals.plos.org/plosone/article?id=10.1371/journal.pone.0253486) (last accessed October 31, 2021).

caused by plastic and who have called on industries to address the issue.

Although these efforts to address plastic waste are less established than earlier private environmental governance schemes such as the Marine Stewardship Council, they nonetheless provide insight into how private environmental governance of plastic pollution could develop and operate in the future.

B Private Environmental Governance and Plastic Pollution

My research has revealed four types of private environmental governance efforts currently being directed at curbing plastic pollution: certification and eco-labels; environmental management systems, plastic industry programs, and voluntary phaseouts on the part of both industries and institutions.

1 Certification and Eco-Labels Eco-labels and certifications "convey information about the sustainability of production and manufacturing processes, the environmental impacts of commercial operations, and the safety of materials in end-products."[4] Both are examples of regulation by information; that is, desired changes in consumer behavior are achieved by providing information designed to prompt those changes. The reasoning is that information about the environmental consequences of certain actions can encourage better environmental outcomes. Thus, eco-labels and certifications have two components: education, through information, to change behavior; and the resulting voluntary changes that arise without a regulatory directive. "An eco-label informational and certification scheme can provide engaged consumers with a measurable analysis created by experts and also provide a single point of product comparison for the less-engaged consumer."[5]

[4] David E. Adelman and Graeme W. Austin, Trademarks and private environmental governance, *Notre Dame Law Review* 93 (2017): 709, 710.

[5] Jason J. Czarnezki and Katrina F. Kuh, Crafting next generation eco-label policy, *Environmental Law* 48 (2018): 409, 417.

Jason Czarneski and co-authors divide eco-labels into three categories: positive, negative, and neutral.[6] A positive eco-label provides a claim that the product is environmentally friendly in some way. A negative eco-label either warns that the product is risky to human health or to the environment, or the label includes instruction for safe use. A neutral eco-label is only meaningful relative to a scale. Eco-labels can also inform about the product itself or about the process by which the product was made.

Eco-labels and certifications can be governed by the producing company, in which case they are "self-declared," or they can be governed by a private third party. Third-party labels are viewed as more favorable: By imposing uniform publicly available standards, third-party labels reduce concerns as to the transparency and accuracy of the information the labels contain. But as with other "tools" used for private environmental governance, eco-labels are voluntary, and private entities are free to forgo both "self-declared" and third-party labels altogether.

While the Mobius strip recycling symbol is a well-known eco-label that appears on materials that can be recycled or contain recycled content, this chapter focuses on private efforts specific to plastic, not sustainability generally. These recycling symbols and some concerns associated with their use are discussed in Chapter 9.

The Plastic Soup Foundation has worked to create two kinds of eco-label to address plastic pollution: the Zero Plastic Inside logo and the Ocean Clean Wash label. The Plastic Soup Foundation was founded in 2011 with the singular goal of stopping plastic pollution from entering water bodies. In 2012, the organization started the Beat the Microbead, a campaign against the use of microbeads in everyday products. The Zero Plastic Inside logo (or Zero logo) builds on these efforts. To receive the Zero logo, cosmetic and personal care brands seeking certification must share their ingredient list with the foundation and must sign a pledge that their products are 100 percent microplastic free.

[6] Ibid.

More recently, the foundation has started the Ocean Clean Wash campaign and label, focused on microfibers found in polyester, acrylic, and nylon clothing. This campaign looks for and promotes solutions to microfiber pollution throughout every stage of a textile's use. To date, only one product – a filter installed in washing machines that removes almost 90 percent of the microfibers in clothing – has earned the Ocean Clean Wash label.

The Surfrider Foundation has devised a labeling scheme to designate plastic-conscious restaurants. Currently more than 672 restaurants in the United States are designated as "ocean-friendly restaurants." To receive the Ocean Friendly Restaurant designation, restaurants agree that they will not use Styrofoam, will recycle properly, will only use reusable food ware for onsite dining, will not offer plastic bags, and will provide plastic utensils and paper straws on request. Restaurants that meet these criteria can pay a small annual membership fee for the Ocean Friendly Restaurant designation. In return, members receive marketing materials – such as window stickers and brochures – to show customers their "ocean-friendly" status. Members are included on the Surfrider Foundation's website and can also post the Ocean Friendly Restaurant logo online and in print material.

While adoption of these three initiatives – Zero logo, the Ocean Clean Wash label, and the Ocean Friendly Restaurant designation – is limited, they illustrate how labeling schemes specific to plastic could be integrated into future private environmental governance practices.

2 Environmental Management Systems Environmental management systems (EMS) are also part of private environmental governance. International Organization for Standardization (ISO) 14001 is perhaps the most well-known EMS, but many other types of EMS are recognized around the globe, including the Eco-Management and Audit Scheme (EMAS) used in the European Union. Environmental management consists of integrating environmental concerns into everyday business decisions, rather than considering environmental concerns as independent of daily business actions. An effective EMS allows companies to improve their environmental performance as well as reduce costs, and certification of the EMS, through ISO or another program, enables companies to inform others about their commitment to achieving a certain level of environmental performance.

Regardless of the industries in which they are adopted, EMS share similar components. These similarities include the establishment of environmental goals that align with the organization's overall objectives including profit, the use of audits to establish baselines and monitor progress, and the incorporation of environmental objectives into day-to-day operations.

Developed in the mid-1990s, the ISO 14001 environmental management system has become the international benchmark by which corporations can voluntarily develop and assess their environmental practices. By the end of 1998, nearly 8,000 organizations in seventy-two countries had formally certified their environmental management systems under ISO 14001. Just over 50 percent of the certificates were held by organizations in Europe. The most recent data numbers, reported September 2021, report that there are more than 15,000 ISO 14001 certificates "for rubber and plastic products," with just under 300 in the United States.[7]

EMS is flexible and can be developed for all businesses and operations, including plastic. An EMS specific to plastic is the Responsible Plastic Management (RPM) standard. Created by experts in ISO certification and accreditation, RPM is a voluntary global plastic management assurance program, an eco-label called Trust Mark, and an online directory for organizations. The RPM standard offers participants guidance in best practices for responsible plastic management by helping organizations develop the following: a baseline review of plastic use; a plastic register documenting use, types, sources and fate of plastic; a plastic management plan; and targets, monitoring, and improvement strategies. If an organization chooses, it can have its RPM program independently certified so that it can carry the RPM

[7] ISO Survey of certifications to management system standards (2020) (available at https://isotc.iso.org/livelink/livelink?func=ll&objId=18808772&objAction=browse&viewType=1) (last accessed April 12, 2021).

Program "Trust Mark" or label. This third-party certification lets consumers and stakeholders know that improvements and claims about plastic are verifiable and credible.

Environmental management systems based on a standard such as ISO 14001 or the RPM program do not guarantee specific outcomes such as reducing waste or improving recycling by certain amounts. Instead, these programs are based on commitments to compliance, environmental protection, pollution prevention, and continual improvement.[8] That EMS do not measure actual environmental performance is perhaps the greatest criticism of EMS programs. Additionally, the process of developing, documenting, and certifying EMS is costly, and critics often point out that many small- and medium-sized companies may be discouraged from seeking certification.

That said, an EMS like ISO or RPM allows individual firms to harmonize and simplify their environmental management practices, thereby reducing the need for multiple environmental registrations and permits. Unlike proscriptive government regulation, EMS give companies the flexibility to develop environmental management practices based on their specific operations. And these commitments can become formalized and enforced by means of contracts put in place at various points along the supply chain. While environmental managers consider EMS to be a good tool, in the end it is up to the individual business to achieve results.

3 Plastic Industry Programs Industry groups (as opposed to individual firms) can also monitor and regulate environmental problems themselves. The plastic industry has taken this approach to private governance as illustrated in *The Declaration of the Global Plastics Associations for Solutions on Marine Litter*.[9] In 2011, forty-seven plastics associations from around the world signed the Declaration, which is

[8] Christopher Bell and John Voorhees, Using standards as a framework for environmental and social governance, *Natural Resources & Environment* 35 Fall (2020): 41.

[9] www.marinelittersolutions.com/about-us/joint-declaration/ (last accessed October 31, 2021).

designed to consolidate and maximize the effect of existing marine litter prevention efforts, as well as to generate additional innovative solutions. The Declaration supports projects in six areas: education, research, best practices, public policy, recycling/recovery, and the containment of plastic pellets. As of 2019, the Declaration was supporting more than 380 projects around the world in these areas.[10] Example projects include the 2018 launch of "This Is Plastics" by the Plastic Industry Association, a campaign created to inspire meaningful discussion about the benefits of plastics and to enable plastics industry employees to become ambassadors for plastics. The Declaration also includes support for research such as the 2019 litter survey of New Jersey's waterways conducted by Environmental Resource Planning, LLC. Signatories of the Declaration also advocate for federal legislation such as Save Our Seas Act 2.0 (discussed in Chapter 4) and state legislation focused on recycling and pellet containment, and fund recycling and recovery projects and campaigns across the globe.

Perhaps the most visible project supported by the Declaration is the industry stewardship program Operation Clean Sweep (OCS). OCS predates the Declaration and was started by the Plastic Industry Association and American Chemistry Council over twenty-five years ago. Today, OCS is an international campaign designed to prevent the release of plastic resins, flakes, and powders into the environment. The campaign targets pellet producers, pellet transporters and packagers, and pellet processers. As part of this voluntary program, producers, transporters, and processors can sign a pledge in recognition of their commitment to OCS principles. These principles include committing to regular trainings on pellet loss, preventing pellet loss and cleaning up after pellet loss, establishing written procedures for minimizing loss and managing clean-ups, conducting internal audits, and sharing best management practices. In return, businesses are given an OCS plaque

[10] Marine Litter Solutions, The declaration of the Global Plastics Associations for solutions on marine litter, 5th Progress Report (June 2020) (available at https://plastics.americanchemistry.com/2020-Marine-Litter-Report.pdf) (last accessed October 31, 2021).

and permission to use the OCS logo on websites and other communications. Businesses are also recognized on the OCS website and in its newsletter.

A significant weakness of OCS is that very few companies, relatively speaking, participate. In Europe, 700 companies along the plastic supply chain had joined OCS by 2019, even though the global plastic supply chain comprises over 60,000 companies. Additionally, in-house industry-based programs are typically not as robust as audits and certifications conducted by an independent third party. Finally, despite the existence of OCS, pellets continue to be released into the environment at all three stages – production, transportation, and processing – suggesting that this method of private governance has not been effective.

This point was exposed in a December 2020 NPR article evaluating nurdles in the environment. In discussing Operation Clean Sweep, Lew Freeman, who was a vice president at the Society of the Plastics Industry at the time OCS was developed, acknowledges that self-interest on the part of the plastic industry was a motivating factor in starting the program.

> "I'd like to think it was because it was the right thing to do," Freeman said. "But I would also be naive if I didn't think that much of the motivation was governed by, you know, keeping the regulators off our backs."[11]

Furthermore, in reviewing the Declaration, its signatories, and the projects they support, it is apparent that the Declaration emphasizes containment, management, recycling, and clean-up of plastic (mid-to-end of life issues). While these are all helpful activities, a critical step is missing, namely, source reduction to reduce the amount of plastic that is consumer in the first place. As explained in Chapter 9, the plastic industry has come under fire recently for not doing more to address the harmful environmental impacts of plastics as well as for

[11] Laura Sullivan, Big oil evaded regulation and plastic pellets kept spilling, *National Public Radio* (December 22, 2020) (available at www.npr.org/2020/12/22/946716058/big-oil-evaded-regulation-and-plastic-pellets-kept-spilling) (last accessed October 31, 2021).

knowingly promoting recycling, not to reduce plastic's harms, but to sell plastic products.[12]

4 Voluntary Phaseouts: Industries and Institutions Because plastic products continue to enter the marketplace, an increasingly vital component of private governance is the voluntary actions taken by individual companies and institutions to actually phase out – and not just recycle or clean-up – plastic products. And these voluntary phaseouts by those industries, institutions, and individuals that use plastic is where most private environmental governance action on plastic is occurring.

Across the globe and across business sectors – travel, leisure and sport, food, and fashion – industries and institutions are making commitments to reduce or eliminate plastic waste. In 2018, for example, Starbucks announced that it would phase out the use of plastic straws by 2020, as did McDonald's. American Airlines and Marriott Hotels and Resorts agreed to eliminate the use of plastic stirrers, as well as straws. In 2018, Marriott and other hotel chains also began to transition away from small single-use plastic toiletry bottles for shampoo, conditioner, and shower gels and to replace them with larger pump-topped bottles. Marriott's action will reportedly prevent about 500 million tiny bottles (or 1.7 million pounds of plastic) from entering landfills each year, which will result in a 30 percent annual reduction in "amenity plastic" usage.

a Leisure and Sport The Lego Group, the manufacturer of Lego bricks, the plastic construction toy, is an example of a business voluntarily and consciously deciding to phase out plastic. Lego came under scrutiny when a 2020 study found that the pieces may persist in the environment for over 1,000 years.[13] Even as they break down, Lego

[12] Ibid.

[13] Andrew Turner, Rob Arnold, and Tracey Williams, Weathering and persistence of plastic in the marine environment: Lessons from LEGO, *Environmental Pollution* 262 (June 2020): 114299.

pieces shed microplastics into the environment. Lego has been responsive in considering both the packaging materials and the materials used for the toy itself. Recently, the company announced that it would replace the plastic packaging that holds the Lego pieces with recycled paper bags. The company is also working to make its Lego bricks out of plant-based raw materials. Currently, 2 percent of Lego pieces – for example, its trees and bushes – are made from sugar-based plastics. Lego has set the ambitious goal of completely switching to sustainable materials by 2030.

In 2018, Club Med launched its Bye-Bye Plastic program, which aims to eliminate single-use plastics in bars, restaurants, and rooms by 2021. Club Med is a signatory of a larger UN voluntary initiative called the Global Tourism Plastic Initiative, which unites the tourism sector behind a common vision to address the root causes of plastic pollution. Launched in January 2020 as part of the United Nations Sustainable Development Goals and in conjunction with the Ellen MacArthur Foundation, the Global Tourism Plastic Initiative currently has forty-six signatories who are leading the shift toward a circular economy in the tourism industry.

The entertainment and sport worlds are also participating in making similar commitments. For example, in 2018, Disney announced that by 2019 it would eliminate single-use plastic straws and plastic stirrers at all its locations across the globe, amounting to a reduction of more than 175 million straws and 13 million stirrers annually. It also announced plans to transition to refillable toiletries in Disney hotels and cruise ships and to eliminate the use of polystyrene cups. Similarly, Sea World has been working to eliminate plastic straws, stirrers, and plastic bags from its entertainment parks.

In 2019, the owner of the Hard Rock Stadium, home to the National Football League's Miami Dolphins, committed to phasing out 99.4 percent of all single-use plastic. That same year, the Milwaukee Brewers, a Major League Baseball Team, partnered with SC Johnson, the Wisconsin manufacturer of household cleaning supplies, for a new recycling program. The biggest source of plastic waste at Miller Park, where the Brewers play, is the 1 million plastic cups that are used each year. Under the new partnership, cups branded with the SC Johnson logo will be placed in specially designed receptacles separate from other waste. SC Johnson will collect the cups and use the recycled plastic in a specific SC Johnson product – Scrubbing Bubbles® bottles. This recycling partnership is the first of its kind and is specifically designed to address one of the criticisms of recycling – the lack of markets for recycled goods.

Other companies are reducing plastic waste through product development and replacement. Adidas, for example, began making sneakers composed of recycled ocean plastic in 2017, and Nestlé, Unilever, Pepsi, and Dasani are switching to using aluminum cans as an alternative to plastic bottles. The increasing use of and switching to nonpetroleum-based raw materials by industries that rely heavily on plastic for their product is discussed further in Chapter 9.

b Grocery Stores Product replacement or voluntary phaseouts has proved more challenging for some industries. Grocery stores, for example, are one of the biggest offenders in terms of generating plastic waste. Consider all the single-use plastic waste resulting from food items wrapped or sold in plastic wrap, plastic containers, and plastic bottles. In the United Kingdom, grocery stores are responsible for 40 percent of all plastic packaging. In the United States, around 23 percent of all material reaching landfills is containers and packaging, most of which is plastic.[14] COVID has only increased the demand for prepackaged food. Even before the pandemic, the plastic packaging market was expected to grow to $412 billion by 2024.[15]

While some countries have attempted to create zero-waste grocery stores, the concept has been slow to catch on in the United States. The first attempt by a US grocery store to be entirely plastic-free, In.gredients, in Austin, Texas, closed in 2018 after six years in operation. Since 2018, more independent grocery stores have opened. Scoop

[14] The Environmental Protection Agency, Facts and figures about materials, waste and recycling (2015) (available at www.epa.gov/sites/production/files/2015-08/documents/reducing_wasted_food_pkg_tool.pdf) (last accessed April 12, 2021).

[15] Mordor Intelligence, Plastic packaging market-growth, trents, Covid-19 impact, and forecast (2021–2026) (2021) (available at www.mordorintelligence.com/industry-reports/plastic-packaging-market) (last accessed October 31, 2021).

Marketplace, in Seattle, for example, is a zero-waste grocery store where customers bring their own reusable containers and "scoop" out their purchases from the store's bins of package-free food, home goods, and personal care products. Some larger grocery stores allow customers to use personal containers to buy specific items such as grains, honey, and olive oil. This model of grocery shopping has limitations. Customers must remember to bring their containers and they often need to shop elsewhere for items that cannot be found in these smaller stores. Additionally, COVID has forced some retailers to close sections of stores where bulk items are located to prevent the spread of the virus and have also prohibited the use of canvas/ personal bags.

Grocery stores in Europe have adopted plastic-free aisles. The Dutch grocery chain, Ekoplaza, unveiled the first #PlasticFreeAisle in February 2018. In these aisles, shoppers can choose from over 700 items whose packaging and labels are plastic-free. All goods in these aisles bear the Plastic Free Trust Mark to help consumers identify products that will not contribute to the world's growing waste problem. While Europe, like the United States, has several independent grocery stores that are plastic-free, all seventy-four Ekoplaza stores in Holland have committed to going plastic-free.

c Fashion Fashion is another industry that, like grocery stores, seems to face an uphill battle when it comes to reducing or eliminating plastic. The amount of clothing made from synthetic fibers has increased over the past twenty years and now accounts for 60 percent of world apparel fiber consumption. A growing number of studies has revealed that apparel made wholly or partially from synthetic textiles is the largest source of microfibers in the environment (and 35 percent of all primary microplastics), shed during both normal use and laundering.[16] A 2011 study found that a single polyester fleece jacket could

[16] Mary Catherine O'Connor, Our clothes are contaminating our planet with tiny plastic threads, Ensia (June 19, 2018) (available at https://ensia.com/features/microfibers/) (last accessed October 31, 2021).

shed as many as 1,900 of these tiny fibers each time it was washed; a later study reported an even higher number: 250,000.

Due to the frequency with which clothes are laundered and the growing fast fashion trend – clothing manufactured at warp speed and sold at a low price point – researchers and policymakers are increasingly focusing attention on the environmental impact of microfibers from clothing. One such project is TextileMission – a three-year partnership among nine organizations from the sporting goods industry, the washing machine industry, and the detergent industry. Initiated in 2017, TextileMission has three goals: creating textiles that emit fewer microfibers, optimizing wastewater treatment technology, and gaining a better understanding of how textile-related plastics move through the production-consumption lifecycle. With 2020 marking the end of the three-year project, the partners are now tasked with developing concrete steps to reduce the input of textile-based microplastics into the environment.

Another initiative is The Fashion Pact, which was introduced at the 2019 G7 by the President of France, Emmanuel Macron. The Fashion Pact is based on the collective ambition of fashion CEOs to commit to sustainability targets that are needed to bend the curve toward sustainability in three areas: climate, biodiversity, oceans. The Fashion Pact is a global coalition of companies in the ready-to-wear, sport, lifestyle, and luxury fashion and textile industry – including their suppliers and distributors – all committed to stopping global warming, restoring biodiversity, and protecting the oceans. The pact is not legally binding and is seen as offering a set of guidelines.

With respect to protecting the oceans, the Fashion Pact initially set two goals: eliminating the use of single-use plastics and supporting innovation to eliminate microfiber pollution from the washing of synthetic materials. However, the first annual report published in 2020 contained revised goals. While acknowledging that microfibers are a problem, the report notes that participating members have decided to focus on an area where they can make the greatest impact: plastic bags and packaging. With that in mind, the actions undertaken are to eliminate "problematic and unnecessary" plastic – retail bags, tags and labels, hangers, e-shopping bags – and to move toward 100 percent recycled plastic with at least half of the remaining plastic used.[17] The annual report notes that 70 percent of coalition members have reduced plastic packaging ("unnecessary and harmful plastic packaging, including single-use") since joining The Fashion Pact.[18]

Designer Stella McCartney has stated that she wants to phase out virgin nylon by 2020 and polyester by 2025. Other fashion designers have voiced similar goals. But like grocery stores, fashion appears to be struggling to adequately address plastic concerns, in part because microfibers are so endemic to fashion.

d Institutions, B Corps, and Socially Responsible Businesses Because plastic pollution is often associated with the harm to animals in the marine environment, many zoos and aquariums have sought to reduce plastic at their institution while educating the public about harms of plastic. As of 2019, 202 aquariums in 41 countries had integrated plastics education into programs and exhibits, while reducing plastic use themselves. The Houston Zoo, for example, is now plastic bag, bottle, and straw free, saving the following annually: ~300,000 plastic bottles, ~80,000 plastic bags, ~23,000 plastic straws. The zoo also recycles single-use gloves through TerraCycle, a waste management system described below. The Monterey Aquarium has stopped using single-use plastic straws, bottles, and bags in the aquarium and has also helped to fund the Aquarium Conservation Partnership – a coalition of US aquariums across that have stopped using disposable plastic straws and bags.

Educational institutions are also demonstrating a commitment to eliminating plastic waste through comprehensive zero-waste initiatives. One often-cited statistic is that the average college student produces 640 pounds of trash each year. The National Wildlife Federation (NWF), a nonprofit organization, spearheaded an eight-week competition among universities and colleges – RecycleMania – to encourage

[17] The Fashion Pact: First steps to transform our industry (2020) (available at https://thefashionpact.org/wp-content/uploads/2020/10/038906e111abca13dce4c77d419e4f21.pdf) (last accessed October 31, 2021).

[18] Ibid.

plastic waste reduction and increase recycling. In 2020, over 300 campuses in Canada and the United States participated in RecycleMania, cutting over 300 million single-use plastic containers from their waste streams.

Several colleges have banned on-campus sale of plastic water bottles and are installing drinking water refilling stations and encouraging the use of reusable bottles. Some schools have partnered with Fill it Forward, a certified B Corp, or business that meets the highest standards of verified social and environmental performance. B Corp certification is relatively new and B Corp businesses – which include Ben & Jerry's and Patagonia – treat environmental and social goals as equal to profit. Fill it Forward users download an app and scan their reusable container when it is used. Every scan helps fund Fill it Forward projects centered on clean water, hygiene, sanitation, and education.

Some companies, such as Burt's Bees, a personal care, lip care, and beauty care business, while not a B Corp, have sustainability as a core business principle and consequently are actively looking for ways to reduce their waste. Indeed, their customers expect that these businesses will be responsive to the growing concern over plastic waste. The Burt's Bees website boasts products that are minimally packaged or packaged using readily recyclable plastic. Also, in addition to promoting traditional curbside recycling, Burt's Bees has partnered with TerraCycle, a waste management company started in 2001 with the goal of eliminating "the idea of waste." Today, TerraCycle offers a variety of user-friendly recycling platforms and has established several partnerships with different businesses. In its partnership with Burt's Bees Recycle on Us Program, Burt's Bees customers can recycle product packaging through TerraCycle's free mail-in program. Once collected, TerraCycle cleans and melts the plastic into new recycled products.

Burt's Bees has also assessed the potential pollution impact of its office environment and employees. The company's website describes a work setting where no one has a trash bin. Instead, employees deposit their trash in a trash station containing five bins with one of the following labels: compost; paper; plastic film; plastic, glass & aluminum; or waste-to-energy. This last bin – waste-to-energy – is also designated as the "bin of last resort." The company reports that only 18.5 percent of its total waste ends up in the waste-to-energy bin. Burt's Bees also engages in efforts to change individual employee behavior and norms by sending company-wide emails that praise successes and shame disappointments.

II ADDITIONAL COMPONENTS OF PRIVATE ENVIRONMENTAL GOVERNANCE

The private environmental governance practices described above are undergirded by information gathering and collaborative efforts led by individuals and nonprofits. What follows are some examples of individuals, nonprofits, and businesses working together to gather information, share best practices, and inspire individual and global action.

A Information Gathering

As is the case with other environmental problems, regulatory failure, or the government's ineffectiveness at address a problem such as plastic pollution, is often the result of "data gaps and informational inadequacies."[19] Professor Dan Esty has argued: "considerable evidence suggests that the most sweeping and serious flaws in our environmental decision processes arise from data gaps and technical shortcomings."[20] This is particularly true in the context of plastic pollution, a relatively new and growing problem. Compounding the issue is the lack of transparency regarding methods and materials on the part of producers and suppliers throughout the plastic supply chain. The plastic industry's ignorance (or evasiveness) has been an obstacle to creating effective plastic pollution policies.

Consequently, enlisting private entities can be extremely useful in closing information gaps that can occur despite the best efforts of

[19] Daniel Esty, *Toward optimal governance*, *New York University Law Review* 74 (1999): 1495.

[20] Ibid. at 1542.

governmental agencies and departments responsible for measuring and studying different public harms. One area where private entities such as businesses, individuals, and NGOs have helped gather information concerns plastic leakage – plastic that is "leaked" into the environment either through mismanagement or disposal. For example, Quantis, a sustainability consulting group, has developed the Plastic Leak Project. Using the Plastic Leak Project Guidelines, companies can pinpoint where plastic leakage is occurring across their supply chains and can quantify their plastic loss and release rates. Sustainability managers, corporate decision-makers, R&D teams, product and packaging designers, marketing teams, and supply chain managers can then use this information to engage in "metric-based decision making" to reduce plastic pollution.

Nonprofits have also been working to help gather data to track and identify where industry can reduce waste. WWF, for example, launched ReSource Plastic in the summer of 2019 to enlist over 100 companies by 2030 to join in the goal of preventing over 50 million metric tons of plastic waste from entering nature. The project asks companies to collect data on, track, and report on their plastic use. Central to this effort is the ReSource Footprint Tracker in which companies complete the following: (1) measure plastic use by country, polymer type, form, and use of sustainable inputs; (2) estimate likely waste management outcomes for this plastic; and (3) track initiatives and investments to reduce plastic pollution beyond supply chains. The ReSource Plastic program is the "first-of-its-kind effort to quantify corporate impact and track company actions and opportunities to reduce plastic waste."

Citizen-scientists also play an important role in gathering information and data. Citizen science has been encouraged as a cost-effective way to increase the amount and scope of data collected, and legal scholars believe that "citizen science and citizen monitoring that meet generally accepted data quality standards can enhance environmental governance."[21] Citizen science projects vary based on the type

[21] George Wyeth, LeRoy C. Paddock, Alison Parker et al., The impact of citizen environmental science in the United States, *Environmental Law Reporter – News & Analysis* 49 (2019): 10237.

of plastic being studied (macro vs. micro), as well as the method of data collection. Some methods involve taking water samples or beach sediment samples, while others include counting and categorizing the plastic debris found on beaches or in waterways. Technology maximizes citizen-scientists' efforts to gather and share data. For example, the Marine Debris Tracker is a free app that allows citizens to report plastic litter wherever they encounter it. The app's website reports that over 1.5 million items have been tracked as of the end of 2020. The Nurdle Patrol, launched in November 2018, helps scientists find and map nurdles released into the environment. The patrol's interactive mapping website allows citizen-scientists to input nurdle data into a mapping system to show where the highest concentrations of nurdles are being found across the United States and Mexico. As of December 2020, over 1 million nurdles have been collected and over 6,000 surveys conducted.[22]

The Big Microplastic Survey is a global citizen science project focused on gathering data on microplastics around the world. A collaboration between the UK nonprofit Just One Ocean and the University of Portsmouth (UK), the survey project, which began in 2018, is now active in over fifty-five countries. As part of this ongoing project, volunteers take samples of sand from a specific area and use a density separation process to remove the microplastics. Citizen-scientists then record the data and take photographs of the microplastics and results.

B Collaboration

Collaboration among nonprofits, individuals, universities, and businesses is also a major component of private environmental governance efforts. The Plastic Pollution Coalition, for example, is a global alliance of more than 1,200 organizations, businesses, and thought-leaders in 75 countries working toward a world free of plastic pollution and of the

[22] Nurdle Patrol (available at https://nurdlepatrol.org/Forms/Home/index.php) (last accessed April 13, 2021).

toxic impact of this pollution on humans, animals, waterways, oceans, and the environment. The Plastic Pollution Coalition provides several informational resources on plastic pollution and its impacts, and also offers guides for living a plastic-free life. Individuals and businesses can sign petitions and take pledges to address the touchstone four Rs: refuse, reduce, reuse, and recycle.

Other collaborations are specific to a type of plastic pollution, such as the Global Ghost Gear Initiative (GGGI), which focuses on ghost gear–that is, fishing nets, lines, and traps that have been abandoned, lost, or otherwise discarded. While ghost gear makes up only 10 percent of ocean plastic pollution, it comprises the majority of macroplastics found in the waters.[23] One study found that fishing nets comprise 86 percent of the Great Pacific Garbage Patch.[24] The Ocean Conservancy reports that ghost gear is "four times more likely to harm marine life through entanglement than all other forms of marine debris combined."[25]

The Global Ghost Gear Initiative was started in 2015 and is a cross-stakeholder alliance of the fishing industry, the private sector, corporations, NGOs, academia, and governments focused on solving the problem of lost and abandoned fishing gear worldwide. The GGGI has three working groups focused on building evidence, defining best practices, and informing policy, each with the goal of catalyzing and replicating solutions.

A final example of collaborative efforts are beach cleanups, like the one sponsored by the Ocean Conservancy, which tend to focus on visible macroplastics. Beach cleanups are also a popular form of citizen engagement that both help raise awareness and remove debris from the environment. As one scholar noted "[b]each cleanups and other coastal litter work helps promote local custodianship and caretaking, with citizen scientists making valuable contributions to coastal

[23] Greenpeace International, Ghost gear: The abandoned fishing nets haunting our oceans (November 6, 2019) (available at www.greenpeace.org/static/planet4-international-stateless/2019/11/8f290a4f-ghostgearfishingreport2019_greenpeace.pdf) (last accessed October 31, 2021).

[24] Ibid.

[25] The Ocean Conservancy, Fighting for trash free seas (2019) (available at https://oceanconservancy.org/trash-free-seas/plastics-in-the-ocean/global-ghost-gear-initiative/) (last accessed April 13, 2021).

knowledge in communities around the world."[26] Other reports show that citizen science efforts enhance awareness about marine debris and can inspire behavior change.[27]

This kind of nonbureaucratic information gathering and collaboration is a critical part of private environmental governance. Data and information are prerequisites to solving a complex, global environmental problem such as plastic pollution and better data and information will allow for better matching of the policies to the problem. Data and information gathered through citizen-science activities can also lead to greater awareness of and spur more action on plastic pollution. Both the public and private sectors must recognize that a better understanding of plastic pollution – from its sources to its harms – is a critical component in the crafting of workable and lasting solutions.

III DRIVERS OF PRIVATE ENVIRONMENTAL GOVERNANCE

So, what drives these private corporations to make voluntary commitments, agree to third-party certifications, or engage in partnerships with NGOs and citizens? While there are many drivers, three are most often cited as motivating change in corporate behavior: new legislation, requests (or demands) by citizen-consumers, and shareholder and investor interest.

Often, companies commit to changing their behavior when legislation is pending or threatened, signaling that some form of regulation is almost certain to be enacted. For example, many states began banning microbeads in cosmetics in the early 2000s. These state bans ultimately prompted federal legislation in 2015. However, rather than waiting for the federal law banning microbeads to be enacted, microbead manufacturers began to voluntarily phase out their use. For these global

[26] Tonyavan der Velde, David A. Milton, T. J. Lawson et al., Comparison of marine debris data collected by researchers and citizen scientists: Is citizen science data worth the effort?, *Biological Conservation* 208 (April 2017): 127–38 (available at www.sciencedirect.com/science/article/pii/S0006320716302063) (last accessed October 31, 2021).

[27] Ibid.

manufacturers, it was more efficient to phase out microbeads than to be in the position of potentially contending with a variety of different state (and international) laws banning microbeads.

Similarly, the decisions of Marriott and other hotels to do away with tiny plastic bottles for toiletries could well be in response to state laws that have been enacted or proposed. For example, in 2020 California enacted a law that would ban small plastic bottles in lodging establishments.[28] Similarly, the New York state senate has passed a law prohibiting hotels from offering small plastic bottles for personal care products.[29]

Pressure from citizen-consumers can also drive companies to make sustainability commitments. A 2020 report from McKinsey & Company notes that "[c]onsumer awareness of packaging waste in oceans and landfills is driving change" in the business sector. McDonald's, for example, which has committed to deriving all its packaging from sustainable sources by 2025, said that reducing packaging is the number one request it hears from customers. The Lego Group also committed to plastic-use reductions after receiving letters from children asking why the company still used single-use plastic.

Greater public awareness of plastic pollution is also driving change. Engagement through specific citizen-science projects helps build this awareness, as explained earlier, but so, too, do broader educational campaigns. For example, raising awareness is an essential part of *National Geographic*'s Planet or Plastic? Campaign. Launched in 2018, the initiative aims to raise awareness regarding the harms of single-use plastic and to engage individuals by encouraging them to track their plastic use and to pledge to use less plastic. These commitments and pledges can be logged and tracked on the National Geographic website. The pledge allows individuals to choose the type or types of plastic they will track (bags, utensils, straws, bottles, etc.), as well as the amount by which the individual seeks to reduce their use (the default is seven fewer items per week). Based on these choices, the

[28] AB-1162; see also Chapter 5.
[29] Senate Bill S5282B; see also Chapter 5.

individual is then told the number of items their actions will remove from the planet's pollution stream. Individuals are then encouraged to share their commitments on social media and to challenge their friends to do the same. To date, over 250,000 pledges have been made which, it is calculated, will eliminate 340,000,000 items from the pollution stream.[30]

Sir David Attenborough's *Blue Planet II* documentary TV series has also been critical in raising awareness about plastic pollution, with some calling the "increased interest in plastic pollution following the series' release 'the Blue Planet II' effect."

Of equal importance with raising general awareness regarding the multiple, global impacts of plastic pollution is the need to heighten individual awareness of the impact of their individual actions and choices. Plastic footprint calculators, such as carbon footprint calculators, have been developed so that individuals can track their individual use. The website Omni Calculator, for example, not only enables individuals to calculate the amount of plastic used each year, but it also offers suggestions for reducing plastic footprints by following the four Rs: refuse, reduce, reuse, and recycle.

Shareholders can also drive companies to focus on the four Rs. For example, in 2019, nearly 40 percent of Kroger shareholders supported a proposal asking the largest US supermarket chain to make all packaging recyclable. Forty-four percent of Starbucks shareholders approved of a proposal asking the company to develop aggressive plans to meet specific packaging reuse and recycling goals.[31] In 2012, shareholders of Proctor & Gamble asked the company to adopt extended producer responsibility principles, shifting financial responsibility of collecting and recycling plastic products from taxpayers and local governments back to the company that benefits from the selling of the products. Shareholders are also pressuring petrochemical companies such as Exxon and Chevron to report publicly on the amounts

[30] National Geographic (available at www.nationalgeographic.com/environment/plastic pledge/) (last accessed April 13, 2021) (last accessed October 31, 2021).

[31] Nearly 40 percent of Kroger shareholders support as you sow proposal on recyclable packaging, *Waste Advantage Magazine* (July 2, 2019) (available at https://wasteadvantagemag.com/nearly-40-percent-of-kroger-shareholders-support-as-you-sow-proposal-on-recyclable-packaging/) (last accessed October 31, 2021).

of plastic pellets (nurdles) released annually into the environment during production.[32] While not all shareholder proposals are as successful as these examples, shareholder activism is on the rise with over 71 percent of shareholder proposals in 2017 asking for action on environmental or social matters.

Asset managers BlackRock – which is heavily invested in climate change solutions – has also committed to funding circular economy projects and started a multimillion dollar fund as part of a partnership with the Ellen MacArthur Foundation. Circulate Capital, a Singapore-based investment management firm pledged to put $19 million in four companies transforming India's waste management and recycling value chain.

Plastic producers and industries that rely on plastic products are experiencing mounting pressure from shareholders, consumers, and NGOs to change business practices.

IV CONCLUSION

Private environmental governance is not without critics. Private efforts are often voluntary; enforcement and compliance depend on a company's willingness to self-monitor, self-regulate, and self-disclose. And as in the example of the Operation Clean Sweep campaign to prevent the release of plastic pellets and flakes, self-policing by the plastic industry has not led to meaningful results. That said, many advocates regard private regulation as more effective and efficient than government regulation, in part because self-governance puts businesses in control of achieving sustainability goals. If the business itself is in charge and has set or helped to set the goal, the goal is more likely to be achieved than if it has been imposed by the government.

[32] David Hasemyer, Investors pressure oil giants on ocean plastics pollution, *Inside Climate News* (May 6, 2019) (available at https://insideclimatenews.org/news/02052019/plastic-oceans-climate-change-pollution-investor-pressure-exxon-chevron-dow-shareholder-resolutions) (last accessed October 31, 2021).

Additionally, when the efforts of all nongovernment actors (i.e., industry, institutions, and individuals) are considered, private environmental governance remains important to amplify an issue. As a result, most scholars agree that while environmental law and policies must be the centerpiece of addressing plastic harms, at the same time, private governance should be employed as a significant complement to these legal remedies.

PART III

Innovation and Design

The final section of this book looks at solutions to our plastic problem through the lens of design. Building on government and business strategies, Part III offers innovation as a complement to the regulatory measures being pursued to address plastic pollution. Part III considers the life cycle of plastic and examines efforts to redesign the composition of plastic, to repurpose and recycle plastic, and to adopt a circular – as opposed to linear – approach to plastic management. In a circular approach, *post-consumer plastic* (or used plastic) would not be considered waste, but rather the feedstock for some other product. Similarly, circular approaches anticipate creating alternatives to petroleum-based plastic that can be more easily repurposed and used again. While the regulatory approaches and business efforts discussed in Part II are central to solving our plastic problem, stakeholders including policymakers, product designers, and manufacturers are urged to think about waste during the design process and to consider ways to boost the circular design efforts discussed in these chapters.

8 PLASTIC ALTERNATIVES

Bioplastics and Material Replacement

Chapter 8 discusses the use of bioplastics as an alternative to petroleum-based plastics. Bioplastics are plant-based, and are either sugars, like those found in corn, or produced by microbes. Proponents of bioplastics argue that bioplastics use fewer fossil fuel resources, have a smaller carbon footprint, and decompose faster that petroleum-based plastics. Bioplastics are also less toxic and do not contain bisphenol A (BPA), a hormone disrupter that is often found in traditional plastics.

Bioplastics, however, require high temperatures to biodegrade, and few cities have the infrastructure necessary to assist in the biodegradation of these plastics. Bioplastics can also contaminate recyclable plastics, thereby necessitating two separate recycling streams – one stream for bioplastics and another for petroleum-based plastics. In addition, many bioplastics still require resources such as land and water to grow the raw biomaterials.

Nonetheless, as concerns over traditional plastic grow, bioplastics have received greater attention. And while the market for bioplastics is expected to increase by 20 percent by 2025, given the low price of crude oil, there is currently little economic incentive to switch to plant-based raw materials. While bioplastics are worth pursuing, this chapter concludes that shifting to bioplastics, alone, will not solve our plastic problem. Thus, innovations in bioplastics should be pursued alongside regulatory and private measures.

I BIOPLASTICS: AN INTRODUCTION

Before diving into the chemistry and use of bioplastics, defining a few terms is important. Bioplastics can be biobased, biodegradable, or both. *Biobased* plastics refer to plastic made at least partially from polymers found in plants and other agricultural products rather than being derived from fossil fuel sources. Biobased plastics may or may not be biodegradable. *Biodegradable* plastics are plastics that can decompose within a few weeks in the presence of certain conditions. Biodegradable plastics may or may not be made of a biobased feedstock. And, depending on the environment, some biodegradable plastics might not biodegrade. Thus, while some bioplastics are biodegradable and some biodegradable plastics are biobased, it is not always the case that bioplastics biodegrade or that biodegradable plastics are biobased. In short, the three terms are not interchangeable. Instead, it is best to remember that the term biobased refers to the starting material for a given plastic, while biodegradable considers a given plastic's end of life.[1] The term bioplastics includes both terms: biobased and biodegradable. Perhaps more importantly, the use of the prefix *bio* does not necessarily equate with a product that is sustainable or environmentally friendly. As this chapter explains, bioplastics are created through energy-intensive processes and may persist in the environment once disposed.

Although there is a biobased alternative for almost every petroleum-based plastic, biobased PET, for example, in 2019 only 1 percent, approximately, of the plastics produced in the world were bioplastics.[2] That said, recent bans on single-use plastic and growing awareness of plastic persistence in the environment, as mentioned above, are prompting greater interest in bioplastics, and production of bioplastics is predicted to grow, reaching a production of 2.44 million tons in 2022. Of this projected bioplastic production, approximately 1.086 million tons will be biodegradable (European Bioplastics).[3] A 2020

[1] Claire Goldsberry, Consumers confused by distinction between biobased and biodegradable plastics, *Plastics Today* (February 8, 2020) (available at www.plasticstoday.com/sustainability/consumers-confused-distinction-between-biobased-and-biodegradable-plastics) (last accessed October 17, 2021).

[2] V. C. Shrutia and Gurusamy Kutralam-Muniasamy, Bioplastics: Missing link in the era of microplastics, *Science of the Total Environment* 697 (December 2019): 134–9 (available at www.sciencedirect.com/science/article/pii/S0048969719341166) (last accessed October 31, 2021).

[3] Tiago M. M. M. Amaro, Davide Rosa, Giuseppe Comi, and Lucilla Iacumin, Prospects for the use of whey for polyhydroxyalkanoate (PHA) production, *Frontiers in Microbiology*

market update reports that the bioplastic industry weathered the COVID-19 economic downturn and the global market for bioplastics is predicted to grow by 36 percent over the next five years.[4]

A PLA and PHA Bioplastics

There are two main types of bioplastic: PLA and PHA.

1 PLA The feedstock or material for PLA (polylactic acid) is typically the sugar molecules found in corn starch, cassava, or sugarcane. When using corn to make PLA, the sugar molecule dextrose is extracted from the starch of a corn kernel. Huge fermenters then convert the dextrose into lactic acid, which is then turned into lactide. Lactide molecules are then linked into long chains or polymers to make polylactic acid. This liquid PLA is then converted into PLA resin (or pellets) that are reshaped into containers, films, and fibers. PLA can look and behave like polyethylene (used in plastic films, packing, and bottles), polystyrene (Styrofoam and plastic cutlery), or polypropylene (packaging, auto parts, textiles).

While corn-based plastic has existed for thirty-five years, for many years, until recently, PLA was too expensive for broad commercial use. Now, what formerly cost $200 per pound to make, currently costs less than $1 pound to manufacture. NatureWorks, a Minnesota-based company, is one of the largest manufactures of PLA marketed as Ingeo. Ingeo feedstock has received several third-party certifications. (See Chapter 7 for an in-depth discussion on certifications and labels). Two of the certifications – the USDA Biobased Certification and the Vincotte certification – confirm that the feedstock derives from renewable agricultural products rather than oil. In addition to these two biobased certifications, Ingeo also carries the International Sustainability & Carbon Certification (ISCC) PLUS – a European

10 (May 9, 2019): 992 (available at www.frontiersin.org/articles/10.3389/fmicb.2019.00992/full) (last accessed October 31, 2021).

[4] Market update 2020: Global bioplastics market set to grow by 36 percent over the next 5 years, *BioPlastics Magazine* (December 2, 2020) (available at www.bioplasticsmagazine.com/en/news/meldungen/20201202-Market-update-2020-global-bioplastics-market-set-to-grow-by-36-percent-over-the-next-5-years.php) (last accessed April 13, 2021).

certification scheme certifying the sustainable production of renewable raw materials.

A study commissioned by NatureWorks before 2006 concluded that producing PLA uses 65 percent less energy than producing petroleum-based plastics. The NatureWorks study also found that PLA generates 68 percent fewer greenhouse gases and contains no toxins.[5] A separate 2016 study not commissioned by NatureWorks included a life cycle analysis that found that less net greenhouse gas generation occurs during PLA production as compared to the production of current petroleum-based plastics.[6] These environmentally improved production impacts, together with biobased feedstock certification and reduced production cost, have made PLA products attractive to such companies as Newman's Own Organics, Whole Foods (formerly Wildoats), and Walmart. It is estimated that overall, PLA production capacities will triple in the next five years.

There are, however, some drawbacks and concerns with PLA. In principle, PLA will biodegrade into harmless natural compounds. But its biodegradability is entirely dependent on certain environmental conditions. PLA will degrade back into carbon dioxide and water within three months when placed in a "controlled composting environment," which currently means a large composting facility that reaches 140 degrees Fahrenheit for ten consecutive days.[7] Further, while some stores and businesses that use PLA may offer consumers the opportunity to return PLA products so they can be composted, most consumers do not have access to such specialized composting facilities. PLA that makes its way into a landfill instead of an industrial composting facility can potentially take as long to break down as do petroleum-based plastics.

PLA is also problematic because it can contaminate recyclable plastics such as soda bottles and milk jugs. Because petroleum-based PET plastic common to these bottles and jugs does not mix well with

[5] Elizabeth Royte, Corn plastic to the rescue, *Smithsonian* (August 2006) (available at www.smithsonianmag.com/science-nature/corn-plastic-to-the-rescue-126404720/) (last accessed October 31, 2021).

[6] Editorial, The future of plastic, *Nature Communications* 9 (2018): 2157 (available at https://doi.org/10.1038/s41467–018-04565-22) (last accessed October 31, 2021).

[7] Royte, Corn plastic to the rescue.

PLA, recycling companies regard PLA as a contaminant that must be sorted out and disposed of separately. Finally, PLA has poor thermal properties that limit its applicability at temperatures greater than 60 degrees Celsius – meaning it has a low melting point and melts more easily than other plastics.[8]

Other complaints regarding PLA center on the use of industrially grown corn as a feedstock. The environmental impacts of industrial farming are well known – from the use of fertilizer, pesticides, and herbicides, to the use of water for irrigation and fossil fuels for planting and plowing the fields. Furthermore, the corn grown for bioplastics is not the same corn grown for human consumption. Similar to the argument against corn grown for fuel, or ethanol, opponents argue that corn grown for plastics is using land that could be used for growing food for human consumption.

Thus, while most environmental advocates agree that corn-based plastic is better than petroleum-based for those plastics necessary to our everyday lives, PLA is not a panacea. Along with the concerns mentioned above, advocates worry that PLA plastics will serve to justify the continued use of single-use plastic items and sale of over-packaged products. Therefore, prioritizing plastic reduction must continue in tandem with investments in PLA plastic, including making composting facilities more widespread and available to the average consumer.

2 PHA Another bioplastic that is often mentioned is PHA (polyhydroxyalkanoate). PHA is made when microorganisms (or bacteria) produce polymer chains from organic materials under certain conditions. Scientists have discovered more than 150 PHAs with different polymer structures.[9]

The process of creating PHA requires depriving the microorganisms of nutrients such as nitrogen, oxygen, and phosphorus while "feeding" them high levels of carbon. In these conditions, the microbes

[8] The future of plastic.

[9] Alexander H. Tullo, PHA: A biopolymer whose time has finally come, *Chemical and Engineering News* (September 8, 2019) (available at https://cen.acs.org/business/biobased-chemicals/PHA-biopolymer-whose-time-finally/97/i35) (last accessed October 31, 2021).

will produce PHA, which has a chemical structure similar to traditional plastics. The kind of bacteria and the nutrients these microorganisms are fed – be it sugars, starches, glycerin, triglycerides, or methane – determine the PHA produced. Companies can then harvest the microbe-made PHA.

Because it is biodegradable and will not harm living tissue, PHA is often used for medical applications such as sutures, slings, bone plates, and skin substitutes; it is also used for single-use food packaging. PHA's biodegradability has led some to say PHA "beats out" PLA bioplastics. Like PLA, PHA is currently being composted industrially, but unlike PLA, PHA can degrade naturally in oceans and landfills. Even so, PHA will not degrade in all environments. For example, PHA will not degrade in the ice-cold water of the Arctic Ocean. Thus, while PHA does not require a special facility to degrade, environmental conditions may still influence its rate of degradation.

The facilities required for the biosynthesis of PHA are expensive and many businesses have limited capacity to scale-up their facilities to a size that is economically viable. Nevertheless, as with PLA, single-use plastic bans around the world have led to greater interest in PHA. In the United States, biotech company, Danimer Scientific, is the leader in the PHA industry. In 2018, it began construction of the world's first commercial production facility and sold its first truckload of PHA resins in January 2020.

In October 2020, Dunkin Donuts started a pilot program in 250 locations to test the use of a straw manufactured by WinCup – a manufacturer of disposable cups, bowls, containers, straws and lids– using Danimer Scientific PHA resins. Danimer Scientific is also working with Bacardi, the rum company, to manufacture packaging that will hold alcohol. Such bottles will not be available to the market until 2023. Both PepsiCo and Nestlé are also working on PHA packaging for their products.

Because PHA is biodegradable and because its production depends on carbon (a common bioproduct of many chemical processes), opportunities for innovative circular designs abound. For example, Mango Materials, a California company, uses methane (CH_4) – a greenhouse gas – to make its own special brand of PHA. Called P_3HP, the PHA product can be used to make biodegradable fibers for apparel or injection mold packaging for phone cases. Mango Materials has embraced circular thinking by locating its operations next to companies that produce methane as a by-product – specifically waste-water treatment plants – thereby using methane that would otherwise be released into the atmosphere as the raw material for PHA.

Another PHA-manufacturer, RWDC Industries, uses discarded cooking oil as its feedstock. It creates PHA that can be used in straws, coffee cups, and fast-food containers. In May 2020, RWDC announced that it had raised $133 million to expand its production capabilities in Athens, Georgia, in advance of the product's commercial launch. Its PHA product, called Solon, has been third-party certified as both biobased and biodegradable. Scientists are also studying how PHA can be made from discarded food waste, which generates methane when discarded in landfills.[10] These innovations could reduce the costs of making PHA while increasing the availability of PHA products.

Bioplastic production could also be increased by manufacturing bioplastics that can be processed with existing equipment that is already used for manufacturing conventional plastic. When bioplastics were first being developed, many of these prototype bioplastics could not be "dropped in" to existing plastic manufacturing equipment and required specialized processing equipment, in which companies were resistant to invest. As bioplastic development matures, PLA and PHA researchers should continue to focus on making bioplastic materials that are compatible with existing equipment so that expansion can happen more quickly.

II MATERIAL REPLACEMENT

An alternative to bioplastics – whereby plastic polymers are "synthesized" from biobased materials – is material replacement or the use of

[10] Yiu Fai Tsang, Vanish Kumar, Pallabiu Samadar et al., Production of bioplastic through food waste valorization, *Environment International* 127 (June 2019): 625–44 (available at www.sciencedirect.com/science/article/pii/S0160412019301357) (last accessed October 31, 2021).

other materials to make products that are typically plastic. The use of jute, seaweed, beeswax, aluminum, and glass are all being explored as materials that could "replace" plastic in different products.

Jute – also called "the golden fiber" – is a naturally occurring vegetable fiber being promoted as an alternative to petroleum-based plastic. Jute naturally grows year-round in South Asian countries such as Bangladesh and India. Together, these two countries account for more than 93 percent of the global jute production.[11] Jute is one of the least expensive natural fibers, second only to cotton, and is 100 percent biodegradable. Jute is durable, and non-toxic, and requires less land and water than other plastic alternatives such as cotton. Additionally, jute cultivation that uses crop rotation techniques improves the fertility of the soil for the next crop. Yet another benefit of jute is that jute plants absorb carbon dioxide and release oxygen at a rate several times higher than trees. According to some estimates, one hectare of jute plants can absorb up to nearly 15 tons of carbon dioxide and discharge 11 tons of oxygen during one growing season, thereby reducing greenhouse gas effects.

Deyute, a Spanish-based company, uses jute in its products. The jute fibers are spun into strong strands making a firm and durable end-product. The main application of jute by Deyute is in burlap, but jute is also used in bags, yarn, and straps.

Seaweed has also shown promise as an alternative to petroleum-plastics and seaweed-based plastics are being developed in Indonesia, China, and the United Kingdom. Seaweed is a desirable raw material because it grows quickly and is less resource intensive. Because it is readily available in the ocean, seaweed does not compete with other crops for land or water.

Seaweed is being promoted by companies as a raw material that can be used in edible plastic packaging. Notpla, a UK start-up that uses brown seaweed to make plastic packaging, is one such company. The plastic-like membrane is made from seaweed farmed in northern France that is dried and ground into powder which is transformed into

[11] Casper Ohm, The case for exploring jute as an alternative to plastic, GreenBiz (April 10, 2020) (available at www.greenbiz.com/article/case-exploring-jute-alternative-plastic) (last accessed October 31, 2021).

a thick liquid that forms a plastic-like substance. The resulting material is both edible and biodegradable. Notpla's website claims that "Notpla biodegrades naturally in 4–6 weeks" and "[u]nlike PLA, it can be composted at home and does not contaminate PET recycling."[12] At the 2019 London Marathon, sport drinks were contained in squishy Notpla pods that were popped into the mouths of runners. Race organizers were able to reduce plastic waste, an otherwise common by-product of a major sporting event. Loliware, a seaweed-based straw company, is another example of a seaweed-based plastic company. Market research expects demand for edible packaging, like those described, to increase on average by 6.9 percent yearly until 2024, eventually becoming a market worth almost $2 billion worldwide.[13]

Still other products are being developed to reduce the need for petroleum-based plastic. For example, Bee's Wrap, developed in 2012, is a durable cotton that is coated in a mixture of beeswax, tree resin, and jojoba oil for use as a replacement to plastic wrap to preserve food and cover bowls. However, like PHA, Bee's Wrap does not perform well at high temperatures. Hemp has also been discussed as a potential substitute to petroleum-based feedstocks, but because its production is controlled by existing drug laws in the United States, there is no large-scale commercial production of this plant as an agricultural commodity.

Aluminum, particularly aluminum cans, has been promoted as a replacement for plastic bottles. As consumer concern for plastic pollution has grown, companies such as Coca-Cola and Pepsi have turned to aluminum – considered a sustainable alternative to the plastic bottle – for their water products: Dasani (Cola-Cola) and Aquafina (Pepsi). Canned Dasani and Aquafina were first marketed in 2020. The appeal of aluminum stems from the fact that aluminum is considered indefinitely recyclable and it does not require a petroleum-based feedstock. As explained in Chapter 9, most plastics cannot be recycled and those that are recyclable are recycled only once or twice before they are no longer

[12] Notpla, www.notpla.com/technology/ (last accessed April 13, 2021).

[13] Prachi Patel, The time is now for edible packaging, *Chemical and Engineering News* (January 26, 2020) (available at https://cen.acs.org/food/food-science/time-edible-packaging/98/i4) (last accessed October 31, 2021).

usable. That said, the carbon footprint of an aluminum can is significantly greater than that of a plastic bottle.[14] Further, the raw material for aluminum is 25–35 percent more expensive than that for a plastic bottle.[15] Even so, market research shows that demand in the United States for "can sheet" aluminum – the type of aluminum used for beverage cans – will grow about 3–5 percent a year through at least 2025, in response to consumer demand. This is compared to growth that has been effectively flat for the last twenty years.

Glass has also been suggested as an alternative to plastic bottles and containers. Glass is manufactured from sand, as opposed to fossil fuels, and is easily, and endless, recyclable. Glass production, however, requires a lot of fossil fuels, and glass is heavier, adding to increased transportation costs. Glass can also break more easily as compared to plastic.

The environmental benefits of aluminum and glass over plastic largely rest with how often consumers recycle the containers. That is, if recycling rates for plastic could increase, the environmental benefits of plastic over some other material could increase. Recycling and other end-of-life options for plastic is the topic of Chapter 9.

III CONCLUSION

Consideration of new materials to replace petroleum-based products is currently being driven mostly by the private sector, and the bioplastic market is still in its infancy. That said, market indicators suggest that experimentation with bioplastics and other raw materials will continue as governments worldwide struggle to address plastic pollution. Until that time when bioplastics will be widely adopted, attention should also be given to the ways in which plastic can be recycled and reused – the topic of Chapter 9.

[14] Eric Onstad, Plastic bottles vs. aluminum cans: Who'll win the global water fight?, *Reuters* (October 17, 2019) (available at www.reuters.com/article/us-environment-plastic-aluminium-insight/plastic-bottles-vs-aluminum-cans-wholl-win-the-global-water-fight-idUSKBN1WW0J5) (last accessed October 31, 2021).

[15] Ibid.

9 PLASTIC'S END

Recycling, Removing, and Revaluing

What if instead of changing the composition of plastic, we changed what happened to plastic at the end of its useful life? Chapter 9 explores end-of-life issues with plastic, focusing on efforts to keep plastic out of landfills and the environment.

As explained in the preceding chapters, the amount of plastic in our environment is a huge problem. To reiterate just a few examples of the extent of plastic pollution: 80 percent of the plastic in our oceans comes from land-based sources, people are unknowingly drinking microplastics, and cows and marine life are ingesting plastic. And this problem of plastic in the environment is the result of several things including ineffective policies, inadequate technologies, and widespread use. Intentional and unintentional actions by individuals and businesses have led to this plastic crisis. For example, when recyclable plastic is sent to a landfill and the landfill is not managed properly, plastic can end up in our environment. When plastic is illegally dumped or carelessly disposed of, plastic can end up in our environment. When we wash our clothes or anything that contains plastic, plastic can end up in our environment. Additionally, factors inherent to the nature of plastic itself – plastics' lightweight and often microscopic size – have made the situation worse.

This chapter explores the collecting and recycling of plastic as well as the removal of plastic from the environment. Specifically, this chapter describes the challenges and inefficiencies inherent to recycling and highlights some novel and creative efforts to capture, collect, repurpose, and revalue used plastic.

I RECYCLING PLASTIC

When industries dependent on plastic are asked about our plastic problem, the customary response is: "we just need to recycle more." Recycling is the process of collecting and processing waste into new products. It is the second most preferred strategy – after source reduction – according to the Environmental Protection Agency's (EPA) hierarchy of preferred waste management strategies. The bans and phaseouts discussed in earlier chapters are examples of methods to achieve source reduction. Disposal by sending something to a landfill is the least preferred, but most common, strategy with respect to used plastic. Energy recovery (converting waste to energy through a process such as combustion) ranks below recycling but above landfilling.

Recycling is a multistep process. It involves collecting used or post-consumer plastic goods, sorting and bundling the plastic by a material recovery facility (MRF), reprocessing by shredding, grinding, and washing the plastic at a separate facility that purchases the plastic bundles, and finally, manufacturing new products using the recycled plastic as feedstock.

This recycling process, sometimes called mechanical recycling, can lessen society's adverse impact on the environment by diverting plastic from the least desired outcome, sending plastic to a landfill, while at the same time providing manufacturers with source materials for new products. Yet despite these environmental and economic benefits, and despite the efforts of environmental groups, state and local governments, and the plastic industry to promote recycling, rates for the recycling of plastic have stayed the same for the past twenty years. The amount of plastic that is recycled has remained less than 10 percent of all the plastic produced in the United States (and is only 2 percent globally).[1] This is significantly less than US recycling rates for paper

[1] Jan Dell, Six times more plastic waste is burned in U.S. than is recycled, Plastic Pollution Coalition (April 30, 2019) (available at www.plasticpollutioncoalition.org/blog/2019/4/29/six-times-more-plastic-waste-is-burned-in-us-than-is-recycled) (last accessed April 13, 2021).

and cardboard (around 66 percent for all paper and cardboard products) and glass (around 27 percent for all glass products).

Why the low recycling rate for plastic? As compared to paper and glass recycling, plastic recycling faces significant logistical, economical, and geopolitical challenges. Any disruption along the recycling process – from the elimination of municipal recycling programs to the lack of markets for recycled plastic – reduces recovery rates for plastic. Further, when these disruptions occur, instead of being recycled, plastic is sent to a landfill or is incinerated. During each process – recycling, disposal, incineration – plastic is often leaked into the environment.

Currently, the United States cannot recycle all the plastic waste that it generates. As one recycling professional noted, the US is "trying to deal with a 21st-century packaging stream based on 20th-century infrastructure."[2] Numerous publications have labeled the US recycling industry as "broken," "garbage," and "in crisis." This criticism has only grown louder as awareness of plastics' harms has increased and the global waste trade has changed dramatically.

In the early 1990s, the United States and other developed countries began exporting their waste, including plastic waste, to China. China was eager for this endless supply of feedstock to support its growing economy, which included manufacturing plastic goods to sell to the United States and other countries. The waste could easily be sent to China on the cargo vessels that are used to deliver goods to countries across the globe. In addition, China would take plastic that had not yet been sorted. China's low contamination standard and favorable shipping rates supported the practice of sending plastic waste to China. And because China was willing to collect and sort mixed waste, waste management companies in the United States developed the practice of "single-stream" recycling, whereby all recyclable material – newspaper, cardboard, plastic, aluminum, junk mail – is placed in a single bin or cart for recycling. This reliance on China to manage US waste discouraged domestic investment in recycling infrastructure and

[2] Edward Humes, The US recycling system is garbage, Sierra (June 26, 2019) (available at www.sierraclub.org/sierra/2019-4-july-august/feature/us-recycling-system-garbage) (last accessed October 31, 2021).

prevented the development of a more robust domestic recycling program. By 2017, the United States was sending 70 percent of its plastic waste to Chinese processors for recycling.[3]

The out of sight, out of mind mentality continued until 2018 when China implemented its "National Sword Policy." Use of plastic throughout the world had proliferated and the numerous types of plastic – with different colors, additives, and compositions – increased contamination rates, making recycling significantly more difficult for China. Pollution concerns and the growing inability to recycle the plastic it was receiving prompted China to reduce both the amount and kind of plastic it imported. The National Sword Policy effectively banned the importation of plastics and other materials from the United States and elsewhere.

As a result of China's ban, the United States was forced to find other markets for its plastic waste such as Malaysia, Thailand, and Senegal. Many of these countries do not have adequate waste management facilities and have also started to refuse plastic waste from the United States.

The Basel Convention Amendments, discussed in Chapter 6, which reclassified plastic as hazardous and subject to rules governing the movement of such waste across international boundaries, are another incentive for changes to waste management policies. For example, in 2021, Plastic Recycling, Inc., a waste management company based in Indianapolis, announced it was investing $2 million to install a system to produce clean recycled flakes from e-plastics. The company cited the Basel Amendments, which took effect on January 1, 2021, as an incentive to install a new system. Changes in the global plastic trade, beginning with China's ban and continuing through the Basel Convention Amendments, have forced the United States to confront its management of plastic waste and, to a lesser degree, its consumption of plastic.

[3] Cheryl Katz, Piling up: How China's ban on importing waste has stalled global recycling, *YaleEnvironment360* (March 7, 2019) (available at https://e360.yale.edu/features/piling-up-how-chinas-ban-on-importing-waste-has-stalled-global-recycling) (last accessed October 31, 2021).

US municipal recycling programs have been a part of its waste management program since the 1960s and 1970s when disposable items became more common, the environmental movement began to take shape, and landfill space was becoming scarce. The plastic industry engaged with recycling when, in the 1980s, the Society of the Plastic Industry developed Resin Identification Codes (RIC) – a series of seven numbers used to identify different kinds of plastic. One (1), for example, stands for polyethylene terephthalate (PET or PETE) plastic and is commonly found on soda bottles and peanut butter jars. Two (2) stands for high-density polyethylene, or HDPE, used in milk jugs, laundry detergent bottles, and some shopping bags. LDPE, or low-density polyethylene, is represented by the number four (4). LDPE is commonly used in plastic films, such as shrink wrap grocery bags, bread bags, and produce bags. The numbers one through seven were placed inside a triangle formed by three arrows – a symbol commonly associated with recycling – that appears on various plastic packaging.

RIC codes were developed to help maintain consistency among manufacturers and to help waste management facilities in sorting the different plastics for recycling. The codes were not developed to aid consumers, despite what many consumers might believe. The American Society for Testing and Materials (ASTM) website, which administers the RIC codes, states that while these codes can assist those involved with recycling, they are not, in fact, recycling codes.[4] Why? Because the use of the code "does not imply that the [plastic] article is recycled or that there are systems in place to effectively process the article for reclamation or re-use."[5] And because such numbers do not exist on paper or glass, most people are not familiar with the different plastic recycling numbers and are unaware of limitations associated with plastic recycling. ASTM International changed the symbol in 2013, replacing the arrows with a solid triangle. But manufacturers were not required to incorporate the new symbol and many plastic

[4] The American Society for Testing and Materials (April 13, 2021) (available at www.astm.org/Standards/D7611.htm) (last accessed October 31, 2021).
[5] Ibid.

products still carry the earlier version of the symbol as shaped by arrows.

Surveys support the claim that consumers are confused about what can and cannot be recycled. This confusion helps to explain, at least to some degree, low recycling rates. A 2014 survey found that 65 percent of respondents did not understand what kind of plastic is acceptable in curbside pickup locations.[6] A 2019 survey conducted by the Consumer Brands Association found that 68 percent of respondents said any item with an RIC would be recyclable.[7]

While plastic is theoretically recyclable, most plastic is never recycled. And while plastic items identified with RIC numbers 1 and 2 are commonly recycled, most material recovery facilities do not recycle the remaining five resin codes. A recent Greenpeace publication, based on a survey of material recovery facilities from all fifty states including Waste Management, the largest material recovery facility in the United States, reported that PET 1 and HDPE 2 are the only plastic groups that are universally accepted by material recovery facilities. Further, only 87 percent of Americans have access to a recycling facility either through curbside pickups or drop-off locations.[8] Of that 87 percent, a much smaller amount (around 30 percent) is collected for recycling, and, an even smaller amount is processed for recycling (around 20 percent).[9] Thus, 87 percent of people have access to recycling facilities, but only 30 percent do recycle, and only 20 percent of what they put out for recycling is actually recycled. This means that people who have access to recycling facilities are not fully participating. And for those who do participate, not all the plastic they put out for recycling is recycled. Regarding RIC 3-7, only around 50 percent of

[6] Lisa Pierce, Confused consumers toss out plastic packaging instead of recycling: Poll, Packaging Digest (August 7, 2014) (available at www.packagingdigest.com/sustainability/confused-consumers-toss-out-plastic-packaging-instead-recycling-poll) (last accessed October 31, 2021).

[7] *Reduce. Reuse. Confuse.*, Consumer Brand Association (2019) (available at https://consumerbrandsassociation.org/wp-content/uploads/2019/04/ConsumerBrands_ReduceReuseConfuse.pdf) (last accessed October 31, 2021).

[8] Greenpeace Reports, Circular claims fall flat: Comprehensive U.S. survey of plastics recyclability (2020) (available at www.greenpeace.org/usa/wp-content/uploads/2020/02/Greenpeace-Report-Circular-Claims-Fall-Flat.pdf) (last accessed October 31, 2021).

[9] Dell, Six times more plastic waste is burned in U.S. than is recycled.

recycling facilities accept plastic group number 5 (plastic tubs), and even fewer facilities accept plastic group numbers 6 and 7. Thus, when plastics bearing the numbers 3-7 are collected, they are either stockpiled, landfilled, or incinerated.[10]

Another problem associated with plastic recycling is contamination. Plastic recycling is compromised when plastic with different RICs are mixed, when plastics are not free of residue from food or other substances, or when labels are not removed. Single-stream recycling has conditioned even well-intentioned citizens to put everything – plastic bags, straws, containers, caps – out for recycling. But these kinds of plastic can jam the recycling machinery. Additionally, the mechanical recycling process cannot remove color and other chemical additives, and the value of the plastic bundles that contain mixed plastics is significantly less than a bundle comprised only of RIC 1 or RIC 2. Still another challenge is that the virgin feedstock for plastic (oil and gas) is inexpensive as compared to the cost of recycled plastic. As a result, there is little economic incentive for companies to use post-consumer recycled plastic.

Additionally, the traditional method of converting recycled plastic into new products – thermomechanical recycling – can only be applied to recycled plastic once or twice before the plastic polymers break down completely. During thermomechanical recycling, plastic is broken down into smaller bits through the mechanical processes of cutting and chopping. The plastic is then cleaned, melted, and converted into some other product. The melting of plastic changes its chemical properties and limits the uses to which recycled plastics can be put. Recycled plastic bottles, for example, are not always made into new plastic bottles. Instead, the recycled plastic from bottles is often converted into "lower grade" plastic and is used in products such as water pipes and traffic cones. In fact, thermomechanical recycling is sometimes referred to as "downcycling."[11]

[10] Circular claims fall flat: Comprehensive U.S. survey of plastics recyclability.

[11] Alexander Tullo, Plastic has a problem; is chemical recycling the solution?, *Chemical and Engineering News* (October 6, 2019) (available at https://cen.acs.org/environment/recycling/Plastic-problem-chemical-recycling-solution/97/i39) (last accessed October 31, 2021).

An alternative to thermomechanical recycling is chemical recycling. In chemical recycling, the chemical bonds that hold the plastic molecules (polymers) together are broken, creating smaller molecules that can be made into new plastics that retain plastic's high-performance qualities. Additionally, chemical recycling processes are more tolerant of imperfect plastic waste streams. As a result, chemical recycling is being offered as a way to avoid mechanical recycling's shortcomings.

Chemical recycling is considered the more difficult and less developed process of the two recycling methods, but it is a growing area of interest for academics, industry, and politicians. Scientists interested in chemical recycling are experimenting with breaking the bonds of long polymer chains using different temperatures and catalysts. For example, a 2021 study was able to achieve a recovery rate of 96 percent of the starting material by creating a polyethylene-like material with chemical bonds that were more easily split.[12] The bond separation process used during chemical recycling better preserves the monomers so that they can be rejoined to create essentially the same kind of plastic. What that means is that the raw material created from chemical recycling can be used in the same manner and can, therefore, replace the virgin petroleum-based raw material used to make high-quality plastic. Unlike the "downcycling" that occurs with thermomechanical recycling, chemical recycling is considered an "upgrading" process because the resulting plastic's quality is not degraded. Some call this process plastic-to-plastic (PTP) recycling or repolymerization because the polymers are recovered. This should not be confused with a plastic-to-fuel (PTF) process, where the plastic is converted to hydrocarbons that are used as fuel, and which is also sometimes called chemical recycling.

Industry is betting big on chemical recycling. Eastman Chemical Company, for example, has invested over $250 million in a plastic-to-plastic chemical recycling facility in Kingsport, Tennessee. The

[12] Chemistry can help make plastics sustainable – But it isn't the whole solution, *Nature* 590 (February 17, 2021): 363–4 (available at www.nature.com/articles/d41586-021-00391-7?WT.ec_id=NATURE-20210218&utm_source=nature_etoc&utm_medium=email&utm_campaign=20210218&sap-outbound-id=AFAA75F4D4E2A698D59BA7A402FF9A2690471E4B#ref-CR3) (last accessed October 31, 2021).

company hopes to recycle 250 million pounds of plastic waste by 2025 and more than 500 million by 2030.

In response to growing consumer pressure and changes to international law, the federal government and state governments have also shown increased interest in both chemical and mechanical recycling projects. Interestingly, recycling is something that garners bipartisan support, and in 2019, federal recycling legislation was a "major trend" rather than a "one-off" event.[13]

In addition to the Break Free from Plastic Pollution Act discussed in Chapter 4, which would require that plastic products contain a minimum amount of recycled content, the RECOVER Act and the RECYCLE Act were introduced in 2020. The RECOVER Act (HR 5115), introduced by Representatives Tony Cárdenas (D-Calif.) and Larry Bucshon (R-Ind.), would establish a recycling infrastructure program within the EPA. Additionally, the bill would designate $500 million in federal funds for states, municipalities, and tribes to improve their collecting and processing infrastructures, from expanding curbside recycling to upgrading material recovery facilities, to encouraging the use of recycled materials in new products. Under the Act, funds could also be used to develop rural recycling programs, to improve consumer education about recycling, and to market recycled materials in the United States.

The RECYCLE Act (S. 2941), introduced by Senators Rob Portman (R-Ohio) and Debbie Stabenow (D-Michigan), would authorize $15 million in grants to states, tribes, nonprofits, public partnerships, and local governments for commercial and municipal recycling outreach and education. The Act also directs the EPA to develop a recycling tool kit to increase recycling participation and decrease contamination rates. Such a tool kit would standardize terms and provide examples of procedures used in residential recycling programs and would develop community self-assessment guides to

[13] E. A. Cruden, 2020 could be the year of legislative boom – or bust – for national recycling policy, *WasteDive* (January 29, 2020) (available at www.wastedive.com/news/2020-legislative-boom-or-bust-national-recycling-policy-congress/571253/) (last accessed October 31, 2021).

identify gaps in existing recycling programs. Additionally, the Act would encourage federal agencies to purchase recycled plastic.

In 2019, the US Department of Energy (DOE) launched the Plastic Innovation Challenge to accelerate innovations in energy-efficient plastic recycling technologies. The Plastic Innovation Challenge has four strategic goals: (1) to develop biological and chemical methods for converting plastic wastes into useful chemicals; (2) to develop technologies to upcycle waste chemical streams into higher-value products, thereby encouraging increased recycling; (3) to design new, renewable plastics and bioplastics that have the properties of modern plastics and are easily upcycled; and (4) to support an energy- and material-efficient plastic supply chain by helping companies scale and deploy new technologies in domestic and global markets while improving existing recycling technologies such as collection, sorting, and mechanical recycling.

In October 2020, the DOE awarded over $27 million to twelve university-based projects focused on improving plastic recycling processes and technologies. Projects will address a variety of research and development areas, including developing plastics that can be cost-effectively recycled or can biodegrade, and developing energy-efficient recycling technologies for both mechanical and chemical recycling that are capable of breaking plastic into smaller parts that can be upgraded into higher-value products. Improvements in recycling technology are a critical part of the circular economy and the DOE Roadmap for the Challenge identifies designing for circularity as an important component of the challenge and DOE activities.

There is also considerable interest in legislation concerning recycling at the state level. In 2019, two states, New Hampshire and Illinois, established committees to study recycling and its changing market conditions. Michigan and Colorado have devoted more funds to recycling – Michigan, by increasing funding to recycling programs to $15 million annually, and Colorado, by increasing user fees at landfills to fund grants focused on increasing recycling and reducing waste. State legislation has also focused on contamination issues. For example, a 2020 Florida law allows waste facilities to refuse contaminated materials that violate the definition of acceptable recyclables as stated in their contracts. Increasing the domestic markets for recycled materials, including plastic, is the focus of laws that were enacted in Washington and New Jersey.

Finally, Texas passed legislation in 2019 to encourage recycling in general, and the chemical recycling of plastic, specifically. House Bill 1953 prohibits the Texas Commission on Environmental Quality from classifying post-consumer plastics or recyclable feedstocks as solid waste "if they were converted using pyrolysis [a plastic-to-plastic process] or gasification [a plastic-to-fuel process] into a valuable product." Advocates maintain that this law will attract new businesses and support job creation by treating post-consumer plastic as raw materials for manufacturing and not as waste. It is expected that this law will further expand chemical recycling facilities in Texas, the largest chemical manufacturing state in the United States. Opponents are concerned that such a law will promote plastic-to-fuel operations, which emit greenhouse gases, rather than plastic-to-plastic efforts. Studies show that the pyrolysis process uses more energy to treat the waste than can be recovered.[14]

Chemical recycling of plastic is emerging technology and there is no consensus in the scientific community on its environmental impacts or benefits. As a result, the EPA has called for further discussions on the processes.

This interest and investment from both the private and public sectors to improve recycling technology will help further efforts to achieve a circular economy, the topic of Chapter 10.

II PREVENTING AND REMOVING PLASTIC

Plastic pollution is not only being addressed through research and development focused on recycling, but also through an expansion of efforts that either: (1) directly prevent plastic leakage into waterways, or (2) collect existing plastic pollution. These efforts span the life cycle of plastic – from the manufacture of plastic through the retrieval of

[14] Andrew Rollinson, Why pyrolysis and "plastic to fuels" is not a solution to the plastics problem, www.lowimpact.org (December 4, 2018) (available at www.lowimpact.org/pyrolysis-not-solution-plastics-problem/) (last accessed October 17, 2021).

discarded plastic products – and can involve both human and technological resources. These human and technological endeavors can complement and work concurrently with regulatory and policy efforts to address plastic pollution.

For example, the volunteer beach cleanup efforts described in Chapter 7 that remove plastic from beaches are useful for raising public awareness of, and gathering data about, plastic pollution, but their impact is limited. For one, beach cleanups do not directly address the plastic already in our oceans. As discussed in Part I, because of ocean currents and temperature changes, ocean plastic that does not sink converges into giant garbage patches – the Western Garbage Patch, located near Japan, and the Eastern Garbage Patch, located near the United States between the US states of Hawaii and California, which are collectively called the Great Pacific Garbage Patch, because the plastic moves between the two smaller patches. These patches are located far from the shoreline and its cleanup is not the responsibility of any one country.

Nevertheless, since their discovery in the late 1990s, these garbage patches have been studied numerous times by scientists, volunteers, and entrepreneurs who have traveled to these garbage patches. For example, Ocean Voyages Institute, a Californian nonprofit, has conducted cleanup missions to the Eastern Garbage Patch nearly every single year since 2009. The organization uses cranes and excavators to pull up discarded fishing nets and employs modified skimming equipment, originally designed to clean up oil spills, to remove smaller plastics such as toothbrushes and laundry detergent bottles. In 2019, the institute collected 42 tons (84,000 pounds) of plastic that was then converted into everything from building materials and insulation to key chains and fuel. In June 2020, the organization collected 206,000 pounds of plastic, more than twice the amount collected the prior year. It aimed to collect 564,000 pounds in 2021, so as to reach a goal of collecting a total of one million pounds from the inception of its recovery efforts.

The Ocean Cleanup is another notable nonprofit working to remove plastic from the ocean. Started in 2013 by Dutch inventor Boyan Slat, who was then eighteen, The Ocean Cleanup today consists of more than ninety engineers, researchers, scientists, and computational modelers who work daily to rid the world's oceans of plastic. The Ocean Cleanup focuses both on ocean plastic and river plastic. Using technology to detect plastic and navigating the ocean patches using the ocean's natural forces, Ocean Cleanup has developed a passive cleanup method that could clean up 50 percent of the plastic in the Garbage Patch every five years. The technology works like a "giant Pac-Man" that scoops up ocean debris using a screen attached to a floating barrier. Plastic from the first cleanup effort, which was completed in 2019, was recycled into useable pellet form and manufactured into the first product made entirely from recycled ocean plastic: UV sunglasses. Proceeds from sunglasses sales help fund future Ocean Cleanup endeavors.

The Ocean Cleanup has also developed the Interceptor, a solar-powered, boat-like device to extract plastic from rivers without the use of human operators. The Interceptor can remove 50,000 kg of plastic per day and is currently deployed in rivers in Malaysia, Indonesia, and the Dominican Republic. Within five years, the Ocean Cleanup hopes to have Interceptors in 1,000 of the world's most polluted rivers.

In addition to these ocean plastic removal innovations, numerous inventions to remove plastic from stormwater and wastewater exist. These products typically use some sort of mesh net system that attaches to stormwater systems and catches larger plastics before they enter our waterways.

More recently, inventors have been focusing on intercepting smaller plastics. For example, in 2015 it was discovered that microplastics can bind to jellyfish mucus. This discovery launched GoJelly, an EU-funded initiative that is studying how jellyfish can be used to create innovative solutions to alleviate microplastic pollution. The desire to remove microfibers from laundry water has also spurred innovations. The Cora Ball is a ball-like object that goes in washing machines and acts the way coral does. Many corals are filter feeders that pick-up plankton from the water that flows past. Similarly, the Cora Ball filters out and collects the microfibers shed in a washing machine when clothes are washed. After several washes, microfibers become visible fuzz on the Cora Ball and can be collected and disposed, thus preventing the microfibers from entering our water system. The Guppyfriend is a washing bag in which laundry is placed before it is placed in a washing machine. Broken fibers collect in the corners of the washing bag after washing and can be easily removed and properly disposed. The Lint LUV-R is a filter that is installed outside laundry machines. Tests have concluded that when these kinds of filter and capture technologies are used, the number of microfibers that end up in washing effluent is significantly reduced.[15]

Scientists have studied these kinds of technologies, and a 2019 article identifies fifty-two technologies that fall into the two categories of (1) prevention of plastic pollution, such as those technologies described for washing machines or (2) collection of plastic pollution, such as those technologies used to remove plastic from the ocean garbage patches.[16] This suggests that in addition to recycling, there are growing options for both intercepting plastic before it enters the environment as well as removing it from the environment.

III REVALUING PLASTIC

Revaluing – or putting a higher monetary value on used plastic – is another novel attempt to reduce plastic waste. The Plastic Bank, for example, offers those who collect plastic waste a means of exchanging the plastic waste for currency at what are called Plastic Banks. Collectors bring the plastic they have gathered to a Plastic Bank location (Plastic Banks are currently located only in Haiti, Indonesia, Brazil, and the Philippines), where the collectors can trade the plastic for money, items, or services. The traded plastic is then recycled and sold at a premium as Social Plastic® to businesses around the world. David Katz, the founder and CEO of The Plastic Bank, writes that "the only way to stop ocean plastic is to reveal the value in plastic by transferring as much value into the hands of our collectors." The

[15] Jeff Kart, Science says laundry balls and filters are effective in keeping microfibers out of waterways, *Forbes* (February 1, 2019) (available at www.forbes.com/sites/jeffkart/2019/02/01/science-says-laundry-balls-and-filters-are-effective-in-removing-microfibers/?sh=16abc504e07a) (last accessed October 31, 2021).

[16] Emma Schmaltz, Plastic pollution solutions: Emerging technologies to prevent and collect marine plastic pollution, *Environment International* 144 (November 2020): 106067 (available at www.sciencedirect.com/science/article/pii/S0160412020320225) (last accessed October 31, 2021).

thought is if used plastic had a greater value, the livelihoods of those who collect plastic would be improved, but also there would be less incentive to discard plastic into the environment, since something of value can be gained if the plastic is returned to the Plastic Bank.

Another emerging strategy to revalue plastic is plastic offset credits. Similar to a carbon offset credit, a plastic credit allows industries to purchase plastic credits to offset their consumption of virgin plastic or related generation of plastic waste, usually on a one-for-one basis (e.g., "for every ton of plastic waste generated, a ton of plastic has been diverted" through a credit purchase). The goal is to generate products that offer a "plastic neutral" or "plastic positive" impact, similar to carbon neutral or carbon positive products. The 3R Initiative is probably the best-known plastic credit undertaking. It involves Danone, the world's largest yogurt producer, Nestlé, Tetra Pak, a packaging company, and Verra, the world's largest greenhouse gas credit program. Launched in 2020, the 3R Initiative, which stands for reduce, recover, and recycle, allows companies "to quantify the effectiveness of their waste recovery and recycling investments" as well as to "buy plastic credits issued by recycling and recovery providers and use them to offset their plastic use."[17] This "circular crediting pathway" aims to catalyze innovating finance to reward and incentivize local circular economy action on plastics.

IV CONCLUSION

Solely focusing on plastic's end of life, however, will not solve our plastic problem. For example, a 2020 study of the method used by the Ocean Cleanup determined that a single device would remove only a small fraction (1 percent) of the plastic in the ocean by 2150. Even with 200 Ocean Cleanup devices continuously working in the world's

[17] Sophia Chi, Danone, Nestlé and Tetra Pak say plastic credits could clean up the ocean, *Barron's* (June 18, 2019) (available at www.barrons.com/articles/danone-nestle-tetra-pak-plastic-recycling-credit-system-verra-51560800095) (last accessed October 31, 2021).

oceans for 120 years, the impact would still be extremely modest.[18] Plastic credits likewise are not a panacea. A formal or standardized definition for plastics crediting is lacking and when uniform standards are lacking the potential for greenwashing, or passing off something as having an environmental impact, when it does not, is high. The World Wildlife Federation's January 2021 position paper on plastic crediting and plastic neutrality echoes this concern. It states, in part: "WWF advocates for companies to pursue a holistic strategy on plastic waste and pollution. Companies should only engage in plastic credits if they have taken action to eliminate unnecessary plastic, move to responsible sources for remaining plastic, and taken steps to increase the reuse, recycling, and composting of their products."[19]

Advocates continue to maintain that the actual reduction of plastic should be the priority, just like source reduction is the preferred EPA approach to waste management. Companies must work to transition to a circular economy wherein unnecessary materials are designed out of the manufacturing process and materials that can be widely recycled are used and prioritized. The theory behind the circular economy approach is the focus of Chapter 10.

[18] Sonke Hohn, The long-term legacy of plastic mass production, *Science of the Total Environment* 746 (December 2020): 141115 (available at www.sciencedirect.com/science/article/pii/S0048969720346441) (last accessed October 31, 2021).

[19] White Paper, WWF Position: Plastic crediting and plastic pollution neutrality (January 2021) (available at https://c402277.ssl.cf1.rackcdn.com/publications/1429/files/original/newWWF_Position_on_Plastic_Crediting_and_Plastic_Neutrality_.pdf?1611957221) (last accessed October 31, 2021).

10 THE CIRCULAR ECONOMY

The innovations discussed in Chapters 8 and 9 are at the heart of what has been called the circular economy, that is, an economy focused on keeping materials and products in use, ideally indefinitely, as the waste materials of a used product become the raw material for a new product. Thus, like other economic theories such as cradle-to-cradle and industrial ecology, the circular economy offers an alternative to the linear make-use-dispose economic system. Chapter 10 will discuss the main principles of a circular economy, an economy that "is restorative by design, and which aims to keep products, components, and materials at their highest utility and value, at all times."[1]

This chapter will also discuss how circular economy principles are beginning to be embraced by both businesses and governments, who increasingly view the circular economy as a way to address sustainability challenges, enhance performance competitiveness and innovation, and stimulate economic growth and development. Proponents of a circular economy regard it not only as a means to conserve and recycle materials, but also as a way to drive new technological, financial, and environmental innovations. In practice, circular economy principles are the essence of zero-waste initiatives that have sprung up across the globe and in the United States, and are increasingly being considered and evaluated by private and public spheres as a way to address our plastic problem.

[1] Martin Geissdoerfer, Paulo Savaget, Nancy M. P. Bocken, and Erik Jan Hultink, The Circular Economy – A new sustainability paradigm?, *Journal of Cleaner Production* (February 2017) (available at www.repository.cam.ac.uk/bitstream/handle/1810/261957/The%20Circular%20Economy%20-%20a%20new%20sustainability%20paradigm_accepted%20version.pdf?sequence=1) (last accessed October 31, 2021).

The circular economy has become a tool for sustainable development, and as applied to plastic, the circular economic theory aims to transform plastic production, consumption, and disposal into a closed-loop and sustainable system. The topics of earlier chapters in Part III – bioplastics and recycling – certainly are compatible with the circular economy. This chapter defines in detail the theory of the circular economy and describes how circular economy principles are being integrated into policy and practice, both generally and as applied to plastic.

I DEFINING THE CIRCULAR ECONOMY

The circular economy is an alternative to a linear economy. In a linear economy, the material flow sequence is: make, use, and dispose. Since the 1950s, when plastic first became commonplace in American households, this linear sequence has been the predominant template for the treatment of plastic material. But the plastics of the 1950s were touted for their durability and long-lasting nature. It was expected that plastic products from that era would be used for years. Today, however, due in large part to the growing demand for single-use plastics, the use stage is much shorter. One study found that the average life span of a plastic bag was 12 minutes.[2]

The circular economy aims to transform the linear economic model into a circular system wherein plastic is in use for a longer period of time and, at the end of its usable life, is recovered and recycled. Significantly, a circular economy framework also aims to minimize waste production and environmental contamination at all phases of plastic's life: from design to disposal. It is the circular economy's comprehensive approach – extending the life of plastic, recovering and recycling at plastic's end-of-life, and minimizing waste and environmental contamination at all stages of plastic's life – that causes

[2] Danielle Chiriguyao, Single use plastic pollution problem, Marketplace (April 22, 2019) (available at www.marketplace.org/2019/04/22/single-use-plastic-pollution-problem/) (last accessed October 31, 2021).

many to view a transition to a circular economy as the optimal approach to combatting plastic pollution.[3]

A circular economy, or one in which waste, emission, and energy leakage are minimized, can be achieved in a variety of ways. Long-lasting design, maintenance, repair, reuse, remanufacturing, refurbishing, and recycling are all actions that encourage a circular economy.[4] Thus, the topics of Chapter 8, Bioplastics, and Chapter 9, Recycling, are central circular economy efforts.

The concept of a circular economy has its foundations in other theories of sustainability, including industrial ecology, cradle-to-cradle, and biomimicry, all of which emerged after the principles of sustainable development were introduced at the United Nations Conference on Development and the Environment in 1992. Shortly thereafter, industrial ecology was developed by Yale Professor Thomas Graedel, as a distinct field of study, one examining industrial operations with a view to designing processes and manufacturing products so as to minimize and optimize their environmental interactions. The cradle-to-cradle concept, developed by an architect and a chemist working together in the early 2000s, was proposed as a way to integrate design and science so as to "provid[e] enduring benefits for society from safe materials, water and energy in circular economies and so as to eliminat[e] the concept of waste."[5] Biomimicry is a "new science that studies nature's models and then imitates or takes inspiration from these designs and processes to solve human problems."[6] Regardless of the term, the objectives and motivations of all of these theories are the same:

[3] Kristian Syberg, Maria Bille Nielsen, Lauge Peter Werstergaard Clausen et al., Regulation of plastic from a circular economy perspective, *Current Opinion in Green and Sustainable Chemistry* (June 2021) (available at www.sciencedirect.com/science/article/pii/S2452223621000183?casa_token=ETXaaIsFczwAAAAA:ZJ27rlQBh4BEy7qcN_0_gTa4iY_HPwz0hRn3nQtBJZpuWo0Agusj-QUGCKbXwzcTFdgI05ioug#bib4) (last accessed October 31, 2021).

[4] Industrial design engineers Martin Geissdorfer et al. offer a similar definition in their article, The Circular Economy – A new sustainability paradigm?.

[5] William McDonough and Michael Braungart, *Cradle to Cradle* ((North Point Press, 2002).

[6] Vincent Blok and Bart Gremmen, Ecological innovation: Biomimicry as a new way of thinking and acting ecologically, *Journal of Agricultural and Environmental Ethics* (January 2016) (available at https://link.springer.com/article/10.1007/s10806–015-9596-1) (last accessed October 31, 2021).

sustainability and waste minimization are the goals; natural systems and cycles are the inspiration.

The term circular economy is most often associated with the Ellen MacArthur Foundation, which since 2012 has authored several reports on the topic. Founded in 2010, the Ellen MacArthur Foundation's goal is to inspire a generation to rethink, redesign, and build a positive future. The foundation defines the circular economy as "an industrial economy that is restorative or regenerative by intention and design and aims to keep products, components, and materials at their highest utility and value at all times."[7] Some of the Foundation's research demonstrates how a circular model could lead to significant economic benefits for certain industries. Thus, the benefits of a circular economy are not only environmental but economic.

The Ellen MacArthur Foundation frames solutions around three circular economy principles: the principle of inputs, the principle of sustainable cycles, and the principle of outputs. The *principle of inputs* focuses on maintaining a constant supply of renewable and nonrenewable sources. The goal is to maintain a balance in the material flow of renewable sources while preserving and increasing natural resource systems. The *principle of sustainable cycles* focuses on a waste-free design by reacquiring resources or by modernizing and improving technological systems. A circular design is incorporated at the early stages to reduce energy consumption throughout the product's life cycle.[8] The *principle of outputs* focuses on working toward identifying positive and negative externalities with certainty, making closed-loop material flows an essential part of the economic system. These three principles are sometimes summarized as keeping products and materials in use (principle of inputs), incorporating regenerative natural systems (principle of sustainable cycles), and designing out waste and pollution (principle of outputs).

To achieve a circular economy in the production of plastic, plastic waste must be prevented, and the consumption of new fossil-fuel based

[7] Ellen MacArthur Foundation, www.ellenmacarthurfoundation.org/circular-economy/concept (last accessed April 14, 2021).

[8] Csaba Fogarassay and David Finger, Theoretical and practical approaches of circular economy for business models and technological solutions, *Resources* (2020) (available at https://doi.org/10.3390/resources9060076) (last accessed October 31, 2021).

plastic products must decline. This will involve extending a product's lifetime (through maintenance and repair) and supporting reuse of plastic through second-hand trading. Transforming consumption patterns will require a fundamental change in business models and the enactment of laws to enable this change to come about. The Foundation has published several reports paving the way for novel business and policy frameworks, in Europe and elsewhere, that would redesign our relationship with plastic and other materials.[9]

II CIRCULAR ECONOMY AND THE LAW

In 2008, a few years before the MacArthur Foundation began studying and promoting the circular economy, China became the first country to enact a law proclaiming an economic model that differs from the linear model.[10] While there are environmental benefits to the circular economy, the motivations behind the Circular Economy Promotion Law of the People's Republic of China were primarily economic. As outlined in its Article I, the purpose of this law is "promoting the development of the circular economy, improving resource utilization efficiency, protecting and improving the environment and realizing sustainable development."[11] In this law, the "circular economy refers to the reduction, reuse, and recycling (3R) activities in the production, circulation, and consumption of products."[12] China's administrative Department of Circular Economy Development is in charge of coordinating and supervising the development of China's circular economy.

[9] Ellen McArthur Foundation, Toward a Circular Economy (2013) (available at www.ellenmacarthurfoundation.org/assets/downloads/publications/Ellen-MacArthur-Foundation-Towards-the-Circular-Economy-vol.1.pdf) (last accessed October 31, 2021).

[10] Yuan Hu, Xuan He, and Mark Poustie, Can legislation promote a circular economy? A material flow-based evaluation of the circular degree of the Chinese economy, *Sustainability* (2018) (available at https://doi.org/10.3390/su10040990).

[11] Available at https://ppp.worldbank.org/public-private-partnership/sites/ppp.worldbank.org/files/documents/China_CircularEconomyLawEnglish.pdf (last accessed April 14, 2021).

[12] We Li and Wenting Lin, 'Circular economy policies in china', in V. Anbumozhi and J. Kim (eds.), *Towards a Circular Economy: Corporate Management and Policy Pathways*. ERIA Research Project Report 2014-44, Jakarta: ERIA (available at www.eria.org/RPR_FY2014_No.44_Chapter_7.pdf) (last accessed October 31, 2021).

China's circular economy practices operate at the enterprise, regional, and social levels, or at the individual business, the group of businesses, and the consumer levels. At the enterprise level, cleaner production through reduced use of materials and energy consumption is promoted. At the regional level, symbiotic relationships are formed among enterprises in eco-industrial parks or zones. At the social level, the recycling and reuse of various industrial wastes are promoted.[13]

While China has, by some estimates, "led the world in promoting the recirculation of waste materials through setting targets and adopting policies, financial measures and legislation,"[14] China is still struggling to recognize the full benefits of a circular economy. A paper published in 2020 identifies several means by which China, and the world, could build up the circular economy. These means include increasing education about the circular economy, devoting more financial and other resources to businesses and firms seeking to convert to the circular economy, and utilizing better metrics for measuring and reporting on the circular economy.[15]

Like China, the European Union has taken a great interest in the circular economy model. In 2020, the European Commission, the executive arm of the European Union, adopted the Circular Economy Action Plan for a Cleaner and More Competitive Europe. The plan introduces legislative and nonlegislative measures and targets for a variety of materials including electronics, batteries, construction materials, and plastic. In terms of plastic, the plan focuses on developing the following: (1) mandatory requirements as to the amount of recycled plastic content in key products such as packaging, construction materials, and vehicles, as well as plastic waste reduction measures for these key products; (2) restrictions on the intentional and unintentional

[13] Ibid.

[14] John A. Mathews and Hao Tan, Lessons from China, *Nature* (2016) (available at www.nature.com/news/circular-economy-lessons-from-china-1.19593) (last accessed October 31, 2021).

[15] Keyou (Emma) Feng and Chun-Yin (Anson) Lam, An overview of circular economy in China: How the current challenges shape the plans for the future, *The Chinese Economy* (2021) (available at https://doi.org/10.1080/10971475.2021.1875156) (last accessed October 31, 2021).

release of microplastics; and (3) a policy framework for biobased plastics and biodegradable or compostable plastics.[16]

Also, in 2020, the United Kingdom adopted the Circular Economy Package (CEP), which introduces a legislative framework for the reduction of waste and establishes a long-term plan for waste management and recycling. The CEP contains recycling targets for plastic as well as targets for reducing the amount of waste sent to landfills.

In the United States, however, in contrast to the situation in China, the European Union, and the United Kingdom, circular economy concepts have yet to play a prominent role in federal legislation. The Break Free from Plastic Pollution Act discussed in Chapter 4 includes an extended producer responsibility (EPR) provisions that would require "responsible parties," that is, manufacturers and retailers of plastic products, to assume responsibility for the cost of collecting, moving, and recycling products at the end of their useful life. EPR schemes are one way to ensure that businesses remain accountable for their products (and any associated packaging), even after the products are sold. As one article notes, EPR "brings manufacturers into the waste management space" and shifts the management and financial responsibility away from taxpayers and the government to the producers.[17] The Break Free from Plastic Pollution Act also included recycling and composting targets to be achieved by these "responsible parties" by 2037 such that: (1) 80 percent of all covered products, (packing and single-use plastics) would be reused or recycled; (2) 90 percent of all beverage containers and paper covered products would be recycled; and (3) 70 percent of all industrially compostable covered products would be composted.[18]

Additionally, several states have considered, and three states have adopted, laws related to EPR. Vermont's law, which was enacted in 2019, focuses on single-use plastic, and creates a working group that

[16] European Commission, The Circular Economy Action Plan (available at https://ec.europa.eu/environment/circular-economy/pdf/new_circular_economy_action_plan.pdf) (last accessed October 31, 2021).

[17] Erin Eastwood, Justin Fisch, and Lara McDonough, Marine Plastic Pollution: How Global Extended Producer Responsibility Can Help, *Environmental Law Reporter* (2020) (available at www.jdsupra.com/legalnews/marine-plastic-pollution-how-global-18364/) (last accessed October 31, 2021).

[18] SWDA § 12105(g)(2)(A)-(B)).

would consider how an EPR would work, if implemented.[19] Maine's law, enacted in 2019, requires the Department of the Environment to draft an EPR scheme for plastic packaging.[20] The proposal includes a shared compensation plan which would require companies responsible for the waste created by single-use packaging to reimburse municipalities for the cost of recycling and discarding single-use packaging.[21] In 2019, Washington passed a law that requires the Department of Ecology to research plastic stewardship programs in an effort to develop a plastic waste management program.[22]

California also proposed a law in 2019, the California Circular Economy and Plastic Pollution Reduction Act, that included EPR principles. California's law, which was not enacted, would have required producers to reduce plastic in packaging and products to the maximum extent possible, and require by 2032, that all plastics be recyclable or compostable.[23]

Although EPR schemes have not yet been implemented at the federal level and are in their infancy at the state level, this activity reflects a growing recognition that producers and manufacturers must take more responsibility for their plastic products. In the meantime, policymakers should consider ways in which EPR programs can be monitored to ensure compliance. No doubt future EPR schemes will harness technology and utilize bar codes and electronic registries to track plastic products so as to recover plastic to the greatest extent possible.

While EPR schemes help cover the costs of collection and recycling programs, if the business seeks to avoid these additional costs, EPR can spur companies to consider the design of and need for plastic in their

[19] S. 113 (Act 69), 2019 Gen. Assemb., Reg. Sess. (Vt. 2019), https://legislature.vermont.gov/bill/status/2020/S.113 (last accessed October 31, 2021).

[20] L.D. 2104 (H.P. 1500), 2019 Leg., 129th Sess. (Me. 2019), www.mainelegislature.org/legis/bills/bills_129th/billtexts/HP150001.asp (last accessed October 31, 2021).

[21] Cole Rosengren, Maine packaging EPR bill, a national bellwether, could re shape municipal funding, *Waste Dive* (February 12, 2020) (available at www.waste dive.com/news/maine-packaging-epr-bill-national-bellwether-recycling/571788/) (last accessed October 31, 2021).

[22] H.B. 1204, 66th Leg., Reg. Sess. (Wash. 2019).

[23] California Legislative Information, SB-54 Solid Waste: Packaging and Products (2019–2020) (update to Cal. Pub. Res. Code §42050(a)(1)(A)-(B)).

products. To create a truly circular economy, manufacturers must consider recyclability and end-of-use in the *initial* product design process. While the EPR provision in the Break Free from Plastic Pollution Act, and at the state levels, would be a step toward a circular economy, the federal legislation has not yet been passed, and only a few states have considered EPR. Fortunately, as mentioned in Chapter 9, there seems to be significant bipartisan support for enacting new recycling laws that would require products with more recycled content and improve recycling infrastructure, both of which would move the United States closer to a circular economy.

III CIRCULAR ECONOMY AND BUSINESSES

Support from the private sector for conducting business in conformity to a circular economy is a critical element in the transition to the circular economy and, encouragingly, examples of private sector buy-in are emerging. One such example is PACE, the Partnership for the Acceleration of the Circular Economy, a collaboration among businesses, governments, and the public. Created in 2018 by the World Economic Forum, PACE is now hosted by the World Resources Institute and employs a full-time team in The Hague, Netherlands. PACE, which focuses on textiles, food, and electronics, in addition to plastic, published its plastics agenda in 2021. The agenda enumerates ten "calls-to-action." These action items include the following: agreeing on which plastics can be eliminated and phased out; incentivizing reuse and recycling for business and consumers alike; setting up functioning collection systems; making recycled plastic competitive in terms of cost as compared with products made of virgin plastic or other materials; and integrating and advancing decent work in the transition to a circular economy for plastics.[24]

The New Plastic Economy is another business-government circular economy effort that addresses plastic, this one supported by the

[24] Partnership for the Acceleration of the Circular Economy, Circular Economy Action Agenda: Plastics (available https://pacecircular.org/sites/default/files/2021-02/circular-agenda-plastics-feb2021_FINAL.pdf) (last accessed October 31, 2021).

MacArthur Foundation. Two of the New Plastic Economy's major initiatives are the Global Commitment and the Plastic Pact.

The New Plastics Economy Global Commitment, which was initiated in 2018 in conjunction with the UN Environmental Programme, unites businesses, governments, and other organizations behind a common vision of a circular economy for plastic and sets targets to address plastic waste and pollution at their sources, starting with packaging. The commitment has gained a number of signatories including over 250 businesses involved in plastic packaging, representing more than 20 percent of all plastic packaging used globally; over 200 institutions, including financial institutions, nonprofits such as National Geographic, World Wildlife Fund for Nature (WWF), and academic and research organizations; and 20 national, subnational, and local-level governments across 5 continents.[25]

In its 2020 Global Commitment Progress report, the New Plastic Economy notes promising progress in several areas among its signatories including the following: 22 percent growth in recycled content in packaging; 31 percent growth in adoption of targets designed to reduce the use of virgin plastic; and an increase in the number of signatories making their total plastic packaging volumes publicly available. The report, however, also identified a few less-promising outcomes, such as significant differences among signatories in their efforts to meet targets and a lack of innovative approaches to rethinking the need for plastic packaging in the first place. As a result, the report noted that it will be difficult to meet the commitment's target of 100 percent reusable, recyclable, or compostable plastic by 2025. The report called on businesses to set rigorous reduction targets and to decide how to address packaging types that are not recyclable today – either by developing and executing a credible road map to make recycling work, or by decisively innovating away from these packaging types. The report further called on governments to adequately fund plastic collection and sorting so that plastic recycling can scale beyond 10 percent, and to create an international framework for action, through the UN

[25] Ellen McArthur Foundation, Global Commitment Progress Report 2020 (www.ellenmacarthurfoundation.org/assets/downloads/Global-Commitment-2020-Progress-Report.pdf) (last accessed October 31, 2021).

Environment Assembly, building on the assembly's vision of a circular economy for plastics.[26]

The other New Plastic Economy initiative, the Plastic Pact, is a global network of local and regional initiatives bringing together key stakeholders to implement solutions aimed at building a circular economy for plastics.[27] Each initiative is led by a local organization and unites governments, businesses, and citizens behind a common vision of ambitious local targets. The United States Plastic Pact was announced in August 2020 and is a collaborative of more than sixty "activators" led by two nonprofits: the Recycling Partnership and the World Wildlife Fund. These activators include private businesses, government agencies, and NGOs across the supply and plastics manufacturing chain. By joining the U.S. Plastics Pact, activators have agreed to work toward four targets: (1) identifying problematic and unnecessary packaging plastics by 2021 and taking measures to eliminate these plastics by 2025; (2) making all plastic packaging 100 percent reusable, recyclable, or compostable by 2025; (3) recycling or composting 50 percent of plastic packaging by 2025; and (4) increasing to 30 percent the average recycled content or responsibly sourced bio-based content in plastic packaging.[28]

To ensure measurable change and transparent reporting, the progress of the U.S. Plastic Pact will be tracked through WWF's ReSource: Plastic Footprint Tracker, which provides a standard methodology for tracking companies' plastic footprints and which is discussed in Chapter 7. Finally, a report of the activators' plastic waste commitments will be made publicly available each year.

Despite these promising collaborations, however, many circular economy laws and programs operate in isolation, and a shift in the global plastic industry at large toward a circular economy is yet to be seen. For example, the New Plastic Economy focuses on plastic packaging, but not on other kinds of plastic. Much like the call to adopt a global treaty on plastic pollution, as discussed in Chapter 6, there are

[26] Ibid.

[27] Ellen McArthur Foundation, The Plastic Pact, www.ellenmacarthurfoundation.org/our-work/activities/new-plastics-economy/plastics-pact (last accessed October 31, 2021).

[28] U.S. Plastic Pact, https://usplasticspact.org/ (last accessed April 14, 2021).

growing calls for global initiatives to advance the circular economy.[29] These initiatives must involve public and private sectors working together to share resources and information and to develop and incentivize circular economies.

In February 2021, the World Economic Forum identified what it termed "three shifts" – three fundamental changes in attitudes and actions – that are essential in scaling up the circular economy.[30] The first shift is to design for circularity by focusing on reuse, repair, refurbishment, and recycling. This includes changing what is produced and how it is produced. Chapters 8 and 9 identified some innovations supportive of this design shift. Legislatures could encourage the use of recycled or reused materials through tax incentives and guidelines for the purchasing of goods and services. Collaborations among governments, businesses, and other institutions could help to develop, harmonize, and standardize the way circular design is measured.

The second shift involves developing new business models where products have an extended useful life. In this model, businesses shift to a "product as a service" model; customers pay for any value or service resulting from the product, but the business retains ownership of the physical product. Bottle deposit and buy-back schemes are an example of this model and extended producer responsibility programs could support these efforts.

The third shift is toward resource management systems that preserve value through reverse design thinking, designing, from the outset, for the impact of the product at the end of its useful life. Such thinking will focus on developing technology that allows for better separation and less contamination of plastic, as well as technology that allows for easier and more complete remanufacturing of plastic. Governments and businesses should invest in innovative recycling technology to

[29] Yong Geng, Joseph Sarkis, and Raimund Bleischwitz, How to globalize the circular economy, *Nature* (January 9, 2019). (available at www.nature.com/articles/d41586-019-00017-z?from=groupmessage&isappinstalled=0) (last accessed October 31, 2021).

[30] Ellen McArthur and Frans Van Houten, 3 shifts can scale the circular economy – triggering a more resilient, prosperous system, World Economic Forum (February 2021) (available at www.weforum.org/agenda/2021/02/3-shifts-can-scale-the-circular-economy-ellen-macarthur-frans-van-houten/) (last accessed October 31, 2021).

ensure that the maximum value of plastic products is maintained for as long as possible. Governments should, as well, invest in collection and sorting facilities to aid in making recycling easier and more efficient. Reverse design thinking also includes planning for the strategic placement of these recycling facilities for maximum use by consumers and industries.

IV CONCLUSION

Realizing a circular economy will require research and innovation at all levels: the product level, the company level, the network level, and the policy level. Designing products for reuse needs to be the standard business practice, and companies and the consumers who use their plastic products need to be better connected so that used plastic is easily kept in use. Government policies should support these efforts by prioritizing waste reduction and discouraging the expansion of fossil-fuel-based plastics. Finally, more research by academics and policymakers is needed to inform businesses and governments as to the feasibility and design of a plastic circular economy and this research needs to be shared. Investing in and growing the circular economy is the next frontier for those seeking to solve our plastic problem.

Underlying the specific call for adopting a circular economy is a broader argument for system thinking as a method for solving complex problems. System thinking requires an understanding of an entire system, achieved by examining the linkages and interactions among all the elements (or stakeholders) that comprise the whole of the system. As this book illustrates, plastic pollution involves many stakeholders; there are many places where change can occur and many ways in which change can happen. Solving our plastic problem will require collaboration among all stakeholders and the integration of theories from diverse disciplines.

INDEX

CPSIA information can be obtained
at www.ICGtesting.com
Printed in the USA
BVHW011654150322
631538BV00007B/61

9 781108 795371